The New Management of British Lo

LEEDS METROPOL   NIVERSITY

The New Management of British Local Governance

Edited by

Gerry Stoker

Foreword by R. A. W. Rhodes

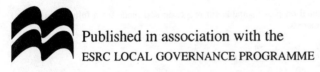

Published in association with the
ESRC LOCAL GOVERNANCE PROGRAMME

E·S·R·C
ECONOMIC
& SOCIAL
RESEARCH
COUNCIL

First published in Great Britain 1999 by
MACMILLAN PRESS LTD
Houndmills, Basingstoke, Hampshire RG21 6XS and London
Companies and representatives throughout the world

A catalogue record for this book is available from the British Library.

ISBN 0–333–72815–7 hardcover
ISBN 0–333–72816–5 paperback

First published in the United States of America 1999 by
ST. MARTIN'S PRESS, INC.,
Scholarly and Reference Division,
175 Fifth Avenue, New York, N.Y. 10010

ISBN 0–312–21970–9

Library of Congress Cataloging-in-Publication Data
The new management of British local governance / edited by Gerry
Stoker.
p. cm.
Includes bibliographical references and index.
ISBN 0–312–21970–9 (cloth)
1. Local government—Great Britain.   I. Stoker, Gerry.
JS3158.N48   1998
352.14'0941—dc21

98–43080
CIP

This book is printed on paper suitable for recycling and made from fully managed and
sustained forest sources.

10   9   8   7   6   5   4   3   2   1
08   07   06   05   04   03   02   01   00   99

Printed in Hong Kong

This book is dedicated to the memory of

Kieron Walsh

who died in May 1995. He was a member of the
ESRC's Local Governance Programme and a good
friend and valued colleague

Contents

List of Tables and Figures

Tables

Figures

List of Contributors

Marian Barnes Department of Social Policy and Social Work, University of Birmingham

John Benington Professor in the Local Government Centre, Warwick Business School, University of Warwick

John Benyon Director of the Centre for the Study of Public Order, University of Leicester

Johnston Birchall Department of Government, Brunel University

Kevin Doogan School for Policy Studies, University of Bristol

Adam Edwards Researcher in Centre for the Study of Public Order, University of Leicester

Shari Garmise Formerly Research Assistant, University of Cardiff

Steve Harrison Nuffield Institute for Health Services, University of Leeds

Neal Geaughan Department of Accountancy, University of Aberdeen

Janet Harvey Senior Research Fellow, Centre for Corporate Strategy and Change, Warwick Business School, University of Warwick

David Heald Professor of Accountancy, University of Aberdeen

Vivien Lowndes Professor of Public Policy and Management, De Montfort University

Maureen Mackintosh Professor in the Faculty of Social Sciences, The Open Unversity

Jane Martin Researcher in the School of Education, University of Birmingham

Penny McKeown School of Education, Queen's University, Belfast

Kevin Morgan Department of City and Regional Planning, University of Wales, Cardiff

Maggie Mort Senior Research Fellow in the School of Management, University of Lancaster

Jon Nixon Professor of Education, University of Stirling

Christopher Pollitt Professor of Government and Co-Director of the Centre for the Evaluation of Public Policy and Practice, Brunel University

Keith Putman Formerly Researcher, Brunel University, now working as a full-time teacher

Stewart Ranson Professor of Education, University of Birmingham

Gareth Rees Professor of Education, University of Cardiff

Barbara Reid Reader in Housing Studies, Sheffield Hallam University

Kathryn Riley Professor and Director, Froebel College, Roehampton Institute, London

Jeffrey Stanyer Department of Politics, University of Exeter

Polly Shardlow Research Fellow in the Department of Sociological Studies, University of Sheffield

Gerry Stoker Professor of Government, University of Strathclyde

Gerald Wistow Professor in the Nuffield Institute for Health Services, University of Leeds

Foreword: Governance and Networks[1]

An Informal History

Date-line London, 15 June 1989

A long, long time ago, or so it seems, there was a research seminar at the Department of the Environment. In two plenary sessions and six workshops, the participants discussed current research interests and priorities for funding, covering such topics as the finance, organisation and management of local government (Department of the Environment 1989). A good time was had by all and, as ever, the real action took place, not in the formal sessions, but in the networking. Conversations between Gerry Stoker, who as entrepreneurial academic fears not publicity, and Martin Kender, who as an Economic and Social Research Council (ESRC) official must ever shun the public glare, decided there must be a way of building on the seminar. There was. The ESRC commissioned Gerry Stoker to write a proposal for a research initiative (as they were then known) on local government (as it was then known).[2] A first draft was circulated in August 1989 and the final report presented to the Society and Politics Research Development Group (RDG) in October 1989.

Date-line Durham, 10-12 April 1990

Gerry Stoker presents his paper on 'Local Government in a Changing Social and Economic System' to the Annual Conference of the Political Studies Association of the United Kingdom at the University of Durham (Stoker, 1990). Rod Rhodes writes a comment on his research agenda (Rhodes, 1990). A lively debate about future research in local government ensued and enthusiastic support for a research initiative was given. The conference was part of a consultation process which lasted nearly two years. It encompassed the annual conferences of the British Sociological Association, the International Studies Association, a second PSA conference (Rhodes, 1991b) and a day-long seminar of the Urban Politics Group of the PSA. The proposal was also circulated to, and discussed with, too many colleagues to cite here.

Rod Rhodes becomes a member of RDG. In the same month, Gerry Stoker emigrates (temporarily) to Wayne State University near Detroit for a year. The two events are related. Rod Rhodes gets to steer the proposal through the bureaucracy under the firm but gentle hand of the ever-present Martin Kender. Local government transmutes into local governance (Rhodes, 1991c, 1992). In 1991 the ESRC Council approves a research initiative of 1.5 million. Gerry Stoker survives urban deprivation and on 1 May 1992 is appointed coordinator. Research Initiatives mutate into Programmes.[3] Rod Rhodes becomes the chair of the Programme Commissioning Panel and its successor Steering Committee.[4] The ubiquitous Martin Kender is no longer with us, elevated to the peerage of head of corporate services (although his delight at carrying this penitential cross was well-disguised). Phil Souben, he of phlegmatic good cheer in the face of Rhodes-ian enthusiasm, succeeds him. The Local Governance Programme is advertised, some 92 bids are received and 34 are short-listed. The Commissioning Panel makes 14 awards.

Date-line London, 24 February 1993

Ever aware of the need to keep up with the times, the RDG has become the Research Programmes Board. Research Coordinators become Programme Directors.[5] Now everything has changed its name at least once. Rod Rhodes is consigned to committee wilderness, but it is too late. At its first meeting the Programmes Board approves a second phase of some £700 000. A further round of advertising produces 110 bids and the Commissioning Panel funds 13 more projects. The deed is done. There are 27 projects, spending £2.3 million. The first-phase projects start in March 1993. The second-phase projects start in January 1994. The Programme finishes in December 1997 – a mere eight years from birth to death. Time disappears when you are having fun.

Aims

The Local Governance Programme had four aims.

• To document the transformation of the structure of government beyond Westminster and Whitehall from a system of local government into a system of local governance involving complex sets of organisations drawn from the public and private sectors.

• To develop a cumulative multi-theoretic approach to the study of local governance by comparing and contrasting the strengths and weaknesses of current theoretical approaches rather than espousing any one approach.

• To identify, encourage and coordinate the participation of a new generation of researchers from the social science disciplines.

• To place the changing British system of local governance in an international context.

Stoker (1996a) describes the scope of the Programme as follows:

> In broad terms all the projects are concerned with changes in the way that public services are managed. In addition there is a focus on the changing nature of decision making within and about localities. The role of government has shifted away from a narrow emphasis on direct service provision to a broader range of activities involving contracting, regulation, enabling and leadership. The boundaries between public, private and voluntary sectors have become less sharp. The local arena is characterised by a complex array of interactive relationships. The broad aim of the Programme is to understand these emerging relationships and assess their significance for government, citizen, public sector provision and local democracy.

Phase 1 had six themes. Theme one provided a historical perspective, examining the history of the institutions of local governance from 1801 onwards. Theme two looked at the changing context of local governance, focusing on: Europeanising local governance; local economic and social restructuring; and the structure and practices of post-Fordist local governance. Theme three focused on the changing map of local power, examining the community power structures of London; and coalition-building between public and private interest in urban development in a comparative study of cities in Denmark, Germany, the Netherlands and the UK. Theme four looked at changes in local politics and specifically: the changing nature of political leadership, parties and decision-making; the recent history of the Conservative party on local government; and the impact of legal change on local government. Theme five was concerned with new forms of service delivery and examined the performance of opted-out schools, hospitals and housing action trusts; and the empowerment of users in health and social care services. Theme six explored the changing role of management in local authorities, looking at emerging patterns of management in local governance; interorganisational cooperation in housing management; and new forms of school and college management.

Phase 2 had four themes. Theme one looked at public opinion and local citizenship. Theme two examined targeting and control in financing local governance and accounting for infrastructure assets. Theme three explored the changing role of the voluntary sector, covering community-based housing organisations and the voluntary sector and local sustainable development. Theme four focused on intergovernmental management and local networks, looking at networks of participation in local planning and local policy networks in Britain and France. Finally, there were six applied strategic projects which were low-cost, short and targeted on issues of direct concern to practitioners. They covered: economic culture; gender; labour market fragmentation; race equality; local strategies for crime prevention; and local economic governance.

Research findings

With such a broad-ranging programme of research spread over five years, it is almost impossible to give a definitive summary of the research themes. Inevitably, the reader draws out certain threads, highlights those aspects of the research of most immediate concern to him or herself. A good place to start is the Programme Director's annual reports and publications (see, for example, Stoker, 1996a and b, 1998a and b).

Gerry Stoker groups the research findings under four headings: the new management of public services; partnership and coalition-building; the political response to the emerging system of local governance; and the context of social and economic change.

This book focuses on the shift from a system of direct management, or hierarchy, towards managerialism and quasi-markets with their emphasis on managerial decentralisation, performance indicators, contracting and purchaser–provider splits. The Local Governance Programme found a complex network of relationships trying to manage this new world. The unintended consequences of complexity, confusion and loss of accountability vie with autonomy, flexibility and competition as the distinctive outcomes of the changes. But perhaps the dominant impression is of the difficulties posed by fragmentation for coordination and the spread of opportunistic behaviour, perverse incentives and inefficient exchange. The new management and the language of managerialism and markets do not fit the culture and logic of public service.

In such strategic issue areas as economic development, environmental protection and crime prevention, the Programme found a growing capacity for networking and partnerships, at local, regional, national and European levels. This activity had two distinguishing characteristics. First, many partnerships were short-term, driven by the need to get access to resources. Second, local public sector actors played the key role in these networks. The 1980s and 1990s saw partnerships and networking rival the unified departments of local authorities as effective mechanisms for integrated action in the emerging system of local governance.

The companion volume on The New Politics of Local Government stresses the emergence of governing coalitions based on many public, private and voluntary sector actors; and the changing organisation and style of party politics. Public managers and private actors now inhabit a strange new world in which the role of government is redefined and a network style of working is paramount. Although party leaders are an integral part of this world, their backbench colleagues are cast adrift in a sea of changes they do not comprehend and which offers them no clear role. Moreover, these changes are a reaction to the changing informational and financial dynamics of local governance. Shifts in the structure of the private sector economy, the effects of globalisation and the complex mechanisms of financial rationing and control interweave to produce an ever-shifting backcloth, the long-term and permanent effects of which remain difficult to judge.

My emphases differ, although they complement rather than contradict Stoker's conspectus. In this Foreword, I want to argue that the Local Governance Programme helped to develop four concepts important for understanding the governance of Britain today, not just local governance: networks, governance, trust and diplomacy (and for a more detailed discussion see Rhodes, 1997b). The language of government in the 1980s and 1990s has been the language of managerialism and institutional economics. The Local Governance Programme challenged and changed that language. To the stark choice between hierarchy and markets, we can now add governance through networks. To an appreciation of the limits to command and control, we can add an understanding of the repertoire of networking; of management by trust and diplomacy.

Governance

The concept which forms the centrepiece of the Local Governance Programme is that of governance which refers to self-organising, interorganisational networks with the following characteristics:

1. Interdependence between organisations. Governance is broader than government, covering non-state actors. Changing the boundaries of the state meant the boundaries between public, private and voluntary sectors became shifting and opaque.
2. Continuing interactions between network members, caused by the need to exchange resources and negotiate shared purposes.
3. Game-like interactions, rooted in trust and regulated by rules of the game negotiated and agreed by network participants.
4. A significant degree of autonomy from the state. Networks are not accountable to the state; they are self-organising. Although the state does not occupy a privileged, sovereign position, it can indirectly and imperfectly steer networks. (Rhodes, 1996, and 1997, ch. 3)

In the 1990s, British government adopted a strategy of 'more control over less'. It privatised the utilities. It contracted out services to the private sector. It introduced quasi-markets through purchaser–provider splits when services could not be privatised. It bypassed local authorities for special-purpose bodies. It removed operational management from central departments and vested it in separate agencies (Rhodes, 1997b, chs 5–7). Central departments rarely delivered services themselves; they were non-executant. Government policy now fragmented service delivery systems. It compensated for its loss of hands-on control by reinforcing its control over resources. Decentralising service delivery has gone with centralising financial control. Such hands-off control may not provide enough leverage for the centre to steer the networks. As networks multiply, so do doubts about the centre's capacity to steer. The shift from line bureaucracies to fragmented service delivery systems can be summarised as the shift from government to governance. Governance has become the defining narrative of British government at the turn of the century, challenging the commonplace notion of Britain as a unitary state with a strong executive. The policy of marketising public services has accelerated the process of differentiation and multiplied networks. To the stark choice between hierarchy and markets, we can now add networks.

The characteristics of networks

If governance as networks now rivals markets and hierarchies as a means of allocating and co-ordinating resources, it is important to identify the distinctive characteristics of these 'governing structures' as shown in the table.[6]

	Markets	Hierarchies	Networks
Basis of Relationships	Contract and property rights	Employment relationship	Resource exchange
Degree of dependence	Independent	Dependent	Interdependent
Medium of exchange	Prices	Authority	Trust
Means of conflict resolution and co-ordination	Haggling and the courts	Rules and commands	Diplomacy
Culture	Competition	Subordination	Reciprocity

Interdependence and resource exchange

Rhodes's (1988) analysis of policy networks in British government shows that British intergovernmental relations are not hierarchical but built on complex resource interdependencies. In brief, local authorities and central departments depend on one another for such resources as legal authority, money and professional expertise to achieve their policy goals. Central-local relations are a 'game' in which both central and local participants manoeuvre for advantage. Each deploys its resources to maximise influence over outcomes while trying to avoid becoming dependent on the other 'players' (see also Kickert *et al.*, 1997).

Policy networks matter. As governments confront a vast array of increasingly differentiated interests, so institutional and sociopolitical differentiation sustain each other. Intermediation is a fact of everyday life in contemporary government. To describe and explain variations in patterns of intermediation is to explore one of the key governmental and political processes. Policy networks analyse aggregation and intermediation – the oligopoly of the political market-place. They are important for six reasons (Marsh and Rhodes, 1992a; Marsh and Smith, 1995):

- They limit participation in the policy process.
- They define the roles of actors.
- They decide which issues will be included and excluded from the policy agenda.
- Through the rules of the game, they shape the behaviour of actors.
- They privilege certain interests, according them access and favouring their preferred outcomes.
- They substitute private government for public accountability.

So, policy networks are about: 'Who rules?', 'How do they rule?', and 'In whose interest do they rule?' They illustrate the process of differentiation of institutions, politics and policies that brings an increase in complexity and loss of central steering capacity.

Initially, central government departments were the fulcrum of this resource dependence but in the 1980s and 1990s the government fragmented service delivery systems and multiplied networks. The networks had two new characteristics which compounded the problems of central steering. First, the membership of networks became broader, incorporating both the private and voluntary sectors. Second, the government swapped direct for indirect controls. Central departments are no longer either necessarily or invariably the fulcrum, or focal organisation, of a network. Power relations may remain asymmetric. The government can set the parameters to network actions. It still funds the services. But it has also increased its own dependence on multifarious networks.

Trust

Networks are a distinctive coordinating mechanism and, therefore, a separate governing structure from markets and hierarchies. The social conception of trust is 'the most important attribute of network operations'. It is the central coordinating mechanism of networks in the same way that commands and price competition are the key mechanisms for bureaucracies and markets respectively (Frances *et al.*, 1991, p. 15). Shared values and norms are the glue which holds the complex set of relationships together; trust is essential for cooperative behaviour and, therefore, the existence of the network.

The social conception of trust sees economic transactions as socially embedded (Granovetter, 1985) and characterised by non-calculative trust (see Williamson, 1993). For example, Tyler and Degoey (1996, p. 347) conclude that non-calculative trust is present even in commercial relations and a central influence on organisational behaviour. They suggest that trust should be seen as 'benevolent intentions' rather than 'calculated risk' (p. 345). In networks, non-calculative trust is important for all transactions, including economic transactions.

However, it would be a mistake to overemphasise the dichotomy between economic and social conceptions of trust. As Powell (1996, p. 63) points out, trust is: 'neither chosen nor embedded but is instead learned and reinforced, hence a product of ongoing interaction and discussion'. Preserving trust is, therefore, a reciprocal and endless task (see Flynn, Williams *et al.*, 1996, p. 136). Fox's (1974, p. 362) conclusions about trust in industrial relations are equally apt for networks. Thus, in networks with high-trust relationships, participants:

> share certain ends or value; bear towards each other a diffuse sense of long-term obligations; offer each other spontaneous support without narrowly calculating the cost or expecting any equivalent short-term reciprocation; communicate freely and honestly; are ready to repose their fortunes in each other's hands; and give each other the benefit of any doubt that may arise with respect to goodwill or motivation.

As a working axiom, therefore, networks are high trust and contracts are low trust. The 'Local Governance' Programme documents the spread of networks and the recurrent tension between contracts and competition on the one hand and cooperative networking behaviour on the other.

Diplomacy[7]

Nicholson (1950, p. 15) defines diplomacy as 'the management of international affairs by negotiation'. He also identifies seven diplomatic virtues: truthfulness; precision; calm; good temper; patience; modesty; and loyalty (to the government one serves). There is a charming quality to Nicholson's account. The budding diplomat is advised that: 'above everything, do not allow yourself to become excited about your work' (p. 116); 'patience and perseverance are also essential to any successful negotiator' (p. 117); and 'personal vanity breeds self-satisfaction which leads to a loss of adaptability and a decline in imagination' (p. 120). He then adds (p. 126):

'But', the reader may object, 'you have forgotten intelligence, knowledge, discernment, prudence, hospitality, charm, industry, courage and even tact.' I have not forgotten them. I have taken them for granted.

For all its slightly old-fashioned, even quaint, air, Nicholson signals an important shift in style to a language which stresses sitting where the other person sits and helping other people to realise their objectives. We relearn old lessons. As de Callierès (1963 [1716]) comments:

'Now, if I were in the place of this Prince, wielding his power, subject to his passions and prejudices, what effect would my mission and my arguments have on me?' The more often he puts himself in the position of others, the more subtle and effective will his arguments be.

The emphasis lies not in imposing one's objectives on another but on finding out about the other. The diplomat must persuade 'another government to accept and perhaps actually help to promote the policies which it is the ambassador's function to advocate' (Watson, 1982, p. 125), and the main technique is 'the maintenance by continual persuasion of order in the midst of change' (p. 223). The literature on diplomatic negotiations contains uncanny parallels with intergovernmental relations in a nation state with its emphasis on negotiation when common interests and issues of conflict coexist. Without common interests there is no interdependence in the differentiated polity and functional conflicts are endemic. One way of resolving conflict in international relations lies in negotiation. Diplomacy may be an old-fashioned word but the arts of negotiation and persuasion are not peculiar to it. As Sir Douglas Wass said, 'finesse and diplomacy are an essential ingredient in public service' (Hennessy, 1989, p. 150). Such skills lie at the heart of steering interorganisational networks. The idea is not new, just misplaced.

Reciprocity

Networks involve friendship, loyalty, even altruism (Thompson, 1993, pp. 54-8) but above all network culture is characterised by reciprocity. As Powell (1991, pp. 272–3) comments, it is an ambiguous concept and, again, there is a sharp disjuncture between the use in economics and the other social sciences. Thus, for economists, 'reciprocity entails exchanges of roughly equivalent value' whereas sociologists and anthropologists emphasise 'the normative standards that sustain exchange', especially indebtedness, obligation and a long-term perspective. So, a lack of equivalence creates a moral sanction, bonds which keep the parties in touch with one another; the books are balanced only in the long term. However, as Thompson (1993, p. 58) points out, reciprocity is also a symbolic relationship and 'in the constant ritual of exchange, deep obligations and duties are established, symbolic statuses confirmed, metaphorical social references invoked'. In this way, network coordination becomes stabilised.

No governing structure works for all services in all conditions. The issue, therefore, is not the superiority of markets and hierarchy over networks but managing networks in the conditions under which they work best. So networks thrive where the following factors combine:

• actors need reliable, 'thicker' information;
• quality cannot be specified or is difficult to define and measure;
• commodities are difficult to price;
• professional discretion and expertise are core values;
• service delivery is localised;
• cross-sectoral, multi-agency cooperation is required;
• monitoring and evaluation incur high political and administrative costs; and
• implementation involves haggling.[8]

Equally networks, like all other resource allocation mechanisms, are not cost-free. They are often closed to outsiders and unaccountable for their actions. They can serve private interests, not the public interest.

They are difficult to steer. For example, Kettl (1993, pp. 206–7) argues that, because of contracting out, government agencies found themselves 'sitting on top of complex public–private relationships whose dimensions they may only vaguely understand'. They had only 'loose leverage' but remained 'responsible for a system over which they had little real control'. Also, the several mechanisms can mix like oil and water. Thus, managerialism undermined the effectiveness of networks. The government promoted competition and contracting out. The result was to 'corrode . . . common values and commitments' and 'to create an atmosphere of mistrust' (Flynn, Williams *et al.*, 1996, p. 115). Market relations had 'corrosive effects' on 'professional networks which depend on co-operation, reciprocity and interdependence' (ibid., pp. 136–7). In short, contracts undermine trust, reciprocity, informality and cooperation.

Conclusions

So, government fragments and networks vie with markets and bureaucracy as key service delivery mechanisms. The consequences of institutional differentiation are many and varied but invariably include complexity and confusion, opaque accountability and a diminished capacity to steer. The phrase 'the hollowing-out of the state' captures many of the changes which have taken, and are taking, place in British government:

1. Privatisation and limiting the scope and forms of public intervention.
2. The loss of functions by central and local government departments to alternative delivery systems.
3. The loss of functions by British government to European Union institutions.
4. A reduced central capacity to steer. (Rhodes, 1994, pp. 138–9; 1997b)

In sum, hollowing out refers to the loss of functions upwards to the European Union and other international bodies, downwards to special-purpose bodies and outwards to agencies. The governance narrative places networks at the heart of the analysis; paints a distinctive picture of British government; identifies important unintended consequences of marketisation; and explores the mix of governing structures.

The core ideas of managerialism and marketisation have restricted the tool kit available to government for managing networks. Networks are pervasive. Government is picking up the skills of indirect management. The new public management, whether in the guise of managerialism or institutional economics, is no longer the challenge confronting government. The challenge is diplomacy in governance (and for a more detailed analysis see Rhodes, 1997b).

Too often academics are all too willing to play the role of ersatz public servant. We are asked to provide data, even solutions, to contemporary problems. But the social sciences offer only provisional knowledge. Prediction is mainly an aspiration and probably an impossibility in the human sciences. But an awareness of our limitations does not render the social sciences useless. If we cannot offer solutions, we can define and redefine problems in novel ways. We can tell the policy makers and administrators distinctive stories about their world and how it is governed. The new public management told a story of economy, efficiency and effectiveness which contrasted sharply with the story of the local government officer as professional with clients and the permanent secretary as policy adviser and fire-fighter for the minister. Governance tells a story of differentiation, hollowing-out, networks, trust and diplomacy which contrasts sharply with the prescriptions of managerialism and the world of markets and contracts. In other words, we provide a language for re-describing the world and the Local Governance Programme has played no small part in challenging the dominant, managerial ideology of the 1980s and arguing for a view of the world in which networks vie with markets and bureaucracy as the appropriate means for delivering services. If there is a simple message it is that for every problem there is a simple solution, and it is always wrong. The language of governance makes no apology for describing a complex world in all its complexity and arguing it is the mix that matters; there is no simple solution based on markets or hierarchies or networks.

R. A. W. RHODES
Professor of Politics, University of Newcastle-upon-Tyne
Chair, ESRC Local Governance Steering Committee

Notes

1. This Foreword draws on the official documentation of the Local Governance Programme and the several annual reports by the Programme Director, Professor Gerry Stoker (University of Strathclyde). Where I have quoted or paraphrased this material, I have not referenced it. This general acknowledgement will suffice.

2. The ESRC is the United Kingdom's leading social science funding agency. It is an independent organisation, financed solely by government. Its activities fall into three groups: research grants, research centres and programmes, and postgraduate training.

3. Research Programmes seek to harness and strengthen the United Kingdom's social science research capacity to address scientific and policy-relevant topics of strategic and national importance. Typically, there will be 10 to 15 projects drawn from several social science disciplines and spread among UK universities. Researchers work independently on individual projects with the support of a Programme Director and his or her advisory Steering Committee.

4. The members of the Steering Committee were: Michael Clarke (Local Government Management Board), Nick Deakin (University of Birmingham), Michael Goldsmith (University of Salford), Peter Jackson (University of Leicester), Marion Kerr (Department of the Environment), Sue Richards (Office of Public Management), John Urry (University of Lancaster) and Robin Wendt (Association of County Councils). Subsequently, Judith Hunt (Local Government Management Board) replaced Michael Clarke, and Maureen Colledge (Department of the Environment) replaced Marion Kerr.

5. The role of Programme Director is subject to constant revision. At the time, he or she represented the Programme, ensured the effective internal communication of the Programme, networked the Programme with the scientific community and non-academic sectors, designed and implemented a communication plan, monitored and advised on the progress of projects, ran the Steering Committee and submitted an annual report.

6. For a more detailed discussion of the distinctive characteristics of networks in delivering public services, and the conditions under which they thrive, see: Flynn, Williams *et al.*, 1996, pp. 139–41; Kramer and Tyler, 1996 chs 4 and 16; Larson, 1992, p. 98; Powell, 1991, pp. 268–74; Rhodes, 1997b ch. 3; Thompson, Frances *et al.*, 1991, Introduction and ch. 21–3; Thompson, 1993, pp. 54–60; and Wistow, Knapp *et al.*, 1994. Initially I used the table in Powell,

1991, p. 269. However, he does not include trust or diplomacy as network characteristics. Also Powell does not explain the dimensions for comparing the three 'forms of organisation' and the labelling varies between text and table. For example, the text discusses sanctions which do not appear in the table. So, my table was prompted by but is only loosely based on Powell.

7. The earliest discussion of diplomatic skills in public management I have found is Keeling (1972, ch. 5) who identifies three species of systems in public services: administration, management and diplomatic systems.

8. See the references in note 6.

1 Introduction: The Unintended Costs and Benefits of New Management Reform for British Local Government

Gerry Stoker

What happened to British local government during the period of Conservative government from 1979 to 1997 was in many respects a brutal illustration of power politics. The funding system was reformed to provide central government with a considerable (and probably unprecedented) level of control over spending. Various functions and responsibilities were stripped away from local authorities or organised in a way that obliged local authorities to work in partnership with other public and private agencies in the carrying out of the functions. The structure of local government itself was reorganised through the abolition of the Greater London council and the six metropolitan counties in the mid-1980s and later the Inner London Education Authority. In the mid-1990s there was a 'single-tier' reorganisation imposed in Scotland and Wales and a more prosaic but nevertheless substantial reform in England. By May 1997 there were over 80 fewer local authorities in Britain than in 1979. The spending, functions and structure of local government had been restructured at the behest of a central government capable of imposing its will against considerable but limited resistance from local authorities.

The story of the 1980s and 1990s in terms of the struggle between central and local government is presented and analysed elsewhere (Stoker and Stewart, 1995; Stoker, 1996; and Wilson and Game, 1998). The focus of this book is on the attempt to reform the management of local government which accompanied the broader processes of reorganisation of finance, function and structure.

The aim of the management reform was to an extent more profound and subtle than the wider system-based reforms. It was to change the

1

way that local authorities worked in terms of the provision of services to the public.

In this introductory chapter a number of key themes are examined. First, the 'new management' revolution is defined and, second, its particular British character identified. What emerges is a portrait of a relatively incoherent, perhaps even contradictory, reform programme imposed by central government prescription and fiat. The Conservatives attempted to impose new management in much the same way as they changed structures, finance and functions. Such a reform style does not provide the best prospect for effective implementation when applied to the more subtle and complex processes of management.

The next section of the chapter launches a discussion on how all major programmes of reform have to confront implementation failure and the 'iron law' of unintended consequences. Purposive social intervention can yield results but not always in the manner prescribed by reformers. Yet it should not be assumed that all unintended consequences are undesirable.

The remainder of the chapter considers, in turn, unintended problems and unintended benefits in the reform process around local governance. The reform process has led to some perverse effects but it has also created the conditions for a redefined role for local authorities in community governance.

A further section considers what lessons might be drawn by future reformers in the light of the experience of the 'revolution' of the past decade or so. A concluding section outlines the structure of the remainder of the book.

New management: hierarchy, market and network prescriptions

'New management' has proved difficult for academics to define, a point explored by Lowndes in her chapter in this volume. There is a growing consensus that the difficulty in part reflects the phenomenon that the doctrines of new management are diverse and perhaps even contradictory. Hood (1995, p. 108) argues that 'many of the critics of contemporary public administration are hostile to conventional bureaucracies, but beyond that what seems to unite them is what they are *against*, not what they are *for*' (emphasis as original). Indeed on that basis Hood goes on to reject the idea that 'new management' is a new global paradigm (as claimed, for example, by Osborne and Gaebler, 1992) on the grounds that it lacks the coherence and consistency to be a paradigm and that it has been applied so differently in various national settings that it could hardly be described as global.

New management advocates do have a clear view of the 'enemy' : traditional bureaucracy and governmental decision-making. The problem with established structures is that they are too inward-looking. They focus on the needs of producers and other actors in the system and not enough on the needs of the public as consumers and citizens. Traditional decision-making structures are perceived as cumbersome and discouraging of creativity and imagination in attempts to tackle social and economic problems. The emphasis is on observing rules and ensuring that procedures are followed and not enough on results and outcomes.

The strength of new management is that few would deny there is some substance in the critique it offers of traditional bureaucracy and government. Another strength – although from an academic viewpoint a source of incoherence – is that new management offers a variety of solutions to the perceived problems of traditional bureaucracies. The diverse prescriptions of new management can be grouped under three headings reflecting broad categories of social coordination (Stoker, 1991, ch. 11; Hood, 1995).

The 'hierarchy' prescription emphasises the value of exemplary and visionary leadership in the reform of public services. The underlying aim is to create a more effective organisation. It also places its faith in the development of strategic visions, both within and across service areas, and values state-of-the-art information technology in providing both information for effective management and better service to the public.

The 'market' prescription emphasises the virtues of introducing direct market competition to provide public services or market-like mechanisms to regulate relationships between 'purchasers' and 'providers'. The emphasis is on replacing relationships controlled by hierarchical structures with contractual ones. Performance-related and individually oriented employee reward structures would also be deemed appropriate. The overarching commitment is to develop a stronger and deeply embedded customer orientation and at the same time create an efficient organisation capable of keeping down public spending.

The 'network' prescription argues for the development of longer-term, non-hierarchical relationships which bring together service providers and users on the basis of trust, mutual understanding and a shared ethical or moral commitment. The emphasis is on empowering both providers and users so that they can work effectively in partnership to achieve shared goals. Quality in service delivery is a key goal. An interest in longer-term 'relational' contracting is characteristic.

Even from the brief descriptions provided so far it is clear that the different prescriptions of new management are in tension with one another. Hierarchical leadership is not easily made compatible with a market-driven system. The former model emphasises the wholeness of the organisation and its linking together under a shared vision. The latter model encourages fragmentation, competition and a culture based on separate 'cost centres'. Competition and formal contracts are not easy bedfellows with the trust and shared ethics of networking. Networks build up partnerships and encourage shared learning. Markets require distance in and 'arms length' regulation of relationships.

The contradictions of new management are not just experienced at an abstract level of analysis but it is clear from various ESRC research projects that they are experienced on the ground by practitioners. Lowndes comments in her chapter on how one interviewee put it: 'we are learning to accommodate mess'.

The research shows that many managers in local authorities have drawn on each of the models and found some way to combine them together, suited to their own organisation and circumstances. Managers have looked at the general prescriptions and attempted to adapt a 'management recipe' which meets the external pressures of legislation and financial restraint and yet makes 'most sense' in their environment. There is a complex process of 'trial and error' and institutionalisation surrounding various reforms. Abstract ideas are translated into practical things 'to do' within their own organisations and in this way managers ease through the tensions and contradictions in the 'new management' models on offer to them. There is a similar process in the spread and development of management thinking in the private sector.

The working through of hierarchy, market and network new management prescriptions is a theme throughout this book. What also needs to be stressed is the particular nature of the British public sector reform programme we are examining.

Public sector reform: the British style

'New management' has developed in different ways in different countries. It is not a global phenomenon but rather it has a particular character in each country in which it has been adopted. Moreover it has not been universally followed. It is important, therefore, to establish the particular character of British public sector reform. Three things mark it out: the scale of change that has been attempted, the centrally imposed and regulated nature of the change and the hyperactive quality of the reformers with one initiative closely followed by another. Only New Zealand rivals the British commitment to this style of public sector reform (Walsh, 1995).

It is difficult to overestimate the scale of change that has been attempted across the public sector. Central government, national quasi-governmental bodies and the NHS have all felt the full force of new management (see Farnham and Horton, 1996). Local governance institutions, local authorities and also other public, private and voluntary sector providers have felt the impact of new management across the full range of service areas and on cross-cutting corporate issues. The chapters in this volume bear out the influence of new management in almost all aspects of local governance.

The British style of change under the Conservatives was of reform initiated and driven by central government. Legislation and ministerial guidance, lectures and threats, backed by centrally sponsored consultants, characterised the reform process. The prominent role of central government in the British case is remarkable not only because of the intensity of its involvement but also because of the manner in which it has sought to develop and implement its programme. The Conservative governments from 1979 kept consultation to a minimum and attempted to impose their reform in a top-down manner. The vision was outlined, structures and financing incentives changed and compliance carefully monitored and checked. The strong hand of central government is a theme in all the chapters of this volume.

A final element in the British style of public sector reform is hyperactivism. Both Thatcher and Major governments launched initiative after initiative in a seemingly endless round of interventions. Dunleavy (1995, p. 61) comments:

> Hyperactivism occurs when politicians individually and collectively gain 'points' with the media and party colleagues from making new initiatives almost for their own sake. They see much less political mileage in efficiently implementing existing policy lines, and none at all in critically evaluating their party's previous policy initiatives.

The legislative load in relation to local government alone between 1979 and 1997 resulted in hundreds of Acts and this is not counting the numerous initiatives, projects and schemes that did not require legislative establishment.

There are probably a number of factors at play which explain why Britain has developed a distinctive style of public sector reform (see Hood, 1995; Dunleavy, 1995). The unitary character of British government and the weakness of any relatively autonomous intermediate tiers allow great scope for domestic policy implementation. The structure of Parliament in the context of sustained majority for one party allows the passage of legislation at a rapid pace and largely unrevised. The fervour of the Conservatives stimulated by Thatcher's political style and influenced by 'New Right' thinking helped to provide ample justification for public sector reform. The arrogance of a political and administrative elite and its search for a new role as its 'grip' on international and economic matters slipped as a result of imperial decline and economic change may also be a factor. Under the guise of a commitment to 'new management', ministers and civil servants alike have shown a greater interest in the 'low' politics of public sector reform in comparison with their previously strong focus on the 'high' politics of foreign affairs and economic policy.

It is not possible to explore further the history of public sector reform here. It can simply be noted that the particular style of British public sector reform has had implications for the unfolding of the process of change. These implications are explored in the next section.

The rhetoric of change, implementation gaps and unintended consequences

The study of processes of change associated with purposive social interventions poses a number of critical questions. What has changed? What is 'new'? What has failed to be achieved? Where are there implementation gaps? What unexpected has happened? The style of British public sector reform makes these questions especially important but very difficult to answer.

A top-down, centrally-driven reform process encourages a rhetoric of change in which the extent of change may be exaggerated. To appease the centre, local authorities and others charged with implementation may over-claim the extent of reform. The centre may over-promote a few exemplary cases in order to provide lessons to others and justify its claims of success.

Analysts need, in the light of such factors to sustain a healthy scepticism about the extent of change. Some things may not have changed all that much. Doogan, for example, in this volume shows how despite the sustained pressure of compulsory competitive tendering since the late 1980s, the basic structure of national wage bargaining and trade union negotiation has remained in place in local government. Morgan and colleagues, again in this volume, argue that although networks of public and private sector actors have developed around economic development, much of the dynamic in the system was provided by central government initiatives and funding programmes. The networks need not have an independent local life.

Assessing how and what has changed, as Pollitt and colleagues point out in their chapter, raises a host of difficult-to-resolve issues. There are three main reasons for caution in assessing the impact of reforms. First, definitions of what is 'better' are inherently contestable. What constitutes better-quality education, for example, is a matter of continuing debate. Second the nature of a reform process means in many instances that the nature of that task and the associated categories of data that are collected change. Constructing reliable 'before' and 'after' measures in such circumstances is problematic. Finally, there are major attribution problems. Given the complexity of the management and operation of local government, to single out a particular reform as responsible for a particular effect is difficult. The discourse is more in terms of a balance of probabilities. In many respects the judgement about the success or failure of a particular new management initiative is as much a matter of faith as proof by good works (Pollitt, 1995).

The style of reform adopted by the Conservatives has led many to comment on the implementation gap they have experienced (Stoker and Mossberger, 1995). Marsh and Rhodes (1992) show how across a range of policy areas there has been a substantial gap between ambition and what has been achieved in practice. The top-down process favoured by the Conservatives requires the following conditions to be effective:

1. knowing what you want to do;
2. the availability of the required resources;
3. the ability to marshal and control these resources to achieve the desired end;
4. if others are to carry out the tasks, communicating what is wanted and controlling their performance.

The difficulty confronting any government adopting such a top-down approach is that the above conditions are likely to be extremely difficult to meet. In short an implementation gap is to be expected because the centre's objectives may become ambiguous and inconsistent, instruments to achieve compliance are absent or limited and other interests may actively oppose or at least be reluctant participants in the process of change. Rhodes and Marsh (1992, p. 9) go as far as to argue:

> Implementation problems may be common to all governments but they were uniquely severe for the Conservative Government because it insisted on an inappropriate (and ill-considered) model of implementation.

The lesson to be drawn is that change imposed from above is likely to have a patchy and complex impact at the implementation stage. The various findings from the ESRC Local Governance Programme certainly bear out that lesson.

In many respects the findings of the ESRC Programme are in tune with the scepticism of the academic community in its response to the rise of new management. There is evidence of the reforms having little or no effect in some areas. There is evidence of implementation failure. Yet academic analysts have pointed to another issue: the unintended consequences of reform. Indeed a general theme in much of the academic literature is that new management reforms not only underachieve but are prone to producing perverse effects which overwhelm or contradict the original ambitions of the reformers.

A host of writers make a powerful case that new management initiatives are prone to such 'policy failures' (Dunleavy, 1995), may solve one problem and simply create another (Peters, G 1993) and are ill-advised 'leaps in the dark' (Jordan, 1994). Hood (1995) takes the argument a stage further by suggesting that the contradictions within new management create the conditions for its failure to provide the basis for a new stable paradigm:

> There would seem to be at least two serious obstacles to the emergence of a stable new paradigm in public management. One is the difficulty that mutual repulsion among different recipes for good public management poses for arriving at a convergent solution. The other is the propensity of polar approaches to public management to turn into 'fatal remedies' producing the opposite of the intended effect. (Hood, 1995, p. 111)

Hood's argument is that the tensions between what were termed earlier the prescriptions of hierarchy, market and network mean that the resolutions reflected in recipes adopted by particular local authorities will fall apart. New management is also prone to 'side effects' (in which additional things happen to those intended) and 'reverse effects' (in which the opposite to what was intended happens), according to Hood because of the inherent weaknesses in its nostrums.

As Hood (1995, p. 112) notes, 'unintended effects of policy and management measures . . . are a recurring theme in social science'. On this point he is supported by Hirschman (1995, p. 61), who comments that 'social scientists are of course forever (and properly) eager to detect unintended effects of social actions and policies'.

However Hirschman goes on to argue that social scientists should beware of the drift in thinking that labels all unintended outcomes as undesirable. Some unintended effects may be socially positive. Further he argues that there is an inherent conservatism in an over-exaggerated concern with perverse effects. The concept of unintended effects should open our eyes to the uncertainty and open-endedness of the world and not to a train of thought that leads to the conclusion that all social intervention is doomed to failure. He concludes : 'many unintended consequences of public policies are not necessarily perverse, and that perverse effects are often such that some positive margin survives their onslaught' (Hirschman, 1995, pp. 63–4; see also Hirschman, 1991).

In the next two sections we take the discussion forward. First, consideration is given to the unintended problems caused by new management. However, in the light of Hirschman's comments, we consider, second, whether there may have been any unintended benefits of new management. What does the evidence from the ESRC Local Governance Programme tell us about such issues?

The unintended problems of new management

Hood (1995, p. 113), following Sieber (1981), identifies seven 'conversion mechanisms' as 'ways in which social interventions can turn into "fatal remedies"'. Evidence from the ESRC Local Governance Programme can be found for each conversion mechanism. New management reforms have produced side-effects or reverse-effects that were not intended. There is evidence of various perverse effects produced by new management interventions.

The first and perhaps most widely commented-on way in which new management has had a perverse effect is labelled 'functional disruption' in which a 'system' need is neglected or threatened by a reform. In the case of local governance, system concerns have been expressed over three issues: (1) fragmentation (Alexander, 1991; Stewart, 1993); (2) loss of accountability (Stewart, 1992); and (3) a decline in the public service ethic (Pratchett and Wingfield, 1996).

Market competition and the contract culture are seen as having exacerbated or stimulated these system-level problems. The evidence from the ESRC Local Governance Programme finds some substance in these concerns. Pollitt and colleagues in this volume suggest that self-management and opting-out initiatives in education, housing and health care may have brought some advantages in terms of managerial accountability and efficiency but have generally led to decreased system coherence and a weakening of broader democratic accountability. Heald and Geaughan, in this volume, note how the commercial confidentiality claims made in the course of private finance initiatives can undermine the basis for public accountability. Lowndes, Mackintosh and Ranson and colleagues, again in this volume, also express and reflect concern about the 'knock-on' implications of market-style reforms in terms of, respectively, democratic accountability, fragmentation and the overall impact on the systems of governance.

A second concern – labelled 'exploitation' – is focused on the way a reform creates openings for opportunistic behaviour which threatens or undermines the ambitions of reformers. Again there is evidence of opportunistic behaviour associated with new management initiatives provided by the ESRC Local Governance Programme. Ranson and colleagues in this volume deals with the issue of schools 'dumping' or 'creaming' 'desirable' pupils in order to improve their overall performance. Barnes and colleagues describe how in community care managers play the 'user card' – making reference to manipulated or controlled user-opinion – in order to justify their policy decisions. Mackintosh deals with the case of a finance department's payroll service – with substantial fixed costs associated with IT – threatened by 'devolved' units in the local governance system being able to opt out to get a better deal for themselves but in the process undermining the overall service.

A third way in public sector reforms can go 'off the rails' is labelled 'goal displacement', in which a technique developed as a means becomes an end in itself. Performance measures designed to improve the quality of a service can become an end in themselves with processes being reformed in order to meet particular performance targets without contributing to an overall better service. Benyon and Edwards, in this volume, argue that the coherence of and commitment to crime prevention initiatives is weakened by demands on police forces to achieve against 'reactive' performance measures such as arrest, detection and clear-up rates. Heald and Geaughan show how a concern to get private finance involved can distort the assessment process of projects leading to a downplaying of environmental and other concerns in order to get a scheme that can attract private finance and generate revenues. The Skye Bridge project is their case in point. Reid in this volume describes how local authority housing organisations have adopted the techniques of competition and partnership working as matters of financial necessity but remain wedded to a fairly traditional view of the role of public housing and local authority provision. Adopting new management has enabled the housing service to survive but it has not produced the customer-orientated and flexible provision envisaged by reformers.

A fourth way in which reform plans can be tripped up is described as 'provocation' where in seeking to increase compliance, the reform measure has stirred up a great deal of antagonism and in so doing led to a loss of cooperation. Doogan's analysis of the impact of compulsory competitive tendering, in this volume, provides evidence of how local authorities and trade unions have worked around the legislation and developed counter-strategies to centrally imposed regulations. As one private contractor remarked to Doogan: 'if a local authority does not want the work to go out, it won't go out – and there is nothing that you can do about it'.

A fifth arena in which reforms can go wrong is where labelling a particular achievement as valuable leaves non-achievers feeling demotivated or excluded. The terminology used by Sieber and Hood is 'classification'. Again, Ranson and colleagues, in their study of market competition in schools, indicate such problems do exist. The competition for urban regeneration, economic development and other prizes can also leave those authorities and organisations that are unsuccessful demotivated. Riley, in this volume, notes the difficulties caused in the further education and training field by the emergence of a substantial group of losers in competitions for funds.

A sixth potential unintended consequence of social reform is 'over-commitment' in which intervention becomes self-defeating because it exhausts resources in pursuit of objectives that cannot be achieved. An illustration here is the tendency for new management reforms to be 'over-hyped' which in turn leads to disillusion. Lowndes and Pollitt and colleagues in this volume show that while claims for the virtues of new management are often expressed in exaggerated terms, the reality of reform is rather more mundane and piecemeal. The reform process has proved neither a triumph nor a disaster. There is evidence of greater managerial creativity but also evidence of continuing and new frustrations among local managers.

Finally reforms can be undermined by the phenomenon of 'placation' through creating the illusion of success and going forward while in practice real problems are left untackled. Riley, Benyon and Edwards, Morgan and colleagues all suggest that in, respectively, training, crime prevention and economic development, the burst of networking and partnership formation characteristic of the new local governance has not resolved underlying problems. Benington, in this volume, suggests that increased euro-networking by some authorities creates the illusion of a dynamic and entrepreneurial local government but in practice the activity is pretty marginal, the preserve of a few authorities, and even within these authorities involving only a small interlocking 'cosmopolitan' elite of members and officers.

The unintended benefits of new management

The ESRC Local Governance Programme provides evidence of the unintended perverse effects of the top-down introduction of new management. Yet equally each of the chapters in this volume contains some evidence of success, of gains as well as losses. Taking each of the new management prescriptions in turn it can be conceded that some gains reflect the impact of better strategic leadership, market-like relationships and improved networking. What can in addition be argued is that some of the improvements – noted by practitioners and researchers alike – reflect unintended benefits of the reform process. The new management reformers have stumbled across three principles of organisational development and change. Ultimately new management has stimulated a new vision of the role of local government.

The first force unleashed by new management but not entirely as intended might be described as the *disharmony* principle. The essence of this principle has a long tradition in political thought and is associated with the 'separation of powers' championed by Montesquieu and others (Held, 1987, pp. 55, 60; Sartori, 1997, pp. 86–91) and the broader constitutional concern with ensuring appropriate 'checks and balances'. Goodin (1996, p. 38) captures the essence of the idea in terms of institutional design:

In designing mechanisms of group decision-making, we are often well advised to designate someone formally to serve as 'devil's advocate', challenging our shared presumptions and telling us things we do not want to hear, as a way of improving the quality of the overall decision that we reach.

The establishment of mechanisms to express disharmony is essential to forcing change. The idea of encouraging, even institutionalising, disharmony does not sit easily with at least two of the three prescriptive frames of new management. Neither the hierarchy nor the network frames would endorse the principle. The market prescription with its focus on competition recognises the value of challenge but sees it as a process external to the organisation. What has given the disharmony principle a cutting edge in public sector reforms is the internal establishment of a range of 'devil's advocates' almost as a by-product that have challenged the organisation's previous ways of working.

The establishment of distinctive 'client' voices, separated processes of service audit and more broadly the purchaser–provider divide has created a focus for change and new thinking within local authorities and other public providers. As Mackintosh shows in this volume, the disharmony principle in operation can prove an uncomfortable experience for local authority personnel used to operating in a less challenging environment. What, however, is also clear is that the establishment of separated and distinctive voices – internal to the organisation – to express users' needs or test the quality of service has proved a valuable catalyst for change as the chapters by Lowndes, Pollitt *et al.* and Barnes *et al.* indicate.

The second principle from which the reform process has gained is the way in which local authorities and other public bodies have been forced to justify their role, actions and performance in public. Goodin (1996, pp. 41–2) refers to the value of the *publicity* principle in institutional design, 'requiring as a test ok all institutions and institutional action that they be (at least in principle) publicly defensible'. Having to render an account – justifying and explaining in different levels of open public forums – has proved a valuable element in the reform process. Words and more broadly shifts in language are powerful tools. As Lowndes and Mackintosh argue, the formal and informal discourses set in train by new management have had a restructuring impact. Talk of customer orientation, user needs, performance measures can to an extent be seen as a gloss or veneer on old institutional practice but the very use of the language opens the organisation to internal and external challenge in a way that was not available before. Barnes and colleagues, in this volume, show how the rhetoric of user involvement has opened out limited but increased potential for influence for disabled and mentally ill people with respect to community care.

A third motor of change which the reform process has stumbled across can be labelled the 'revisability/robustness' principle. To survive, institutions need both to respond to changes in their 'factual or evaluated universe' and at the same time to be 'capable of adapting to new situations: not brittle and easily destroyed by them' (Goodin, 1996, pp. 40–1). The challenge of New Management has produced effective reform not necessarily because of the validity of its prescriptions but because the threat that it posed has unleashed forces of creativity and innovation previously dormant in local authorities and other service providers. As Desveaux (1995, pp. 33–4) argues, crisis can be a stimulant to change in bureaucracies and can in turn encourage bureaucracies to seek to more actively influence and construct their environment. A sense of crisis helps to generate policy ideas that 'would otherwise not be considered technically feasible or politically desirable'. It also 'involves generating new skills, changing decision-making processes, improving administrative co-ordination and communication, and . . . even altering standards and incentives for hiring'.

There is plenty of evidence in the chapters in this volume, especially those by Lowndes, Pollitt *et al.*, Mackintosh, Ranson *et al.*, and Reid, of organisations feeling the pressure to change in order to survive. As one local authority informant told Lowndes: 'the questions that are being asked in almost every service are challenging, confrontational and basic. The major question is whether local government can and should continue in its present form.' What is also clear in the chapters by Benyon and Edwards, Morgan and colleagues, Riley and Benington and Harvey is that local authorities have responded to the challenge of change by developing new foci for activity and new skills and processes. The phoenix rising from the ashes of traditional local government is community governance.

The rise of community governance

A paradox in the developments of the mid-1990s is that although local authorities have found many of their traditional service delivery tasks squeezed by financial constraints and challenged in their management by competitive tendering, opting out and performance targets, they have begun to develop a leadership role in some of the broader challenges of community governance. Economic development, urban regeneration, environmental protection, community safety and anti-crime measures, anti-poverty initiatives, preventative health case schemes and anti-domestic violence projects are among the areas where local authorities have sought to take forward the vision of community governance. Central government has encouraged such developments in part through giving local authorities particular responsibilities in areas such as environmental protection and in part through a series of funding schemes that enable local authorities to bid for monies to undertake initiatives in these areas in partnership with other stakeholders.

The starting point for community governance involves setting a wider role for local authorities. The task is not the delivery of a discrete set of services but a concern with the well-being of the locality for which they are responsible. The key issue is not how to deliver services but rather how to maximise the well-being of the citizens of the area. A second feature of the new vision is its emphasis on working in partnership with other actors and agencies. The aim is not only to work with others in the formulation of shared strategic objectives but also to work with and through them to achieve implementation. A third feature of community governance is a concern with outcomes of service delivery and diverse interests within any community. Community governance asks: who gains, who loses?

There have been problems, as Chapters 8–12 show. Developing a shared vision is challenging and it is even more demanding to find the capacity and resources to implement projects, and get things done. Too many projects because of the time-limited nature of their funding, have lacked the staying power and capacity to make a major long-term impact. Tensions have been identified in the relationships between key stakeholders. There remains a degree of uncertainty about the legitimacy and appropriateness of local authorities in the broader agenda of community governance.

It is in some respects ironic that the pressures unleashed by new management have encouraged local authorities to rethink and redefine their role. The vision of the new management reformers aimed at more efficient and customer-oriented service delivery by local authorities has been challenged by a broader vision of a new community governance.

For community governance to become established, local authorities will have to develop further new ways of working and reaching out to their communities. Painter (1996) argues that local authorities need to develop a targeted approach. Given the range of appointed bodies it is vital for local authorities to be strategic and focus on a few key agencies that can be influenced and that have a major impact in the locality. Beyond developing a strategic approach local authorities will need to release and mobilise the resources of influence at their disposal: legal, regulatory, financial, physical, staff skills and expertise and information. Releasing resources to take on the wider role of community leadership may in turn require changes in internal organisational and decision-making structures. Time and organisational space for both officers and councillors will have to be created so that local authorities can pursue concerns beyond their immediate service delivery responsibilities.

Above all local authorities will need to extend and enrich the legitimacy they have as elected bodies by demonstrating a capacity to develop new ways of engaging with local communities and developing the local democratic discourse. There are a considerable range of options for democratic innovation within existing legislative arrangements (open forums, scrutiny committees, citizens' juries, market research and so on). Local authorities might be able to utilise further existing planning responsibilities to provide the umbrella for drawing together different stakeholders in a number of policy areas (transport, community care, economic development, land use and so on).

There would also be a need for central government to encourage or even instruct the appointed bodies to cooperate with local authorities in the development of community coordination. Ted Cantle, Chief Executive, of Nottingham, suggests that quangos should be placed under a 'duty of partnership'. They would have to consult the local authority(ies) in the area they operated. They would have to reconcile their plans with those of the local authority as far as possible. They would be expected to cooperate with specific partnership projects in their local area. Strong messages of support for an integrating role for local authorities from central government could transform the environment for partnership.

Ultimately local authorities might need some statutory backing for a more developed community governance role. The Labour government elected in May 1997 has begun to take up this challenge.

Public sector reform has been about creating a leaner and more responsive service delivery system. However there is alongside such developments a growing vision and practice of local authorities which takes them beyond a role in service delivery. The term 'community governance' has been used to capture the embryonic conception of a shift in the purpose and rationale of British local government.

The future of reform?

The ESRC Local Governance Programme has provided an assessment of a dramatic era of change for local government in Britain. From the early 1980s through to and beyond the mid-1990s, four consecutive Conservative governments drove through a nationally inspired and centrally imposed management revolution. The impact of reform has been considerable, it has been argued, but not always in the manner intended by the reformers.

The Labour government elected in May 1997 has shown a strong interest in continuing the process of management change and reform for local government. It has, however, committed itself to developing a different reform style, one that is more experimental, involves more consultation and is less top-down. As Labour's Local Government and Housing Minister, Hilary Armstrong (1997, p. 18) comments: 'it is vital that we lose the skills of battle and find the skills and organisation of partnership . . . One of the ways in which we can achieve this is to meet and discuss ideas and policies . . . another is through the use of pilot studies to develop and test ideas in the real world. To ensure lessons are learned before we legislate – not after.' It would appear that Labour has already latched on to the major lesson of the ESRC Local Governance Programme which is that change imposed in an across-the-board heavy-handed, non-consultative manner is prone to considerable implementation failure and the production of a range of unintended effects.

Yet this judgement needs to be qualified. While the restructured Department of the Environment, Transport and the Regions – the central government department broadly responsible for local government matters – is led by ministers committed to a more experimental, 'bottom-up' style, other departments and ministers appear less willing to give up the prescriptive, regulatory style developed by the Conservatives. In education, employment and welfare policy arenas, legislation and ministerial interventions seem designed to ensure that local government delivers the national objectives of the new government. In the words of the Education Minister, Stephen Byers, local authorities 'have to prove they are part of the solution rather than part of the problem'. It would appear that New Labour is interested in revisiting some of the tough reform principles stumbled across by the Conservatives.

The substantial shocks to the system of local government in Britain have delivered a reformulated and challenging redefinition of local self-government. The value of local government is not to be judged by the services it delivers (the dominant paradigm of the 1970s) but by its capacity to lead to a process of social, economic and political development in our communities. The vision and virtue of this community governance role is widely accepted. What is far from clear is whether central government – under the new Labour leadership – is prepared to will the means for local authorities to take on that role. They might, in turn, suggest that it is not clear to them that most local authorities have the will, capacity and imagination to open themselves up in the way the community governance role demands. The debate on local self-government in Britain runs the risk of becoming stuck on a catch-22: to perform, local authorities need to be trusted but to be trusted, they need to perform.

Outline of the book

The next four chapters provide a general assessment of the impact of new management on local governance. In Chapter 2 Vivien Lowndes examines how and to what extent change has occurred. She reveals a complex pattern of formal and informal processes in the implementation of reforms. She also shows the limits to change and argues that many traditional practices continue to exist alongside new elements. In a concluding section she notes how councillors – and with them the process of formal democratic accountability – have been left behind by many of the changes. Ambiguity and uncertainty over the future role of councillors is a by-product of the processes of change set in motion by new management.

In Chapter 3 Christopher Pollitt and colleagues look at the experience of devolved management, and in particular, that of 'opted-out' schools, hospitals and former local authority housing providers. A general assessment of the impact of change leads to a balance sheet of gains and losses. Managerial accountability and autonomy have been enhanced and along with them more activity and more initiative. However the changes have not necessarily delivered better performance to the public and have exacerbated the difficulties of public accountability and system coordination.

Kevin Doogan's focus in Chapter 4 is on the impact of competitive tendering, especially on employment patterns and rights within local government. The study shows that there were between 1979 and 1994 almost 300 000 job losses. Male full-time employment in various manual occupations was the greatest casualty. The analysis, however, also provides evidence of continuity in bargaining arrangements and a continuing role for trade unions. It also demonstrates the salience of various local factors in explaining the impact of contracting-out.

Maureen Mackintosh in Chapter 5 explores the impact of competition, devolved management and contracting on the culture and understandings embedded inside local authorities. She identifies two economic 'discourses' that have risen in response to new management. The 'trading' discourse sees the new world as driven by contracts in which units within and outside the local authority pay for each other's services at an agreed price. This discourse is closest to the 'official' ideology of the market version of new management. However Mackintosh finds a second discourse which she labels 'public business' which has emerged in part because of the fears of fragmentation and the collapse of a distinctive public service ethic. The 'public business' discourse argues for developing a longer-term and more flexible set of relationships between the purchaser and a few providers.

The next three chapters examine each of the main service areas that are the responsibility of local government. Stewart Ranson and colleagues in Chapter 6 deal with the education service. They show that schools – even those in deprived communities – have responded to the forces of competition and the ideas of new management in a variety of positive ways. Yet 'the market' in which these schools are forced to operate is powerful enough to destroy many of the achievements and efforts of individual schools. Without the protection of more system management, provided by a democratic process organised by local authorities, Ranson and colleagues argue that schools will continue to fail those from more disadvantaged areas.

Marian Barnes and colleagues, in Chapter 7, focus on community care and the push for greater involvement of user groups. They conclude that collective action on the part of mental health service users and disabled people has the capacity to challenge the assumptions of welfare professions. Yet much of the rhetoric about a greater concern with customers can be seen as empty in part because resources are missing to match demands and the process of participation itself can be manipulated by professionals for their own ends.

Housing is the focus of Chapter 8 in which Barbara Reid draws on her research into the reframing of housing services. She argues that the management of housing has undergone substantial reform with a huge explosion of partnership and joint-working schemes. The fundamental public sector orientation of housing managers has remained intact but they have adapted their ways of working in order to survive.

The next four chapters show how in response to the demands from a variety of sources local authorities have begun to develop a broader community governance role. John Benyon and Adam Edwards, in Chapter 9, provide an account of local authority involvement in crime prevention partnership based on case studies in Leicester and Nottingham. They argue that such arrangements have considerable value in bringing together a range of public agencies with community groups. The main difficulty they identify is the fringe character of such initiatives so that their coherence and durability is undermined by short-term, competitive funding arrangements.

Kathryn Riley explores in Chapter 10 the emergence of networks of provision in further education and training, drawing on a case study of South East London. Networking has considerable benefits in bringing together various agencies to provide more effective service to the public. However it does have some costs in terms of the time and effort it takes. There are also problems around the accountability and transparency of network relations.

Kevin Morgan and colleagues in Chapter 11 examine networking for local economic development. They argue that networking is deceptively simple in principle but profoundly demanding in practice. They compare the networks around economic development in South East Wales and the West of England. They conclude that although networks have grown over the 1990s neither region could be considered close to the model of an integrated and cohesive 'networked region'. The hand of national government looms large over much economic development activity. However the authors identify a number of pointers to successful networking. They also argue that the vertical networks fostered by the Welsh Office hindered the development of horizontal networks in South East Wales, disempowering to a degree local actors and giving a more hierarchical character to the Welsh networks than those that emerged in the West of England.

John Benington and Janet Harvey explore in Chapter 12 the role of local authorities in Europe. They examine the range and variety of networks in which local authorities are involved. They consider why local authorities join transnational networks. They explore how networks work and what are the main tensions associated with them. Finally they provide an overall assessment of the impact of euronetworking.

In Chapter 13 David Heald and Neal Geaughan examine the private financing of public infrastructure. They argue that there are some good arguments for using private financing but also some arguments which are less satisfactory. In the latter category, for example, is the view that private finance enables projects to go ahead that the public sector could not afford while in practice what is generally happening is a delay in the cost to the public purse, not a saving. The chapter proceeds to explore the incentives and effects created by private finance schemes. The authors conclude that there is a danger of being carried away with the rhetoric of private finance and not drawing the proper lessons about its appropriate use.

In Chapter 14 Jeffrey Stanyer winds up the book by reminding us of some of the lessons of history. Problems of fragmentation, complexity and policy failure are not new. Local governance has, he argues, always been a messy business.

The final drafts of the chapters were mostly completed in the summer of 1997. With the election of a Labour government in May 1997 the world has moved on with considerable pace. The chapters in this book have little to say directly about this new world. However they do analysis the Conservatives' reform schemes and provide food-for-thought for would-be reformers.

2 Management Change in Local Governance

Vivien Lowndes

Introduction

This chapter discusses findings from research into management change in local governance. Its distinctive contribution to the literature on management change lies in:

- linking levels of analysis, through an exploration of change in management ideas, management within individual organisations, and the management of interorganisational networks;
- analysing the political implications of management change, through an exploration of consequences for local citizenship and democracy;
- developing new theoretical tools for analysing management change, through an exploration of the utility of 'new institutionalism'.

The chapter starts by introducing key concepts from new institutional theory, indicating how they can be used to analyse management change in local governance. The main part of the chapter brings theory and research findings together to present four core arguments about the changing management of local governance:

- There is no one 'new management' but different, and potentially contradictory, streams of ideas and practices.
- There is no one process of 'management change', as individual organisations and service sectors respond differently to system-wide triggers for change.
- Management change is non-linear, involving continuities between old and new approaches, movements forwards and backwards, and change at different levels.
- Management change has political significance, impacting upon relationships between government and citizens at the local level.

Analysing management change in local governance: building new institutions

The 'common sense' in putting institutions at the heart of political science and public administration has led to a curious silence surrounding the theory and method of institutionalism (Rhodes, 1995, p. 55). Institutional analysis traditionally restricted itself to descriptive and historical accounts of constitutions and government structures, and displayed a distrust of 'theory'. The emergence of 'new institutionalism' provides an opportunity to develop a theoretically informed approach to understanding institutions and institutional change in local governance. However, while the 'old' institutionalism was distrustful of theory, the 'new institutionalism' has frequently been dismissed as overly abstract, even arcane (Jordan, 1990, pp. 183–4). There are many different 'disciplinary' varieties of new institutionalism; confusion over terminology and levels of analysis is rife (Lowndes, 1996a). We adopt a multi-theoretic approach based on key organising concepts. We set out our key concepts below, indicating how they can be used to analyse management change in local governance.

Institutions as sets of formal and informal rules

As Fox and Miller (1995, p. 91) note: 'Institutions are habits, not things'. We are not concerned here with 'brass name-plate institutions' (Fox and Miller, 1995, p. 92) but with the formal and informal rules that guide and constrain people's action. Such rules provide information on others' likely future behaviour and on sanctions for non-compliance (Knight, 1992, p. 17). Rules embody a 'logic of appropriateness' which simplifies the choices facing actors (March and Olsen, 1989, p. 38). Institutions embody power relations by privileging certain courses of action over others; they express 'patterns of distributional advantage' (Knight, 1992, p. 9). Rules may be consciously designed and clearly specified (contracts, job descriptions, structure plans, operating procedures, terms of reference) or take the form of unwritten custom or convention (as in aspects of professionalism, departmentalism, commercialism or user orientation). New institutionalism allows us to analyse 'new management' in terms of several different streams of new rules (with formal and informal elements), each embodying particular sets of power relations and impacting on managerial and political behaviour in different ways.

The institutional environment

Institutions exist at different levels (Ostrom, 1986, p. 21). They may be specific to a particular organisation (or part of an organisation) or shared in a specific community or locality, or exist society-wide. Fox and Miller (1995, p. 92) note that institutions exist 'within' and 'between' organisations, 'as well as under, over and around them'. In local governance, society-wide rules impact upon what happens in individual organisations, either formally through legislation and regulation, or informally through 'organising templates' (DiMaggio and Powell, 1991, p. 13) derived from education and training, cultural preferences, the media and public opinion. Locality-specific institutions ('how things are done around here') may either reinforce or undermine institutional templates circulating in the wider environment (Clegg, 1990, p. 163). The influence of the local institutional environment is potentially of particular importance in local governance where the legitimacy of organisations may derive at least in part through their 'rootedness' in local communities. A focus on institutions allows us 'to blur, and make permeable, what are often taken to be the fixed boundaries' between local government and its environment (Fox and Miller, 1995, p. 92).

Institutionalisation and deinstitutionalisation

Institutions are associated with stability and tend to adapt slowly (North, 1990, p. 83). Purposive attempts at reform are hard to achieve (March and Olsen, 1989, p. 91; Brunnson and Olsen, 1993, p. 3). Because institutions reflect patterns of distributional advantage, institutional change is likely to be resisted by those who benefit from existing arrangements or see new rules as hostile to their interests (Knight, 1992). At the same time, rooted as they are in culture and convention, informal rules may persist in the face of change in formal rules (North, 1990, p. 36). 'Old' and 'new' institutions coexist, often in tension. In local governance as elsewhere, institutional change is not achieved simply through producing structures or rule-books; it requires a reworking of what is considered 'appropriate' – it involves processes of 'social production' (Stone, 1989). Institutional change involves both strategic action to create new rules and incentives, and norm-governed behaviour to embed and sustain new rules over time (Lowndes, 1996a, pp. 194–5). New institutionalism allows us to analyse management change in terms of many disparate processes of institutionalisation and deinstitutionalisation, whilst also highlighting the inherently political nature of institutional change.

The value of the 'new institutional' approach for our research can be summarised as follows:

- the focus on underlying institutional frameworks facilitates analysis across organisational boundaries and across the management/politics divide;
- the focus on component institutions avoids reifying 'new management' as a more or less coherent entity existing in opposition to 'old management';
- the understanding of change in terms of many and disparate processes of institutionalisation and deinstitutionalisation avoids a 'once and for all' perspective which sees 'change' as an event with a prescribed outcome (which can either succeed or fail).

'We are learning to accommodate mess': four propositions about management change in local governance

In this section of the chapter we bring theory and research findings together in presenting four propositions about management change in local governance.

1. There is no one 'new management' but different, and potentially contradictory, streams of ideas and practices

Narratives about the 'new management' are frequently structured 'through sets of dualities and oppositions' (Clarke and Newman, 1997, p. 48). Features of 'old' and 'new' management are listed in pairs, with the assumption that management change involves a (beneficial) movement from one column to the other (see Osborne and Gaebler, 1992, for example). Typical pairings include: centralisation versus decentralisation, producer versus user orientation, hierarchy versus empowerment, uniformity versus diversity, monopoly versus competition, and so on. Our research suggests that this form of debate imposes an artificial coherence on both 'old' and 'new' management and overemphasises the discontinuity between old and new.

Our survey of practitioner journals confirmed that public management is being rethought. The survey showed that the coverage of management items *per se* (as opposed to policy or professional issues, for instance) had increased dramatically between 1980 and 1992 (the number of articles almost doubled). The spread of 'managerialism' in a broad sense was captured in a remark by one of our interviewees: 'We use this word 'management' – that is not something that would have been understood before in any kind of positive sense.' The journal survey also pointed to the danger of referring to a single 'new public management'. Using our sixfold classification of management topics (see p. 38), it was clear that the focus of management debate varied over time and between service areas. 'Commercialism' and 'user involvement' were the topics that received the most attention, with coverage of the former increasing dramatically after 1987, and coverage of the latter being strongest in health and social care journals.

However, as Fox and Miller (1995, p. 107) note: 'Ideas are brought into 'good currency' through interaction in a particular setting with others.' When we surveyed practitioners to find out about the management ideas that they themselves felt to be important, a mixture of 'traditional' and 'new' elements were stressed. The ideas accorded the highest priority were: accountability to the public; efficient service delivery; delivering services to a high professional standard; and listening to users. Different clusters of opinion were evident; for example, those who emphasised ideas around efficiency, control and performance were less likely to emphasise user and accountability ideas. The survey also asked practitioners about the management innovations that were actually being put into place in their organisations. It was clear that some of the ideas felt by respondents to be particularly important were not in practice well-developed (notably user involvement). The survey results also showed that some of the ideas which were at the heart of the debates reviewed in the journal survey had limited support among practitioners as approaches to local governance management (notably internal markets and purchaser/provider splits).

Interviews in our case study organisations demonstrated that managers saw a clear distinction between 'old' and 'new' management at the level of words and ideas. Asked to list key words to describe each, the 'old' management list invariably included: departmentalism, professionalism, paternalistic, centralised and bureaucratic. The 'new' list typically included: devolution, enabling, customer-or user-focused, strategic and corporate. However, in commenting on the new management in practice, interviewees drew attention to the persistence of 'old' cultures and practices, the sheer volume of different new initiatives, and the conflict between different elements of the 'new management' – for instance, between corporate strategy and devolution, internal markets and 'flexibility', economy and quality, 'right sizing' and 'caring for staff'.

Our research shows that, despite the coherence implied by many analyses, 'new' management in practice is a complex and differentiated body of ideas and practices. Some 'new management' ideas lose currency quickly and are dismissed as 'fads' ('business process re-engineering' was offered as an example); other ideas are rapidly accepted and acquire the status of 'common sense' (like cost centre management and elements of 'customer care'). Some aspects of the new management are relatively easy to implement (such as aspects of performance monitoring), while others require a much longer time-frame and are more likely to be adapted in implementation (such as internal trading systems). Changing circumstances and changing ideas mean that 'new management' has not stayed still but evolved and acquired new dimensions – it is dynamic and internally differentiated and, moreover, contains potentially contradictory elements.

Academic commentators have responded to the shortcomings of the 'dualism' of dominant narratives on management change by proposing a series of models or stages in the development of 'new management' (see, for instance, Pollitt, 1993; Ferlie *et al.*, 1996; and Walsh, 1995). Our own research revealed three key orientations among local authorities pursuing management innovation: an efficiency orientation (stressing 'value for money' and performance measurement); a market orientation (stressing contracting, externalisation and internal trading); and a user and/or community orientation (stressing 'customer care', 'citizen's charters' and forms of user and community involvement) (see Lowndes, 1997, pp. 52–3). However, it was also clear that the organisations we looked at were seeking to combine a wide range of new management initiatives, both in the context of internal management and inter-agency working. As one interviewee put it: 'We are learning to accommodate mess.' Different authorities used different 'organising images' to express their own particular blend of new management initiatives – for example, 'strategic enabling', 'business-like management', 'positive management', and 'community leadership'.

Rather than using the language of models – which has become ever more complicated as numerous 'hybrids' are introduced (see Ferlie *et al.*, 1996; or Hood and James, 1996) – it is more helpful to see individual local authorities as adopting particular 'management recipes'. Adapting Whitely's (1992, pp. 120–7) concept of 'business recipes', our argument is that different arrangements of management rules and norms become institutionalised and relatively successful in different contexts. As we shall show below, 'recipes' vary because they are 'embedded' in different patterns of social relations (Granovetter, 1985), relating to the distinctiveness of local contexts. Such recipes are not static. Organisations change their particular mix of management ideas and practices over time, depending on the success or failure of previous innovations, and on changing internal and external pressures – including legislation, resources, community demands, and managerial and political preferences.

2. There is no one process of 'management change', as individual organisations and service sectors respond differently to system-wide triggers for change

The particular 'management recipes' taken up by different local authorities relate in part to the internal differentiation of the 'new management' as a body of ideas, and in part to the varied responses of different local authorities to system-wide triggers for change. Our research showed that internal power relations (and the role of leadership), service characteristics, and 'locality effects' (Urry, 1987) all played a role in structuring local authorities' repertoire of responses to management change.

The importance of external triggers or stimuli to management change was highlighted in all the local authorities we studied. Most frequently mentioned was the impact of compulsory competitive tendering (CCT), although Local Government Review was important in some organisations. At the level of ideas, interviewees referred to the 'transfer of private sector ideas' (often via consultants) and – more importantly – the impact of a 'general push' from central government to 'do things differently'. As one chief executive put it:

> The questions that are being asked in almost every service are challenging, confrontational and basic. The major question is whether local government can and should continue in its present form. There are strong pressures to move away from direct provision to an enabling, monitoring, standard-setting organisation. These pressures are both direct in the form of legislation and indirect in the form of financial structures.

A general climate of resource constraint was identified as a trigger to economy- and efficiency-oriented management change, and for some local authorities a specific resource crisis was a spur to significant change. Resource constraint was, however, also identified as an obstacle to forms of management innovation which required investment. One interviewee explained the positive and negative aspects of central government pressure thus:

> In the past we were badly managed and useless in direction. Local government was given a good shake-up by the Tories and it did a lot of good. It's continued so far that it became destructive. At first we got leaner and meaner. Now we've just got a lack of resources.

While legislation, resource availability and new management ideas were, on balance, the main drivers for change, we found that the susceptibility of organisations to change and the direction of that change were intimately linked to 'internal' factors. The strength and style of leadership were highly significant, with the appointment of a new chief executive being the most common internal trigger to management change. 'Newness' itself was seen as a trigger to change – often a new chief executive was appointed specifically to 'shake things up' and was able to play this role because he or she was not embroiled in 'things as they are'. The same argument applied to the role of other new senior appointments, and to the use of external consultants to 'drive change'. As one interviewee explained: 'The people inside the system just don't know what needs to be done – they just can't see it.' One of the women chief executives we interviewed felt that 'newness' was only part of the story. Because traditional management practices are embedded in broader social relations, effective leadership required a challenge to fundamental norms of behaviour:

> If you want to introduce change, then you need women and black people on the staff who have no investment in the old system and who will want change and be prepared to threaten the old male culture.

The identification of change programmes with particular individuals had negative effects in some of our case study organisations. Management innovations were perceived as individuals' 'hobby horses' or as being the business only of the particular department whose leader had initiated the programme. Some interviewees felt the power of paid officers to stimulate major change in the organisation was 'undemocratic', as it did not always have councillors' support or – more often – their full understanding. In some local authorities, management change was very definitely politically led, associated with a change in party control, or in dominant factions of the controlling party, or by the selection of a new leader .

As suggested by the journal survey, our case study research showed that the embedding of new management approaches varied across services. This related to differences in each service's existing institutional framework – in levels of technology, degrees of professionalisation, legal and regulatory arrangements, resource demands, and the nature of relationships with the public – and to their power resources within the organisation as a whole. Different innovations were prioritised in different departments and various departments played the role of pioneer or pilot (notably housing, education and 'blue collar' services subject to CCT). Some services had a reputation within their organisations, or even across the board, for being resistant to change (notably planning and environmental health). Within individual organisations, some departments maintained an 'island' status, working according to their own rules, relatively unaffected by change programmes. Sometimes this was part of a change strategy – that 'difficult' departments should be left to themselves until some later date; sometimes it was a result of outright resistance or studied inertia on the part of those concerned. The different stances of different services to management change presented particular challenges in the context of cross-service and inter-agency working.

Patterns of leadership and relationships between different services and departments are all part of a local authority's 'organisational biography' (Lowndes, 1997, p. 47). Our research showed that long-held organisational traditions – for instance, of strong leadership or public participation – and the continuing influence of past events affected local authorities' susceptibility to, and interpretation of, change. A particular organisational event (like a budget crisis or a political scandal) was often decisive in positioning a local authority with respect to management change. Local authorities also appeared to go through a 'life cycle' of innovation, involving periods when they were more or less susceptible to change. A local authority's general image of itself – and the way it was seen by the outside world – seemed to affect the impact and interpretation of external triggers to change.

It was clear from the research that local authorities are not free-floating entities but are grounded, to a greater or lesser extent, in their localities. 'Objective' characteristics of a locality – its social and economic character, its geography, its demography and settlement patterns – placed particular demands (and opportunities) upon a local authority. 'Subjective' elements of the local environment, like political and civic traditions, local conventions and the cultures of different communities, were also important. Locally-specific 'ways of doing things' were sometimes formally articulated and vigorously promoted as part of a local authority's identity and heritage; sometimes they impacted subtly and informally upon perceptions of what was possible and impossible, desirable and undesirable (Lowndes, 1996b). One local authority we studied explained that partnership approaches 'fitted' in their area because of the large number of active community groups; another favoured neighbourhood decentralisation because of the distinct identities of different communities in its area; another stressed working with local firms, in the context of a sharp increase in unemployment.

We noted earlier that locally-specific institutions may either reinforce or undermine institutional templates circulating in the wider environment (Clegg, 1990, p. 163). Our research shows how the impact of external pressures for change (from legislation, resource constraint, and new management ideas) is mediated within individual local authorities by organisational politics and 'biography' and by the objective and subjective characteristics of different services and different localities.

3.   Management change is non-linear, involving continuities between old and new approaches, movements forwards and backwards, and change at different levels

We argued above that practitioner debates tend to overestimate the discontinuity between old and new management approaches. There is also a tendency to portray 'change' as an event which can either succeed or fail. Such accounts tend to stress the role of individual 'champions' and the importance of 'communication' and 'culture building'. There is a strong assumption that 'hearts and minds' can be won over and that change is a positive-sum game – all can be 'winners' once convinced to 'sign up' (see, for instance, Moss Kanter *et al.*, 1992; Peters, T. 1993; Osborne and Gaebler, 1992). Findings from our research challenge these assumptions, pointing to the tenacity of 'old' management practices and vested interests, and the difficulty of 'embedding' change within an organisation.

Our interviewees identified the persistence of old management practices as a barrier to change, pointing particularly to 'departmentalism', 'professionalism' and 'bureaucracy'. Our practitioner survey found that 62 per cent of respondents perceived a conflict between old and new management approaches in their organisation. At the same time, it was clear that many practitioners did not regard the persistence of traditional approaches negatively. The practitioner survey found, for instance, that 'delivering services to a high professional standard' was among the top four management beliefs. Our interview data revealed that 'old' approaches were seen as having strengths as well as weaknesses (for example, stability, clear roles, an emphasis on basic services); and 'new' management as having weaknesses as well as strengths (for example, 'macho style', fragmented and finance-led).

Interviewees commented on the tendency of traditional approaches to 'incorporate' new management ideas. 'Old' approaches were seen as tenacious, their persistence leading to the 'bureaucratisation' of management change and the implementation of new ideas in 'old' ways, often directly undermining their purpose (for example, 'top-down', control-oriented approaches to devolution). The tenacity of old approaches related to actors' vested interests in maintaining them; frequently new language simply obscured old practices – terms like 'corporate' and 'strategic' were often a guise for continued centralisation, and the territorialism of departmental structures was often simply subdivided into the mini-fiefdoms of new 'service units'.

The change process was managed differently in different organisations, depending on particular leadership styles (political and managerial) and levels and patterns of resistance. 'Cultural' strategies (via 'launches', image-making, 'visioning' and 'communication') were combined to varying degrees with the manipulation of incentives (via reorganisations, regradings and redeployment/redundancies). Informal as well as formal methods were used to circulate new ideas. As one chief executive explained:

> We have to recognise the informality of the place . . . What we'll do is set up a rumour line to try and get the facts across. You have to live with rumour and it shows that people talk to each other.

In many organisations, introducing new management involved an equal mixture of commitments and threats. One local authority policy statement explained that:

> It is vital that everyone who works for the Council is equipped and willing to promote these core values in their everyday work. The

Council will ensure that all current and new staff are informed, trained and supported in the implementation of these values. Any failure to follow these values will damage our relationship with our customers and will not be accepted.

The vast majority of respondents to our staff survey believed there had been real change in the way their organisation operated, with 94 per cent disagreeing with the statement that 'nothing had changed'. However, interviewees showed an awareness of different levels of management change, distinguishing between change in the 'formal' and 'real' organisation, at the 'surface' and 'deeper down', and between 'leaders' and 'laggards' among departments. In some cases, 'surface'-level change was seen by interviewees as constituting an end in itself ('You have a lot of words and terminology bandied about – but it's rhetoric and people often don't understand'); in other cases, different levels of change were seen in terms of stages of a long-term process. Across the board, interviewees were keenly sensitive to the difference between putting new structures and language in place and the process of developing and 'embedding' new codes of conduct. 'Communication' about the reasons and nature of change was not enough. As one officer explained: 'Newsletters come down for staff to explain what is going on, but their tasks haven't really changed'. Interviewees noted a relative lack of attention paid to developing 'systems' to support new management approaches. A middle manager explained that:

Beneath the top layer of big issues like budgets and service plans, there are no mechanisms to translate things down the hierarchy. Heads of Service come out of meetings and have to make things happen, but have no method below them for doing so.

Interviewees made judgements about 'how far' their organisation had gone in the change process – 'about half-way there' or 'stalled for the moment' – but also recognised that different parts of the organisation moved at different speeds and that there were reversals as well as movements forward. The costs of 'undoing' old ways of doing things were sharply recognised by many. One interviewee commented that management change was 'very uncomfortable and alien to the way that we've been brought up'; another noted that 'there is a breakdown of social values in the way that people treat each other – reorganisation is very traumatic'. In our practitioner survey, 80 per cent of respondents felt that staff were resistant to change.

The research shows that 'old' management ideas and approaches existed alongside new developments, either in parallel or direct contradiction. Innovations often became effectively 'incorporated' – reinterpreted and implemented in ways which did not threaten the existing institutional framework. It was clear that institutional change could not be achieved simply through introducing new language and structures: it required a reworking of what is considered 'appropriate' within the organisation. As the council statement cited earlier noted, staff needed to be 'informed, trained and supported' in the introduction of new rules, and clear about the sanctions for non-compliance. The institutionalisation of new rules and the deinstitutionalisation of old ways of doing things was clearly a long-term process, with movements forwards and backwards, and change at different levels.

4. Management change has political significance, impacting upon relationships between government and citizens at the local level

Debates about management change and local democracy are frequently held in isolation from one another. As one of our interviewees put it: 'There is a problem of how you emphasise the governance side. So far we have developed the service dimension.' The research shows, however, that management change has far-reaching implications for local citizenship and democracy. New management innovations present a new set of constraints and opportunities for the exercise of local democracy and citizenship, just as the institutions of bureaucracy and professsionalism have traditionally structured local politics (Lowndes, 1995; Prior, Stewart and Walsh, 1995).

Management change in local governance has been associated with a view of local democracy in terms of responsiveness to service users (see the seminal statement by Waldegrave, 1993). Our research found that management innovations had mixed effects in terms of access. In our practitioner survey, a large majority of respondents (87 per cent) felt that their organisations had succeeded in improving their responsiveness. Interviewees stressed the contribution of new facilities (like one-stop shops bringing together different front-line services) and a new 'customer first' ethos in many services. There was some scepticism about an emphasis on 'public relations' rather than better or extra services. Those who were involved in delivering services via interorganisational networks were concerned that: 'If we make the bureaucracy too 'flexible', the people out there don't know who to deal with and how.'

Our research highlighted the difficulties encountered by front-line staff in seeking to meet rising public expectations as access to services improved: rationing decisions were becoming both harder (as demands increased) and more transparent. Some interviewees simply expressed frustration at being 'attacked' by angry members of the public, while others were concerned about the equity issues raised by a stress on responsiveness to individual 'customers'. How could the local authority meet its responsibilities to the wider community and particularly to those groups least likely to take advantage of new access opportunities (like elderly and disabled people, non-users of services and some members of minority ethnic groups)?

The stress on 'direct accountability' to the public led to tensions between local authority members and officers. Some interviewees were concerned that they were making what should be member-level decisions; others felt that members did not understand (or respect) the new emphasis on responsiveness. As one officer explained: 'You have to put the customer first now – but elected members are dubious. They say you shouldn't ask the public questions, because of the answers you'll get.' There was a perception in many of our case study organisations of members and officers occupying separate cultures, with the former seen as conservative, out of touch, and self-seeking. An interviewee argued that:

> They [the councillors] are in a Morris Minor, while the officers race past. The members have no positive view, they are always stopping things. They won't let go . . . They have a very parochial view . . . they're only interested in the person who talked to them last.

In addition to innovations to improve access for individual service users, local authorities were experimenting with new forms of citizen consultation and participation. Sometimes these were linked to specific issues or service developments (often stimulated by legislation); sometimes consultation was being developed as part of a general attempt to 'open up' the council's decision-making, or to exercise 'community leadership' within an organisationally more fragmented system of local governance. The research highlighted the different views held by different organisations (including different parts of the same local authority) on what constituted meaningful participation. In social care, there was a marked contrast between housing officers' focus on project-based consultation and social services' concern to consult on 'process' issues. At the same time, a user group we interviewed expressed frustration that 'the way things are structured doesn't enable personal issues to become policy issues'.

The growing need to operate through inter-agency networks brought great scope for conflict and communication difficulties among 'representatives' of different types – councillors, board members, managers exercising devolved powers, and community or voluntary sector leaders. The legitimacy of each type of representative came from a different source – from election, appointment, professionalism, or common experience. These different legitimacies or mandates were not always mutually recognised, and there was a lack of clarity about their relative value. In social care, for instance, health officials mistrusted the 'political' approach of the local authority, while councillors were reluctant to share power with health 'quangos'. The 'representativeness' of community leaders, user groups and voluntary organisations was frequently questioned by our interviewees.

Some councillors we spoke to felt that their democratic mandate should secure them a 'first among equals' role in inter-agency settings. The research highlighted, however, the difficulties encountered by councillors in operating within networks – they could not rely on 'normal' forms of officer support or on clear direction from their party group; decision-making timetables were out of 'synch' with council committee cycles; and skills of listening, influencing and negotiation were all-important. Tellingly, there was little evidence of special training or back-up for councillors to allow them to operate effectively in inter-agency settings. We did observe that, by default, officers were becoming the dominant force in such decision-making environments.

Our research showed considerable confusion – indeed a widespread sense of crisis – concerning the role of local authority members. New management was according local authority officers new roles in terms of securing 'responsiveness' to individual service users and consultation with communities; it was also casting officers in the lead role within the ever-increasing number of inter-agency partnerships and contractual relationships. Members' roles in relation both to service delivery and strategy were being squeezed. In the words of one of our interviewees: 'The elected member's position is being eaten away at both ends.' Many of the councillors we interviewed recognised the challenge that faced them but bemoaned the absence of appropriate 'mechanisms' through which to develop new roles. As one leader explained:

> Members are going through an identity crisis about what their role is
> . . . We are elected by people to deliver things. People think that we

control things that we don't . . . The agencies are the ones with power and we try and work with them . . . We recognise the need to talk to people in a more hands-on way. We need to find mechanisms that give a reasonable representation of what people think. We don't really have ways of doing this.

Our research demonstrated little evidence of any fundamental review of political institutions. At the same time it was evident that many 'new management' developments (particularly around 'responsiveness' and inter-agency working) were having 'political' impacts, in the sense that they were destabilising power relations within the locality – relations between elected members and paid officers, between local authorities and non-elected bodies, and between the users and providers of local services. New approaches to local governance management were, in effect, restructuring constraints and opportunities for the exercise of local democracy and citizenship. The research highlighted the need to develop new political institutions in local governance, given the palpable sense of crisis over members' roles and deep-seated tensions around responsiveness and consultation.

Conclusion

Drawing upon a robust theoretical framework and extensive empirical investigation, this chapter has shown that, despite the coherence implied by many analyses, there is no one 'new management' nor one process of management change. 'New management' is made up of different, and potentially contradictory, streams of ideas and practices. These elements are combined by different organisations into relatively stable and distinct 'management recipes'. While external triggers to management change are important, the susceptibility of individual authorities to change, and the direction of that change, is related to internal power relations and to local sensibilities and circumstances.

The research shows that management change is a non-linear process, involving continuities between old and new approaches, movements forwards and backwards, and change at different levels. Change is not produced simply through introducing new language and structures; it involves a reworking of what is considered 'appropriate' behaviour. The research shows the 'knock-on' effects of changing management behaviour on local political processes. New management approaches present a new set of constraints and opportunities for the exercise of local democracy and citizenship. The research highlights the importance of developing a 'new politics' alongside the 'new management' in local governance – a challenge expressed in the Labour government's White Paper, *Modern Local Government: In Touch with the People* (July 1998).

About this study

Thanks are due to the other members of the research team, namely the late Kieron Walsh, Kathryn Riley, Jackie Woollam and Paula Smith.

The four elements of our multi-level research strategy are outlined below:

- Changing ideas about public management were researched through a content analysis of four leading practitioner journals: *Local Government Chronicle, Community Care, Education and Health Service Journal*. We studied issues of the journals for the first six months of the following years: 1980, 1984, 1988 and 1992. Articles, including editorial material, were coded into six categories: commercialism, user involvement, evaluation, strategy, collaboration and staffing. We analysed change in terms of the coverage of 'management' issues in general, the significance of different management topics over time, and variation between service areas (see Walsh *et al.*, 1996).
- A questionnaire was used to survey individual local government managers about their views on how their organisations should operate, on how management innovations were actually being introduced, and on the impacts of management change. Working in 31 case study organisations (see below), we received 210 completed questionnaires, in which managers made judgements about 33 structured statements (see Walsh *et al.*, 1995).
- Case study analysis was used to compare 'old' and 'new' management within individual organisations, to study the triggers, barriers and process of management change, and to consider impacts in terms of service delivery and local politics. Our 31 case study organisations were all in the process of introducing specific innovations. There was a rough balance in terms of political control, type of authority and regional spread (within England). Interviews were undertaken with 230 officers and members (individually and in groups), and supplemented by analysis of key documents.

- Management within interorganisational networks was researched through locality-specific studies in education, social care, waste management and community safety. Interviewees were identified on a rolling basis, as the shape and focal points of each network became clear. We interviewed 150 individuals from public, private and voluntary and community organisations (see Lowndes and Riley, 1998).

3 Letting Managers Manage: Decentralisation and Opting Out

Christopher Pollitt, Johnston Birchall and Keith Putman

This chapter examines the experience of opting out in health, education and housing services. After an initial discussion of the issues raised by opting out and the context in which it took place the chapter addresses a series of questions about the impact of opting out. Did it increase management freedom? What impact was there on accountability? Did the performance of the organisations improve?

Issues context

Since the 1980s the UK public sector has been restructured to a greater extent than any other OECD country except New Zealand (OECD, 1995, p. 135; Pollitt *et al.*, 1997). Two central themes in the UK reforms carried out by the Conservative administrations of 1979–97 were decentralisation ('power and responsibility down to the local level') and better management ('freeing managers to manage'). These themes have been reflected throughout a very long list of changes in central and local government, among non-departmental public bodies, in the National Health Service (NHS) and elsewhere. They were most powerfully combined and exemplified in central government's attempts to create a series of self-managed local service delivery organisations – grant-maintained (GM) schools, NHS trust hospitals and housing associations formed by large-scale transfers of what was previously local authority housing. These three types of organisation provided a focus for our research.

The Conservative governments of the 1980s and 1990s imposed a 'maelstrom of legislation' upon local government (Burns *et al.*, 1994, p. 3). Ministers believed that the freedoms given to self-managed organisations, combined with an increasingly competitive environment, would generate major improvements in performance.

The creation of these new types of local unit raised a whole series of questions. In our research we were able to look at only a subset of these. We attempted to:

(a) discover what were the consequences of opting out for the managers in a sample of schools, hospitals and housing associations;
(b) compare the experiences of these managers with those of similar organisations which had not 'opted out' or which had done so only reluctantly and/or well after the new policies were put in place;
(c) enquire what arrangements were in place to ensure public accountability, and how well these seemed to be working;
(d) explore what information and views were available concerning the performance of self-managing organisations.

The ideas driving the reforms

At the very generalised level of ministerial speeches, decentralisation and better management were frequently made to sound as though they were straightforward and self-evident virtues. In these broad terms the 'message' given by ministers was clear. The previous arrangements were inflexible, inefficient, bureaucratic and unresponsive. Delegating or decentralising authority and strengthening local management would lead to more locally responsive services and greater creativity and productivity.

In the academic literature, however, 'decentralisation' is seen as a complex concept with a long history and a wide variety of possible meanings (for example, Burns *et al.*, 1994; Mintzberg, 1979). The connection between decentralisation and the introduction of market-type mechanisms (MTMs), enthusiastically pursued by the Conservative government, is recognised as problematic (Burns *et al.,* 1991; Fitz *et al.,* 1993; Hoggett, 1996).

In our own work we found it useful to recognise a number of distinctions within the broad concept of decentralisation. Defining decentralisation as the spreading out of formal authority from the few to the many, one can immediately draw a distinction between decentralisation within a given organisation (for example, by allowing middle-management authority to spend money or hire staff without consulting the budget chief or director of personnel) and decentralisation from one (hierarchically superior) organisation to another (hierarchically subordinate) one (for example, when a GM school acquires authority previously wielded by an local education authority (LEA).

We refer to this latter type of decentralisation (from one organisation to another) as devolution.

A second important distinction is between political decentralisation and administrative decentralisation. Political decentralisation (or devolution) entails the transfer of representative political authority from one group of representatives to another. This may occur through the devolution of power from central governments to elected local authorities. Alternatively, political devolution may involve some delegation of political authority from elected local politicians to local citizens (for example, to a committee of local tenants or to parents elected to the governing body of a school). By contrast, administrative devolution involves no shift in formal political authority but rather the delegation of specific powers and responsibilities from one level of management to another. An example would be the delegation of a specific spending authority (up to a specified sum) from a central finance division to a local manager. The creation of executive agencies in central government offers a large-scale example of administrative decentralisation in so far as the setting up since 1988 of more than 120 'next steps' agencies employing more than 70 per cent of the Civil Service has not, according to the government, changed the constitutional position and responsibilities of ministers (O'Toole and Jordan, 1995). Whilst decentralisation has taken place in many European countries during the 1980s and 1990s the UK is unusual in the extent to which it has favoured administrative over political reforms (Pollitt *et al.*, 1997).

A final distinction is that between vertical and horizontal decentralisation. Most discussions of the topic refer only to vertical decentralisation, where authority is passed 'down the line'. However, as Mintzberg (1979, p. 186) has pointed out, authority can also be spread out horizontally. Mintzberg defined horizontal decentralisation as 'the extent to which non-managers control decision processes'. Thus, for example, if within a hospital, doctors gained authority over decisions which had previously been controlled by managers, that could be seen as a piece of horizontal decentralisation.

Drawing on the above distinctions it is possible more accurately to classify the forms of decentralisation covered by our research. NHS trusts were examples of vertical administrative devolution. No additional political authority was passed to the trusts, political control being represented by the Secretary of State for Health, as previously. Trusts represent devolved administrative authority, however, because they are new, corporate institutions which are no longer 'part of' a district health authority.

The creation of GM schools involves the transfer of both administrative and some political authority. Administrative powers that were formerly exercised by the LEA now become a matter for the head teacher and the board of governors. However, some shift in political arrangements also took place. The line of political accountability that used to run through local councillors and the local Education Committee was severed. In its place was put the board of governors.

Finally, housing associations formed through large-scale voluntary transfer (LSVT) also entail the devolution of authority from local authorities to new organisations. This devolved authority includes both administrative and political components. As in the case of GM schools the line of political accountability through the local council is broken.

These more sophisticated ideas about decentralisation and devolution helped us to understand that what was happening in the three sectors was very far from being just a simple downward flow of vertical decentralisation and devolution. In respect of the vertical dimension what seems to have happened is that political and administrative bodies with jurisdictions for particular geographical areas have devolved some of their authority downwards to local service providers. Thus local authorities handed over authority to housing associations and GM schools (as well as to LEA schools operating LMS (local management of schools)) while district health authorities ceded authority to NHS trusts. But further 'up' and 'down' the vertical chain of authority centralisation took place – not in every instance, but frequently and significantly. On the 'up' side central government enlarged its own repertoire of authority and/or gave additional authority to bodies it controlled (such as the Funding Authority for Schools and the Housing Corporation). To give some brief but important examples, in education the centre took control of the curriculum and, through the 1988 Education Act, gave itself many additional specific powers. In the health sector the powers of the NHS Executive were considerably strengthened, partly at the expense of the regional health authorities. As many of the respondents in our four NHS trusts pointed out, central government has continued to develop initiatives which impose very considerable new constraints and requirements on all NHS Trusts. Two clear examples were the new arrangements for junior doctors' hours and training and the imposition of Patient's Charter indicators throughout the NHS. In housing centralisation was less marked, but the role of the Housing Corporation began to grow as that of local authority housing departments dwindled. In short, local autonomy was offset by new measures of central government control.

If, instead of moving up the vertical dimension we move down, further centralising tendencies become clear. Within the newly autonomous schools, hospitals and housing associations, the authority of top management over less senior staff seems in many cases to have grown. Enhanced financial and personnel powers strengthened the hands of chief executives and head teachers *vis-à-vis* their staff.

Our research has also identified some evidence that the sphere of professional autonomy from line management (that is, the horizontal dimension) has continued to shrink. In schools teachers were used to being managed by head teachers so the vertical line was already fairly clear. In housing departments professionals such as architects and quantity surveyors were never particularly interested in general management anyway, and tended to focus their attention on development work. The new freedoms of housing association status have not fundamentally altered this orientation but have, if anything, increased both the vertical and horizontal authority of the Chief Executive. In NHS Trusts the testimony of the consultants we interviewed varied somewhat, but none of them suggested that managerial authority over their activities had decreased. On the contrary, a number asserted that there was now much more active management of the medical staff.

The reforms themselves

NHS trusts were the flagships of the reforms announced in the 1989 White Paper *Working for Patients* (Secretaries of State for Health, Wales, Northern Ireland and Scotland, 1989). Following the publication of the White Paper the Department produced a Working Paper on trusts which listed the advantages they were supposed to enjoy:

> They will have far more freedom to take their own decisions on matters that affect them most without detailed supervision from above. This new development will give patients more choice, produce a better quality service and encourage other hospitals to do even better in order to compete. (Department of Health, 1989, p. 3)

Later in the same document a list of more specific benefits was presented (pp. 5–6). The powers and responsibilities of NHS Trusts were to be formally vested in new and separate legal corporate entities, run by boards of directors.

The first opted-out GM school opened in September 1989. Over 50 clauses of the 1988 Education Reform Act were concerned with opting out. GM schools opted out of the control of their LEAs in order to become separately incorporated institutions funded directly by central rather than local government. The original opting-out process could be initiated either by the school governors or by 20 per cent of parents petitioning the governing body. Secret ballots of parents then determined whether the application for GM status would go forward to the Secretary of State for Education. Once a school achieved GM status the composition of its governing body changed so that it no longer included party political nominees. A GM school is able to invest money, acquire and dispose of property and enter into contracts with staff and with other agencies. In the process of policy development, however, some of the more radical features of the original concept of opting out were modified so that the differences between GM and LEA schools with LMS were lessened (Fitz *et al.*, 1993, pp. 25–7). After 1989, however, a number of changes took place which were clearly intended to enhance the advantages enjoyed by GM schools (Fitz *et al.*, 1993, pp. 29–31). Such detailed changes were continued up to the 1997 election – for example, during 1996 the government, faced with a decline in the number of schools voting for self-governing status, moved to allow GM schools to borrow against their assets. By November 1996 there were 1147 operating GM schools, of which 649 were secondary schools.

Unlike trust status in the NHS or grant-maintained status in education, LSVTs in housing were not the direct product of central government legislation. Rather they were a strategy devised by local authorities in response to central government legislation. Central government's own preferred strategy had originally been that of 'tenants' choice' but that policy was generally acknowledged to have been a failure. LSVTs proved much more popular, and the role of the Department of the Environment was mainly reactive – making up new rules to govern the transfers, partly in response to Treasury pressure to limit the numbers which could transfer in a given year. By the end of 1996 over 50 transfers had taken place, consisting of more than 223 000 homes and generating more than £3.6 billion in private finance.

The financial freedoms granted to housing associations (including the powers to borrow on their assets, to retain surpluses and to build up reserves) were particularly significant in a context where local authority housing departments were becoming more and more constrained by central government regulations. The 1989 Local Government and Housing Act made the housing revenue account responsible for paying housing benefits to council tenants and so central govern-

ment grant aid was once more needed. This enabled increased pressure
to be put by central government on housing management costs. On the
capital side, strict housing investment rules had made it impossible for
councils to go on building new homes. Finally, the right to buy for
individual council tenants continually reduced the stock and made it
difficult for authorities to meet their statutory duties towards the
homeless. After LSVT new tenants did not have this right.

The case studies

Because some of the information we were given was locally
sensitive we decided to identify each of the 12 fieldwork sites by
pseudonym, as follows:

> *Starling* – Small NHS acute trust hospital in the north of
> England. Fourth-wave trust
> *Pigeon* – Medium-sized NHS acute trust hospital in the same
> sub-region as Starling. Second-wave trust
> *Duck* – Medium-sized NHS acute trust hospital in the south of
> England. Second-wave trust
> *Eagle* – Large NHS acute teaching trust hospital in the south of
> England. Fourth-wave trust
> *Trout* – Local authority housing department where voluntary
> transfer had been rejected by a ballot of tenants
> *Pike* – A large housing association created by a large-scale
> voluntary transfer (LSVT) of housing stock from a local
> authority
> *Flounder* – Local authority housing department where volun-
> tary transfer had not been pursued by local councillors, follow-
> ing a preliminary testing of tenants' views
> *Carp* – Housing association created by LSVT [All four housing
> organisations were located in the south of England.]
> *Rabbit* – GM secondary school in the Midlands
> *Badger* – LEA secondary school in prosperous Home Counties
> town
> *Dog* – GM secondary school in Midlands inner city area (early
> opt-out)
> *Fox* – LEA secondary school in the same Midlands area as Dog,
> but in more prosperous suburban locality

Motives for opting out

In the health sector it was quite clear that local contextual factors were very important in influencing attitudes towards becoming a trust. The most prominent and frequently mentioned of these factors were:

(a) the quality of the previous relationship with the district health authority;
(b) the moves (or lack of them) towards trust status made by neighbouring acute hospitals;
(c) The state of internal readiness for autonomy, the degree of opposition from local consultants being one important element here.

Amid this diversity, by far the most frequently (and fervently) mentioned reason for seeking trust status was a negative rather than a positive one. The aim was to escape 'interference' from the district and/or regional health authority (Pigeon, Duck, Eagle). The quality of the existing relationship with the district health authority was quite a good predictor of the tendency to go for an early opt-out. The two hospitals which had waited until the fourth wave before applying for trust status had both been influenced by the result of the 1992 general election. After that, consultant opposition to Trust status had dwindled rapidly – it had become clear that a Conservative government was going to be in power for some time and hospitals that had not yet begun to apply for trust status began to worry about being left behind by those that had. At Eagle, for example, the doctors and managers were closely watching a number of other hospitals in the locality and consultant opposition had virtually evaporated once it was seen that others were becoming trusts and that an early Labour government was no longer a possibility. The other fourth-wave trust (Starling) was situated in a strongly Labour area and had been reluctant to put forward an application until the 1992 election (third-wave applications had had to be made just a few days before that election). Also the hospital was completing a sizeable capital investment programme and had decided that it did not want to leave the shelter of its district health authority until this was complete. The hospital was a relatively small one that had never regarded itself as a 'glamorous outfit' and the then chief executive had pursued a cautious, consultative style. Interestingly, a new chief executive was appointed to lead the shadow trust.

In the education sector it was interesting to note that the head teacher's opinion on the issue of applying for GM status had prevailed in each of the four schools where our research was conducted. In Rabbit and Dog the head teachers had been instrumental in orchestrating the change process, despite vigorous campaigns opposing the change of status. Indeed, at Dog the head had gone ahead despite a roughly 50/50 split between staff for and against. In Badger and Fox the heads had decided that caution was the better policy. In the former case relations with the LEA were good and both the head and deputy told us that there had been little or no educational political desire on the part of staff, governors or parents to opt out. In the latter case (Fox) the senior management team had been in favour of opting out but the local political climate had seemed to be against it and the head was reluctant to risk alienating parents. A vote against opting out could have created a serious rift between the school and the parents. In both the non-opted-out cases there was evidence that the LEA had become somewhat more responsive and supportive since the possibility of opting out had become a factor to be reckoned with. It was noticeable that fresh LEA investment projects had taken place or were in progress at both Badger and Fox.

Relations with the respective LEAs had been much poorer at the schools which had chosen to opt out. At one of these schools the LEA funding strategy had appeared to disadvantage the school, and the Head had become increasingly dissatisfied with local education policy. It had seemed that amalgamation or closure in the not-too-distant future was a possibility. The other GM school had definitely anticipated amalgamation (or even closure) and, together with the possibility of financial advantage, these considerations drove the campaign for GM status. The staff had been concerned at the proposed changes but had accepted the judgement of the head that the move was in the best long-term interests of the schools. The chairperson of the governing body had resigned, but without any public animosity. Interestingly, the head teacher who carried this through was not personally a believer in the principle of opting out and was opposed to the general tenor of the government's policy on education. Nevertheless, under the particular circumstances faced by his school he judged that GM status was the best route to survival. The immediate cash benefits of GM status had been appreciated at both Rabbit and Dog, but were probably insufficient by themselves to account for the original impetus to opt out.

The benefits of a change of status were probably more immediate, tangible and direct in the housing sector than in either health care or education. At both Pike and Carp councillors and managers were apprehensive about the increasing restrictions being laid on local authority housing departments by central government. They foresaw rapid increases in rents (in the case of Carp by as much as 50 per cent) and an increasing inability to undertake major repairs or new build. 'Everything was going against the local authority' (manager, Carp). On the other hand housing association status held out the possibility of cash relief and access to borrowing. From the managers' point of view there was also the fact that housing association status held out 'bigger money and a chance to improve their careers' (Pike).

On the other hand there were two main reasons for not going for LSVT. The first was a lack of political consensus (vigorous opposition by some Labour councillors and a lack of cohesion on the Conservative side in Flounder). Second, a negative vote by tenants or the expectation of such a vote can prove fatal. In Trout a tenants' vote went against the recommendation from the Conservative Group that the LSVT route should be adopted. Although the council had initially been in agreement it subsequently split, leading to conflicting information and arguments being presented to tenants and sufficient alarm among the latter for the vote to be lost.

Consequences of opting out: freedom to manage?

The great majority of the individuals we interviewed, across all three sectors, believed that local managements had gained greater autonomy by moving their organisations to self-managing status. Few believed that it was either desirable or possible to go back to the previous arrangements. In this important sense the policies of the Conservative administration since the late 1980s may be said to have achieved a considerable measure of success.

The benefits that were perceived to have derived from greater autonomy varied from sector to sector. In the NHS the financial benefits were thought by most to be meagre, but there was a real sense of relief that decisions no longer had to be cleared with allegedly bureaucractic district health authorities. A subsidiary argument – believable but hard to prove – was that many hospital staff now identified more strongly with their particular institution ('sink or swim together': Eagle, Duck, Starling). One clear gain was the ability that trusts had to reshape their own management structures (although repetitive reorganisations could easily lead to 'reorganisation fatigue'). Examples of the use of the new managerial freedoms were forthcoming, though they tended to be of modest scale and relatively mundane. Refurbishing the hospital entrance-way and retaining a trust's own kitchen service instead of having to go into the region's 'cook–chill' system were two fairly typical examples (Duck). The rapid contruction of a new geriatric ward was an example of a more substantial initiative. Towards the end of our research period more exciting examples, such as the development of hospital 'home care' and outreach services, began to appear. What had not occurred (at least by the end of our fieldwork period) was the kind of major developments of new services which some managers and consultants had hoped would be possible within the freedoms of trust status (Pigeon, Starling, Duck). The main reason for this was the general tightness of resources throughout the NHS. Decentralisation can be a vehicle through which local managers are accorded the doubtful privilege of performing cutback operations themselves rather than having them imposed from above (Hoggett, 1996, p. 25).

With respect to human resource management (HRM), the predominant mood appeared to be cautious or even sceptical. Duck was the most advanced site, in that it had managed to get a high percentage of its staff (except for the doctors) to join a performance-related pay scheme, while the remainder stuck to Whitley terms and conditions. Many of our respondents were of the view that trusts were being pressed to use their notional freedoms to set pay and conditions but did not really want to. One chief executive described the pay and reward side of the reforms as 'a total flop'. During 1995 central government pushed hard for the development of local pay deals in the NHS. However, the government's efforts to orchestrate the situation caused considerable frustration among many trust managements.

The financial benefits of self-management were much clearer in the education sector than in the NHS. If we look across the responses to all the questions that we put to GM and LEA schools the most frequent difference between them relates to comments about what one GM school head referred to as 'the major cash boost at the start' (Rabbit). However, it is important to note that this was a once-only injection implying that, once the money was spent, the freedoms of GM schools would not be strikingly different from the freedoms enjoyed by LEA schools under mature LMS systems.

A large number of the GM staff that we interviewed were of the opinion that the additional money had helped raise morale and improve performance (Rabbit, Dog). Senior staff in GM schools also emphasised the improvement in 'job satisfaction' as they were able to exercise increased responsibility, for example, in arranging contracts with outside organisations or in the purchase of materials from a local supplier instead of the authorised LEA suppliers.

Another important area was that of the development and mission of the schools. Whilst schools in the LEA sector were constrained by the organisational and strategic demands of being part of a corporate group of institutions, GM schools believed themselves able to respond and develop separately in a way that enhanced a sense of ownership and mission (Dog, Rabbit).

Both GM schools had stuck to basically the same pay and conditions of service as were being applied by the LEA. Head teachers in all schools acknowledged the value of rewarding good performance, but expressed concern about the dangers of performance-related pay. There was evidence of a 'softer' approach to HRM in the schools than in the NHS trusts. In the trusts managers were prepared to 'let go' staff who were no longer regarded as valuable, whereas in schools we found head teachers using their flexibilities in order to create new roles.

Some disadvantages of opted-out status were acknowledged by many of the staff we interviewed. There was a sense of loss of being part of a 'community of LEA schools' and, more practically, a sense of isolation from LEA amenities. It was evident that relations between a GM school and its LEA could vary considerably. In the case of Rabbit they were reasonably cooperative but in the case of Dog there had been mutual sniping and deliberate exclusion from LEA events.

Interestingly, there seemed to be little desire for further autonomy. Quite a few of the staff in the GM schools registered surprise that we should even ask such questions (Rabbit, Dog). Head teachers and members of senior management teams generally expressed the view that, whilst it was theoretically possible further to extend the autonomy of GM schools, this would be undesirable. Most respondents believed that it was necessary for reasons of accountability that all schools in the state sector, whether LEA or GM, should remain within a clearly defined framework.

In the housing sector the benefits of LSVT were both substantial and clear:

(a) an immediate cash injection and ongoing control over borrowings against a strong asset base, all subject only to monitoring by the lending institutions;
(b) following from this, the ability to pursue a vigorous housing developmen strategy, including improvement of existing stock, new developments and partnerships with local housing authorities;

(c) tangible change in organisational structures and cultures;
(d) increased tenant participation and representation;
(e) measurable improvements in housing management performance.

LSVTs got an immediate cash injection – several million pounds to undertake catch-up repairs on the existing stock, plus a rolling programme which would, in two or three years, add central heating, new double-glazed windows and sometimes roofs. In addition, they obtained low-interest loans based on their asset values, immediate grant aid via the local authority's capital receipt and a further annual housing association grant, together producing hundreds of new homes per year (Pike was already producing more than 500 and Carp about 200). The more aggressive of our two housing associations had begun new builds for several local authorities and had found it necessary to open regional offices. The contrast with the cash-strapped NHS trusts was sharp. Housing associations have become almost completely autonomous businesses. They have therefore needed to develop more business planning, more monitoring of cash flows and a regular system of meetings with lenders and local authority partners. The associations are also attempting to get closer to the 'customer' with satisfaction surveys and initiatives to foster tenant involvement. Hardly any of our respondents in the housing associations could identify disadvantages from opting out.

Consequences of opting out: local responsiveness and accountability?

Although local responsiveness was much emphasised in ministerial rhetoric concerning self-management, it is by no means clear that there had in fact been any major shift in this regard in any of our three sectors. Of course, much depends on how 'responsiveness' is defined. In this regard it is important to draw the distinction between, on the one hand, political decentralisation and, on the other, managerial or administrative decentralisation (Birchall, 1996). Of the three types of self-management covered by our research, only one (GM schools) could be construed as significant political decentralisation (in so far as GM schools are now responsible to boards of governors rather than an LEA). However, such evidence as is available does not seem to indicate that governing bodies have become any more 'representative' of parents and other local interests as a result of achieving GM status (Fitz *et al.*, 1993). In so far as the reforms contain a mechanism for improving responsiveness it is therefore managerial in character, that is, the model is that by giving local managers more authority and increasing the competitiveness of the environment in which the service-providing organisation operates, a situation will be produced in which those managers feel obliged to pay greater attention to the views of the users of their services.

It is also important to bear in mind that the three different sectors begin from different starting lines. Housing and education, though significantly different from one another, both start from a local authority environment in which broad supervision (and sometimes much more detailed intervention) by elected representatives was a constant fact of life. The NHS, by contrast, has never been run by democratically elected representatives.

It was striking how rarely the issue of public accountability was referred to by any of our respondents. Almost always this was an issue that we had to raise with them. When we did so, we encountered some highly critical comments about the performance of elected politicians under the old local authority system for schools. Some teachers at GM schools expressed relief that their new status had allowed them to 'escape from politics'. In the NHS, although local authority nominees had only played a limited role on the old district health authorities, a number of NHS managers nevertheless applauded the removal of this modest political influence. One manager at Starling was fairly typical when he said that 'the political members were often there to make political points rather than to improve health care'. At another hospital the chief executive, when asked to whom he felt the Trust was accountable, thought for a moment and then replied, reflectively, 'we're not accountable to anyone'. Overall, democratic accountability was a subject that was conspicuous mainly by its absence from the responses to our questions about the advantages and disadvantages of self-managed status. This was true both at the self-managing and the non-self-managing sites, across all three sectors.

Consequences of opting out: improved performance?

Our research shows that the connection between self-management and performance is by no means simple and that in many cases it is extremely hard to know whether performance improvements have resulted from the introduction of self-management. Many, but by no means all, of those that we interviewed believed that performance improvements had taken place, and this is an important finding by itself. However, the more we pressed questions concerning the evidence for significant or radical performance changes – and the links between performance change and self-management – the more complexities began to appear. In most cases it seemed that those who believe that self-management has significantly improved performance do so more on the basis of faith or general impressions than on a foundation of systematic, valid evidence.

There was plenty of evidence that activity had intensified – that more service users had been processed more quickly and/or with lower unit resources. There were also many signs that local managers were obliged to take certain types of performance measure more seriously than ever before (NHS Patient's Charter, waiting times; school SAT and exam scores; rent arrears; and so on).

However, to conclude from this evidence alone that self-management had stimulated better-performing services would be unwarranted. On the contrary, the particular reforms that we have looked at exhibit all the typical problems of evaluating management reform (Pollitt, 1995).

The first of these problems is that of deciding what constitutes 'better performance'. Is it a question of efficiency, quality, effectiveness, user satisfaction or what? Quite different answers may emerge depending on which criteria of improved performance are given precedence. In the case of the NHS, for example, there is no shortage of evidence that individual trusts have become more adept at treating more patients per annum in a series of specific categories. However, there is a very considerable shortage of public domain information about the clinical quality and clinical effectiveness of the services concerned, as well as anxiety about possibly increasing inequities in the way in which services are provided. So if performance is defined as treating more patients within a limited period of time, one would say that many NHS hospitals have improved. However, if performance is defined as clinical effectiveness, then one can only record a question mark, and if performance is defined as making an equitable response to the health-care needs of the community, then the situation is unclear and may actually have deteriorated. In short, performance is a multidimensional concept (like quality) and different stakeholders may give priority to different aspects (see the discussion in Monnier, 1997).

A second problem is that it is rare to find a continuous time series of reliable performance information that covers the period from before the self-management reforms until after the reforms were implemented. None of the institutions in which we conducted fieldwork could produce much information of this kind. In many cases the categories of data that are collected (and the institutions themselves) have changed with the reforms, so that no before and after time series can be constructed. In other cases the kinds of data in which we would be most interested have only been collected since the reforms anyway. Some basic activity data is available over a longer term, but to a considerable extent the data connections that would allow us to establish the extent of reform-induced change have been broken. Furthermore, in many cases there have been extensive changes in senior staff (especially in the NHS) so that even qualitative comparisons with the past may not be particularly reliable.

A third problem is to know how to explain any performance improvements for which there is good evidence. There are often a number of possible causes. In health care and education one spur to improved performance has been the increasingly centralised system of imposing published performance measures, such as Patient's Charter indicators and school 'league tables'. A second possible cause has been the introduction of MTMs, generating a certain amount of competition between different local service-providing organisations. Paradoxically, both the performance indicator system and the MTMs have been imposed on local service-providing organisations by central government. To describe this kind of increased performance-consciousness as principally a product of self-management would be quite misleading. Finally, the proportion of our respondents who believed that self-management had produced better performance in the sense of effectiveness varied from sector to sector. It was lowest in the NHS. It was somewhat higher in GM schools, but most of these examples revolved around one-off injections of transitional money. It was highest in housing associations, where managerial freedom appeared to have been greatest.

Sectoral and local differences

Although at a general level self-management was a policy promoted by central government right across the public domian, our research has confirmed that there are major differences in the ways in which it has been implemented within particular sectors. Housing, for example, is significantly different from schools and hospitals, partly because it is a capital-dominated operation but mainly because it is much closer to being a real competitive market than either education or health care. In any case, council housing had always existed alongside a large and vibrant private sector. Housing association managers can raise capital and raise or lower rents. The service they provide depends less on individualised face-to-face contacts than does most education and health care. Their primary 'product' is physical and measurable (houses and flats) in ways that education and health care are only rarely. Most housing association managers were on performance-related pay (Pike and Carp).

There are also significant differences between schools and hospitals. A major one is size. Hospitals are much larger entities. For example, one of our LEA secondary schools had an annual budget of 2.2 million and employed about 70 staff. Compare this with one of the acute hospitals (not the largest) which had an annual budget of 45 million and employed 2700 staff. Hospitals are more differentiated organisations, with a much wider range of functions and occupational groups. This tends to produce a need for more formalised and more elaborate rules and procedures to bind together the different parts of the organisation. The larger size may also mean that the effects of change take longer to reach the majority of staff in a hospital. In a school most of the staff are quite close to the 'outside world' and are therefore more likely to notice when there is a change in the messages coming in from 'outside'. It could therefore be argued that the gains from self-management are more likely to be recognised and appreciated throughout the staff of a school than of a large hospital. Housing associations fall somewhere between hospitals and schools in size. One of the larger associations had received a capital stock valued at nearly 50 million and was currently managing more than 8 000 properties with a staff of more than 180.

In addition to sectoral differences there were also important local factors. These seem particularly important in explaining the initial decision to apply, or refrain from applying, for grant-maintained status/trust status/voluntary transfer. They could include the relations a particular service delivery organisation had experienced with other neighbouring units; whether its relationship with its superior authority (local or health authority) had been harmonious or otherwise, and local party political factors. Each of these factors could predispose or deter an organisation from putting itself forward as a candidate for self-management. Very often we found that in making the decision to apply or not apply, the leaders of the organisations where we researched had been looking very closely at what other provider organisations in their particular localities were likely to do. There had often been a concern not to be the 'odd one out' either by rushing forward with an application when no one else in the area was doing so or by hanging back when the majority were seeking to gain new freedoms.

Conclusions

The story of central government-induced self-management among local service-providing organisations under the Conservatives was one of neither triumph nor disaster. Easy claims that most public service managers have been 'energised' and service users 'empowered' did not stand up to close scrutiny. Our research shows very little evidence of user 'empowerment' and plenty of examples of both continuing and

TABLE 3.1 Local self-management: freedom and constraint

Type of organisation	General financial climate	Devolution/ decentralisation of spending authority	Ability to restructure	Ability to set local pay and conditions
LA housing departments	Bleak	Increasingly tight central government controls	Moderate	Moderate
LVST housing Associations	Buoyant	Extensive freedoms, both capital and current	High	High
GM schools	One-off cash boost	Extensive freedoms	High	Mainly national terms and conditions
Second-wave NHS trusts	Very tight	Significant freedom, but within tight overall climate	High	In theory, but much central government intervention
Fourth-wave NHS Trusts	Very tight	Significant freedom, but within tight overall climate	High	In theory, but much central government intervention

TABLE 3.2   **Local self-management: some results**

Type of organisation	Managerial accountability	Political accountability	Efficiency and quality	Effectiveness	System coherence
LA housing departments	Increased	Unchanged	Largely unchanged	Probably static or decreasing	Probably decreased
LSVT housing associations	Increased	Decreased	Increased	Probably increased	Probably decreased
LEA schools	Increased	Unchanged	Probably increased	Unknown	Probably decreased
GM schools	Increased	Decreased	Probably increased	Unknown	Probably decreased
Second-wave NHS trusts	Increased	Marginally decreased	Increased	Unknown	Probably decreased
Fourth-wave NHS trusts	Increased	Marginally decreased	Increased	Unknown	Probably decreased

new frustrations among local managers. But at the same time, those critics who bitterly write off the new public management and market-type mechanisms as doctrinaire disasters are guilty of exaggeration and over-simplification. Many of our interviews indicated that new energies had been released and that greater managerial creativity was being practised in all three sectors. The true picture is therefore a complex one, with gains and losses, increased clarity in some aspects and continuing obscurity in others. In Tables 3.1 and 3.2 we have attempted to summarise this complexity in tabular form. Obviously any summary of 12 different organisations is bound to do some injustices to local colour and detail. Furthermore, the entries in the different cells are not all made with equal confidence. Our evidence in respect of the two right-hand columns in Table 3.2 is particularly incomplete and should therefore be treated with considerable circumspection. Within these caveats, however, Tables 3.1 and 3.2 give a broad indication of the progress of self-management over the three years 1994–6. A lengthier account is given in our book *Decentralising Public Service Management* (Pollitt *et al.*, 1998).

Finally, we conclude (as academics frequently do) that continuing research in this area would be highly desirable. We would suggest that our own work has pointed to some of the crucial issues that such further research could focus upon. We hope that our successors will be able to develop different research designs that will enable them to concentrate on those effects of self-management that our project could only touch upon lightly. Prominent among these relative unknowns are changes in the core quality and effectiveness of local services and in the overall coherence of service provision within the health, education and housing sectors. These are issues which the new Labour government will find as unavoidable as did their Conservative predecessors. If evaluation research can be built in to further reforms from the outset then Parliament and public will stand a better chance of being able to assess the value of management reform than was possible under the Thatcher and Major administrations.

About this study

We are extremely grateful to the very large number of people – most of them very busy – who generously gave their time for interviews and who also supplied us with documents and made arrangements for us to visit their organisations. We were struck by the keenness with which most of the individuals whom we met wished to debate the issues of self-management. We have completed our research quite convinced that the 'improvement ethic' of most public service providers has survived what has now been a long period of intense pressure and change.

The project was based mainly, but not exclusively, on intensive semi-structured interviewing and documentary analysis carried out at 12 fieldwork sites. More than 160 interviews were carried out, averaging over an hour in length. The bulk of these were conducted in a 'first wave', between late 1994 and mid-1995. A smaller number of interviews were completed in a 'second wave' between September 1995 and February 1996. The purpose of the 'second wave' was to provide a longitudinal check (had anything changed since the first round?); to explore certain key issues in greater depth (especially concepts of performance and accountability); and to secure a measure of respondent validation for the picture of the organisation's circumstances which we had formed as a result of the first wave of fieldwork. A semi-structured interview schedule was designed and piloted for the first wave and a different, more focused schedule was created for the second wave.

The interviews were concentrated at fairly senior levels – we never intended to focus on the 'rank and file'. In each hospital we approached the chief executive, other executive directors and a sample of other senior managers and consultants. We also sought interviews with the main local purchasing authority, with non-executive directors and, where appropriate, with the local GP fund-holders and the Community Health Council. These latter interviews helped to give us some perspective from 'outside–in' to complement the main thrust of the research which was essentially concerned with an 'inside–out' perspective. In the secondary schools we interviewed the head teacher, other senior teachers, governors and, in some cases, officers of the LEA. In the housing associations we interviewed chief executives and their top management team, plus members of the board (the chair, councillor and tenant representatives). In the non-opted-out housing departments we interviewed deputy chief executives, directors of housing and their management teams, together with councillors on the Housing Committee and tenant representatives.

Foreseeing the amount of data the interview programme would generate (approximately 3000 separate responses) we decided at an early stage to pre-code our questions and employ software (Textbase Alpha) that would permit us to sort out themes and patterns automatically.

The 12 fieldwork sites were carefully chosen. We selected two pairs (four in all) in each of the three sectors (health care, education and housing). To give a reasonable geographical spread each pair was drawn from a different part of the country although we excluded Greater London on the grounds that the capital suffered from some unique problems (at least in degree) which we did not see as central to our research.

One factor that posed a problem for our original research design was the rapid emergence within the NHS of a position where virtually all hospitals were becoming trusts (this had not been the original policy intention, however). This meant that we could no longer pursue our plan of contrasting a pair of acute trusts with a pair of directly managed units that had not opted to become trusts. We therefore selected two 'early' trust applicants (second-wave) and two 'late' trust applicants (fourth-wave).

In addition to our interview programme we collected a large number of institutional documents (Annual Reports, Citizen's Charter publications, accounts, management handbooks, etc.) and conducted a general literature search on the subjects of managerial autonomy, decentralisation and devolution in public service contexts.

4 The Contracting-Out of Local Government Services: Its Impact on Jobs, Conditions of Service and Labour Markets

Kevin Doogan

Introduction

This chapter discusses employment and labour market change as cause and as consequence of the introduction of market forces into local government services. In doing so it seeks to shed a particular light on the evolution of local governance processes, and also considers the adaptability of employment patterns and labour market systems in response to the commercialisation of municipal services. In examining the labour market impacts of the restructuring of municipal services the research has attempted to ascertain the extent of changes in employment patterns and in the bargaining position of the workforce. More specifically, the investigation has sought to examine 'dualism' within the workforce in the creation of core groups and peripheral groups of employees. The literature on the subject to date has described a growing polarisation within the local authority workforce and the related loss of trade union bargaining strength. In the first instance, the position of trade unions is said to have been severely weakened, either in terms of their bargaining capacity or their membership base (Walker, 1987; Walsh and Davis, 1993; Deakin and Walsh, 1994; Foster, 1993; and Walsh, 1995). This is explained as an outcome of the pursuit of flexible labour markets and the polarisation of the workforce that allegedly ensues. Thus notions of a 'two-tier' labour market, or of a core and periphery, evolving out of the replacement of full-time with part-time jobs, is found in the work of Farnham and Horton (1992). Related to this is the view that women employees have been particularly disadvantaged in the privatisation process (Painter, 1991; Walsh and Davis, 1993; Escott and Whitfield, 1995).

Not surprisingly such views have their detractors and studies of the reforms of health and education services suggest different labour market outcomes. Research into the restructuring of the health service, whose reorganisation has parallels with local government restructuring, examines the impact of trade unions in relation to local bargaining outcomes (Lloyd and Seifert, 1995). Elsewhere, a recent study of the tertiary education sector has drawn attention to the durability of trade union organisation during the restructuring of higher education establishments (Arthur, 1994). Finally, Fairbrother (1994) also points to very different scenarios for workforce representation and even entertains the possibility of trade union 'renewal' with the development of a local bargaining capacity.

Privatisation, marketisation and the new institutionalism

The term 'marketisation' is most often used in this chapter to describe a reworking of relationships between the public and private sectors rather than the more restricted notion of privatisation.. The latter reinforces the apparent dichotomy between public and private organisations and operating environments and imputes to the process of transfer a single and irrevocable shift in sectoral position and identity. The preference expressed here for marketisation is based upon the permeability of the boundary between public and private, and on the need to explore the relationships that transmit service culture both to and from the public sector. Marketisation is discussed here as a process marked in stages or contractual waves and as a set of labour market and employment outcomes. Moreover, the sectoral distinctions often implied in the notion of privatisation deserve careful consideration in respect of labour market and employment position. It is suggested here that workers are not 'beamed down' from the mother ship of the local authority to the alien landscape of the private sector.

This 'quantum leap' notion of privatisation is particularly inappropriate for the study of employment change, both in terms of the short time-frame embedded in the concept, and also in terms of the organisational consequences of sectoral relocation. Research into other public services such as the telecommunications and water industries shows that privatisation, *per se*, is not necessarily the principal catalyst for labour market change. Studies of the water industry show that far greater levels of job losses took place in the ten years before privatisation in 1989 than since that time. This research usefully points out that between 1979 and 1989 responsibility for water provision was taken from the local authorities and placed under the auspices of ten regional boards, and in the process employment levels in the industry fell by some 20 per cent in this period (Harris, 1994). Employment change in this sector has been of much smaller magnitude since privatisation than occurred in the previous decade. Elsewhere, in relation to the telecommunications industry, research also shows that as far as employment was concerned privatisation initially represented little more than 'a change of ownership' (Sinden, 1995). Rather, it was the exposure to competition some years later, in BT's case principally with the entry of Mercury into the market-place, that drove the reorganisation of employment practices and the restructuring of labour markets.

The question of time-frame therefore assumes some significance in studying the employment consequences of marketisation. To restrict the discussion to pre- and post-privatisation differences over a short time period can place significant limitations on the analysis. Thus it is often said that privatisation is the spur for institutional decentralisation involving a transfer from a large centralised public bureaucracy to a smaller private sector organisation. In some sectors this may be accurate in the first instance, but it becomes less appropriate over time as processes of regroupment and recentralisation take place in waves of mergers and corporate reorganisations. In other services, such as water and electricity, the break-up of public bureaucracies has given way to the reconstitution of those services with the formation of 'super utilities' which cut across sector boundaries, providing water and electricity within one corporation (Smith, 1995). Such downstream restructuring, involving the horizontal integration of service providers, represents a reconstitution of private capital that is driven by the search for economies of scale. Thus to associate privatisation with institutional decentralisation and a shift from large to small employing organisations is less than accurate in the contemporary restructuring of many public services.

A third component of marketisation emerges out of the 'new institutionalist literature' that considers markets as social constructs in important respects. In addition to the renewal of interest in Polanyi's notion of the 'market as an instituted process', recent developments in economic sociology and geography conceive of markets as 'embedded' within (local) culture and history and 'situated' in space and time (Polanyi, 1944; Granovetter, 1985; Harvey, 1996). In this branch of the public sector the local authority is the key purchaser and/or provider of goods and services and has a constitutive role in market formation. With compulsory competitive tendering (CCT), contract specification rests in the hands of the local authority and, as such, local government has a key role in determining the operating conditions and the access to local markets.

Employment change in local government in England and Wales

As Table 4.1 shows, employment in local government in England and Wales fell by 377 000 or by 15 per cent of the workforce between 1979 and 1994. Of particular interest is the fact that some 80 per cent or 313 000 of these job losses took place in the 1990s during the period examined in detail by the locality studies. It should be noted, however, that adjustments in employment levels for the sector conceal processes of service contraction and expansion and perhaps more accurately represent the net stock of jobs involved in the provision of a changing portfolio of local services.

Nonetheless, it is clear from Table 4.1 that manual job losses have contributed in large measure to the loss of local authority employment and account for 90 per cent of the employment decline since 1979. What is also revealing is that job losses have been much greater for men than for women. Of the 361 000 job losses between December 1979 and March 1994 some 296 000 (81 per cent) have been male and 65 000 (19 per cent) have been female. The result of these changes has been the long term shift towards non-manual female employment. Where men accounted for almost 40 per cent of the workforce in 1979 they now account for little over 30 per cent and, relatedly, the proportion of manual employment fell from 44 per cent to 36 per cent over the same period. Male full-time employment has been the greatest casualty of employment restructuring. Between December 1979 and March 1994 almost 300 000 job losses occurred, representing a 34 per cent decrease in male full-time employment and accounting for 82 per cent of total job losses in local government over this period.

More recent evidence since 1990 offers a slightly different perspective, but also confirms many of the longer-run trends. In the 1990s marketisation has begun to embrace administrative, professional,

TABLE 4.1   Employment change in local government, 1979—94 (England and Wales, December figures in thousands unless otherwise stated)

	1979	1990	1994	Change since 1979	Change since 1990
Total					
employment	2481	2417	2104	−377 (−15%)	−313 (−12%)
Manual staff	1097	902	758	−339 (−31%)	−144 (−15%)
Non-manual					
staff	1384	1515	1346	−38 (−3%)	−169 (−11%)
Male full-time	876	726	579*	−297 (−34%)	−147 (−20%)
Male part-time	93	97	94*	+1 (1%)	−3 (−3%)
Female full-time	680	680	629*	−51 (−8%)	− 51 (−8%)
Female part-time	833	914	821*	−12 (−1%)	−93 (−10%)
Male:female					
ratio	39:61	34:66	31:69		
Manual:non-					
manual ratio	44:56	37:63	36:64		
Full-time:					
part-time ratio	63:37	58:42	57:43		

* Gender breakdown in 1994 refers to March figures, the latest available data, which are not wholly compatible with manual and non-manual totals.
*Source:*based on information provided by the Local Government Management Board.

technical and clerical (APTC) services and the relative share of non-manual job loss has increased as a consequence. Overall the local authority workforce has experienced 313 000 job losses between December 1990 and December 1994, representing some 12 per cent of the workforce in this period. In absolute terms job losses among non-manual employees have been larger than those of manual employees (169 000 compared to 144 000), but in relative terms there has been a 15 per cent cut in the manual workforce and a cut of 11 per cent in the non-manual workforce. In absolute terms there have been 150 000 job losses among men and 144 000 job losses among women since 1990. However, relative declines show that the rate of job loss for men was double that for women, with male employment falling by 18 per cent compared with 9 per cent for women. Once again, male full-time employment is the largest casualty in this latest phase of the restructuring of municipal services, with a 20 per cent decline of male full-time workers, consisting of 147000 job losses which accounted for 46 per cent of total job losses for the sector in this period.

Change and continuity in the local government labour market

This evidence suggests that the core and periphery model of employment and labour market restructuring has little explanatory power in the contemporary reorganisation of the local authority workforce. Job losses are evident across a spectrum of employee groups, but particularly among male full-time workers and those in manual employment. Evidence from the national survey and case studies strongly supports the view that, in most instances, part-time work has not replaced full-time employment amongst those services that remain within the local authority. In those services which remain within the public sector, marketisation has served to drive an intensification of the work regime rather than a restructuring or a polarisation within the municipal workforce. Full-time and part-time differences cannot therefore support a distinction between primary and secondary labour markets in respect of employment status and security. Moves towards temporary contracts are not confined to lower manual or non-manual grades and are significant in middle and senior managers and policy officer grades. Furthermore, the wider programme of local government reorganisation and the creation of unitary authorities also conspires to spread insecurity of employment across a wide range of occupation categories.

Because discussions of dual labour markets and 'core' and 'periphery' often take on a gender dimension, it is worth noting that the account of the gender impact of marketisation in local government provided here offers a very different perspective to that of other recently published research. In particular, it would appear to contrast with research published by the Equal Opportunities Commission, which, *inter alia*, argues that job losses have been particularly prevalent amongst women workers as a result of the introduction of competitive tendering for local government services (Escott and Whitfield, 1995). It should be stressed that the concern here is with the wider process of marketisation rather than with CCT. However, the findings presented here have a broader empirical base because, in contrast to the Escott and Whitfield study, they are derived from national and local evidence of employment and cover a wider range of service changes. Although there are areas of agreement between the two research projects, there are contrasting views about employment change in local government in respect of gender.

Explanations for the decline in male full-time employees and the changing gender composition of the local authority workforce relate to the form of productivity gains that have accompanied the introduction of market forces. The employment impact of competition has been uneven across the services, depending on the nature of the service and the employee groups engaged in their delivery. The productivity gains in municipal services that are largely provided by men have been based in significant measure on job losses or transfers. For services largely provided by women the evidence suggests that labour have been driven down by greater flexibilities secured in terms and conditions of employment. For refuse collection or grounds maintenance, marketisation prompts the reduction in the numbers of men on work teams. For catering and cleaning staff the more competitive regime is reflected in adjustments in a variety of measures from cuts in hours to changes to sick pay schemes.

Another factor that may make a small contribution to the reduction of male full-time employees is found in the voluntary externalisation of technical and professional services. It is interesting to discover the key role played by senior managers in professional groups such as engineers, architects and other design staff in promoting the voluntary transfer of units or departments to the private sector. There is insufficient evidence to provide robust generalisations on gender and voluntary transfers, but a significant feature of our evidence is that where it did take place it affected staff groups with a large proportion of male full-time employees. On this basis it seems not unreasonable to consider the separate effects of gender and voluntary transfer on the change in male full-timers in the local government workforce.

Overall, the evidence does not suggest that labour market fragmentation has precipitated a process of localisation of bargaining arrangements within local government. Although central government has in some measure promoted the break-up of national employment systems, they have proved remarkably durable mechanisms for labour market regulation. This durability derives not only from the corporatist interests of the bargaining partners, but also from the fact that reference to national terms and conditions continues to provide a useful and efficient framework for wage negotiation and the mutual recognition of grading systems. Furthermore, the national system has a capacity to make small adjustments in grading structures and to build in enhancements which allow some degree of flexibility to respond to local market conditions. Through this system of national negotiation, contrary to any trends towards polarisation within labour market groups, the policy objective of harmonisation between manual and craft groups and APTC groups has been established. Thus in the 1994 round of wage negotiations management and unions agreed in principle to the promotion of the harmonisation of terms and conditions for blue- and white-collar staff groups.

Finally, it is worth stressing that the analysis of employment change invites a careful assessment of general trends and the particular instances. The generalities expressed here are offered in the awareness that scenarios of minimum and maximum change compete for inclusion in the research summation. The discussion must therefore address both change and continuity and be aware that, as the field of vision moves from the local to the national level, different perspectives are provided with a possible diminishing sense of the pace of change. For instance, this investigation has encountered an example of extreme fragmentation in which a local authority has maintained its grounds maintenance operation by cutting its permanent workforce to a handful of staff and engaging a small army of pensioners, some 250-strong, on a seasonal and casual basis to carry out the service. To many manual workers in this authority it might appear that labour markets and traditional employment practices have been completely overhauled. Yet trends derived from the national survey and case studies suggest that such an example is exceptional. The larger picture, of experience from different parts of the country, suggests the survival and continuity of employment practice and, more significantly, that the structure of the local authority labour market remains intact. Overall, the system is under pressure but national terms and conditions apply to the large majority of the workforce and national wage bargaining, albeit bolstered by greater local flexibility, has survived the first waves of marketisation. Or, to draw the wider conclusion, while market forces may have altered market structures have remained intact.

Labour market fragmentation and the transfer of services to the private sector

In this section labour market fragmentation is discussed, first, in terms of local variations in marketisation outcomes and, second, in connection with the subcontracting of local services. So far the research findings have dwelled on the continuity of employment and labour market practice. However, the concept of labour market fragmentation is more obviously expressed in the transfer of work across statutory boundaries. Whereas the preceding discussion stressed the generality of trends and patterns and the continuity with previous regimes, with the transfer to the private sector greater stress is placed on the specificity and discontinuity of experience. Such an emphasis is necessary, in the first instance, because there is considerable local variation in the extent and pace of externalisation. From locality to locality and from service to service there is a large variation in the degree to which contracts have remained in-house (LGMB, 1993; Patterson and Pinch, 1995). The salience of local processes and the impact of local actors are suggested by the extent of this service and locality variation. Central government has laid down procedures by which services are to be subject to competition, but what follow are not pure market outcomes. Local determinants such as the political culture of the locality, the role of corporate senior managers or departmental heads in contract packaging and specification and the bargaining strength of trade unions, either at departmental level or authority-wide, have significant impacts on marketisation outcomes.

In the course of the research a private contractor remarked that:

> If a local authority does not want the work to go out, it won't go out – and there is nothing that you can do about it . . . In theory you can appeal to the Department of the Environment, but the local author-ity can block the transfer if they want to.

Clearly the role of the local authority in contract specification was crucial for this contractor. The private sector can be discouraged from competing with in-house providers in a variety of ways. Bureaucratic procedures can discourage smaller local private contractors (stories are told off the record of 700-page health and safety documents issued with the tendering instructions). Services can be packaged in ways that also deter competition. Housing maintenance contracts were 'put out' for very large numbers of units which included old housing stock, both of which tend to discourage the private sector. On the other hand the research encountered an enthusiastic enabling authority, ideologically committed to the externalisation of services, actually providing training for competitors to go against the in-house bid.

Locality and service variations are further explained by institutional adaptation within the local authority. It would create a false impression to portray marketisation outcomes as the result of clearly defined local strategies and policies. Although there are well-known cases of, for example, 'traditional' labour authorities whose policies are broadly supported by members and staff and endorsed by their trade union representatives, they are less common than might have been deduced from analysis of the political character of local government in the 1990s. Fieldwork evidence produced in this research corroborates the findings of other researchers in the Local Governance Programme. In Chapter 2 of this volume Lowndes discusses a fragmented world of local government management and disparate processes of institutional change. The research discussed here contained numerous examples of authorities without a clear strategy towards CCT. A sense of 'muddling through' in *ad hoc* policy responses to service tendering was reinforced in numerous case studies. This is less surprising, however, if due consideration is given to the external environment of local government reorganisation (LGR) with the creation of unitary authorities and the internal management impacts of marketisation. During the life of this project LGR cast a long shadow over many authorities and instilled a sense of 'planning blight'. This uncertainty was amplified by the fact that personnel management services were also to be subjected to CCT. This seemed to impair the development of corporate policy towards CCT and to reinforce the role of departmental managers which added to a sense of service specificity in policy-making.

Second, the discussion of labour market fragmentation developed here provides an alternative or a complement to notions of subcontracting or external decentralisation (Hoggett, 1994). Fragmentation captures the sense in which work is packaged in discrete ways and 'put out' to tender. A workforce is attached to a contract which is awarded for specific periods. In many accounts, however, subcontracting implies a shift from the large to the small employer and, in this setting, from public to private or charitable organisations (Blackburn, 1992; Drucker and Macallan, 1994). While this may have a specific relevance for the construction industry, in the majority of instances in the local government sector the notion of subcontracting is less than helpful in the local government sector as the successful bidders from the private sector are usually large companies, sometimes part of a multi-national corporation, and not the small local firm. This is a point made forcibly, if not exaggeratedly, in other discussions of the 'globalization of public services' (Dunleavy, 1994). Thus the relocated staff often become part of an organisation which is itself undergoing a process of expansion. As with many housing associations and some colleges of further education, the organisations may enlarge through acquisitions or mergers. More generally, the business services industries have experienced a process of concentration and are becoming increasingly dominated by the larger players (Purnell, 1995). In terms of labour markets it is helpful to consider the transfer of services involving not only fragmentation, but a repositioning across sectors often accompanied by agglomeration. For example, in two of our case studies in the southwest and the north-west of England, grounds maintenance contracts were awarded to Brophys Ltd, which had become a large employer in this sector. Interestingly, Brophys was a subsidiary of one of the privatised water companies. The same trends were observed in computing services for local authorities with national and international players, including the giant American corporation AT&T, acquiring the companies that have become successful bidders for financial services contracts. Hence, the notion of an activity being subcontracted fails to capture the way in which the corporate world is reorganising in response to the opportunities provided by marketisation.

New labour market patterns: contract-bound employment

The separation of the planning and delivery of municipal services has established new norms and frameworks for wage-setting and industrial relations. Upon transfer to the private sector it would appear that wage-setting derives more from the contract than from an employee's position within the corporate labour market of the new host organisation, and for this reason the term 'contract-bound employment' has been adopted. The research discovered several instances in which trade unions were not recognised for wage negotiation purposes in their new corporate location (although they might have been recognised for other issues such as Health and Safety). This situation was justified on the grounds that labour costs and therefore wages were seen to derive from contract specifications. Accordingly, transferred staff were often given a wage increase that matched the local authority offer, but it was often imposed unilaterally instead of being negotiated with the trade unions. Again, for the sake of balance, it should be pointed out that the unions have secured recognition with some firms, and there is growing evidence that private sector companies are reviewing their position with the unions as part of a concerted effort to change public perceptions about this sector. However, interviews with business service contractors provide evidence of 'truncated trade unionism' which involves a carry-over of union recognition from the public sector but which often does not fully extend to wage-bargaining in the host organisation.

The previous discussion of internal employment outcomes stressed the importance of a balanced assessment of change and continuity in the marketisation process. With the transfer of activities to another sector it is similarly necessary to achieve a sense of proportion in discussing labour market outcomes. It is often the case that little might appear to have changed with the repositioning of services. Thus, in one large county council, which had externalised many of its financial services, the transferred staff continued to work in the same building, be paid the same wage rates as before and retain membership of the local trade union branch. The only symbol of change was the appearance of the corporate logo of Touche Ross on the office door. Other minimum-change scenarios were obtained from the example of a voluntary transfer of a highways department. In this case some three or four hundred staff 'went over', but to little immediate effect. The manager of the private company observed that the staff still thought they were part of the council and noted that 'You are not going to change the culture of a large group of staff like that.'

On all sides, but particularly in the private sector, employment protection legislation in the form of the Transfer of Undertakings – Protection of Employment or TUPE legislation – was perceived to have had a significant impact on the transfer process. However, it was most noticeable that there were local and service variations in the time period covered by the legislation's protection. On the one hand, in some of the construction-related services it was felt that protection lasted from 'contract to contract', whereas other personnel managers felt that, 'as soon as the ink is dry on the contract', the employer has the right to change terms and conditions.

There are contradictory effects in respect of the predictability conferred upon the wage-setting system. Before work goes out, in the preparation for bids, labour costs and relatedly wage costs are determined by factors *other than the rate for the job*. Instead, the rate for the contract, that is, the perceived market rate, features in the bidding process and engenders an unpredictability in wage-setting. Workers are thereby more exposed to the *blind* forces of competition, which are uncertain and appear beyond the control of local wage bargainers. Wage expectations, in this more precarious environment, are subject to downward pressures arising from the threat of open competition.

However, in some post-transfer situations, by contrast, the wage-setting environment might be more predictable than in previous circumstances. Once the contract has been won, it is known that there is money for possibly a three- or five-year period, and certainties are introduced in the private sector that might not pertain in the public sector. It is difficult for employers to argue that they do not have the money in the bank when the terms of the contracts specify the allocation for labour costs for the life of the project.

The question of predictability and stability in contractual relations is important to the discussion of fragmentation. In most of our case studies local agencies engaged in a tendering process with identifiable outcomes and were offered some scope for forward planning within reasonable parameters. Thus work was packaged, specified for certain periods, usually three to five years, and then priced. Depending on bidding outcomes the work transferred out or remained in-house for determinate periods. However, more recent evidence, particularly from the externalisation of white-collar services, suggests a less predictable relationship between purchasers and providers. Case study evidence suggests that in certain services work can be transferred into the private sector without a market guarantee from the public authority. Where the purchaser–provider relationship is less predictable it is possible that greater insecurity of employment will prevail and wages and conditions will be subject to downward pressure. Thus a direct service organisation (DSO) manager complained that, under the new system of local management, schools are not obliged to look to the local authority to provide cleaning services and that they can shop around for other, cheaper alternatives. In this case it led directly to the greater use of casual cleaning staff within the DSO. In other examples of externalised social services, for exmple, particularly in residential care, the private contractors complained that planning was exceedingly difficult because the local authority was offering 'spot contracts', buying individual bed spaces on an *ad hoc* basis. In health services, too, there was evidence of externalisation without market guarantee from the public authority. Thus the stability of the relationship between purchaser and provider, particularly in the extent to which market guarantees are provided to the private contractor, is of key importance to the relocation of work across statutory boundaries. The extent of this market guarantee confers on the new employment position a stability or precariousness that impacts directly on bargaining capacity. This view is pursued in the following chapter where Mackintosh discusses flexibility as a discourse of control of risk management.

For the most part the research findings are based upon the more stable purchaser–provider relationships and this exploration of contract-bound employment has revealed two elements. One is the transmission of public service culture and work organisation into the private sector; the other is the potential for change in the individual labour market position as a result of transfer processes. People might be replaced on new contracts with different terms and conditions when filling the posts vacated by old local authority staff, and in other cases private companies might offer to 'buy out' the old local authority contracts. Transference outcomes may be observed over time which involve the gradual evolution of new forms of work organisation and the inculcation of a private sector company culture and business practices.

Conclusions

To say that there is nothing 'new under the sun' is both intellectually conservative and ill-informed. To argue, however, 'that the sun has never risen before' is a far greater error. While acknowledging long-term cultural shifts and adjustments in employment practices, it is important to retain the sense of continuity and the remarkable resilience of local agencies and practices against this sea change in public policy. The 'Ridley model' of the enabling authority meeting once a year to allocate contracts has failed to materialise and it is not unreasonable to speculate that municipal services will survive in a recognisable form for the foreseeable future. National arrangements for determining pay and conditions will probably continue to dominate local bargaining systems, precisely because they have a greater local flexibility and responsiveness than is widely assumed. Thus the introduction of market forces has served to bring about changes in employment patterns while labour market systems have survived largely intact (Doogan, 1997, 1998).

It is worth considering who, if anyone, is in control of this process of marketisation. The state makes the rules by which local public services are exposed to the forces of the market, yet central government policy-makers could never have anticipated the developments that have subsequently transpired. Central government may set the rules, but it cannot be said to be in control of the marketisation programme. In other words it might be in the driving seat, but it does not have a firm grip on the wheel. Market behaviour is mediated by local agencies and conditioned by local and national bargaining capacities. This conclusion, however, might well be at odds with the subjective impressions of many local actors in our case studies. The fieldwork gained the strong impression that services were being submitted to economic and political forces that appeared beyond the control of local managers or trade unions. It is important to acknowledge this sense of powerlessness. After all the 'hand' of market forces is indeed hidden and serves to introduce unknown quantities into local planning and bargaining processes. However, the extent of locality and service variation in marketisation outcomes testifies to the salience of local processes. Bargaining strength differs from area to area and the political culture and the industrial relations culture of the locality condition the responses to marketisation.

The neo-liberal discourse of 'deregulation' or privatisation conceals the ways in which the state governs access to markets, specifies the products and services that are traded, establishes the legal codes that enforce contractual governance, and is the key purchaser and, to a lesser extent, provider of goods and services. In the context of the competitive tendering of municipal services these roles have important local and national dimensions. Our research shows, on the one hand, that local authorities have been forced to compete by central government; on the other hand, through contract specification and packaging the local authority can affect market access for private contractors and retain a very large part of service provision on an in-house basis.

Clearly, therefore, the operation of markets is conditioned by both central and local agencies. In this regard there are interesting questions raised by changes in central and local relations after the 1997 general election. The new Labour government has promised to replace CCT with a 'best value' system of local service delivery. This will impose a duty on local authorities to achieve best value although it is unclear as to how this is to be realised. It has been noted, however, that competition was an important management tool for achieving best value, but it was not the only tool. In interviews in one local authority and with several national experts, the view was expressed that opposition to CCT was focused on the element of compulsion rather than competition. Accordingly it will be difficult to predict how much will change with the new government. It is interesting to consider that one outcome of Labour replacing the Conservative Party in central government might be that new lines of tensions are generated within local authorities rather than between central and local government.

About this study

This chapter differs from other accounts of the employment implications of public service restructuring in terms of research focus and methodology. The scope of the study is relatively broad in terms of the spectrum of services covered and in the forms of restructuring investigated. This approach is adopted, first, because the introduction of market forces is achieved by a variety of mechanisms, and second, because of the difficulties associated with the attempt to specify the precise impacts of policy changes. Thus marketisation might arise from the voluntary externalisation or the compulsory tendering of local services, or the incorporation of further education colleges. Moreover marketisation can become entangled with other aspects of policy and structural change, such as the creation of unitary local authorities or the general impact of central government spending restrictions. Finally, because marketisation captures both a repositioning of service delivery in the private sector as well as the commercialisation of the public sector, the research strategy has opted for breadth of vision rather than narrowness of focus. Accordingly, this account stresses the evolutionary nature of the marketisation process while other studies dwell on more immediate privatisation outcomes.

In this respect this investigation has been very fortunate in that it has been possible to collect data at local and national level. In particular the Local Government Management Board (LGMB) has been very supportive of this research and has provided statistics on the local authority workforce in different categories of male and female, full-time and part-time, and manual and non-manual employee groups over a long time period. The research is able to draw on this national survey material and to complement it with case study evidence in different local areas. The local-level studies consist of semi-structured interviews with local authority personnel managers and trade union representatives in 14 localities. Furthermore, in many local authorities additional interviews were conducted with CCT policy officers and the managers of the direct service organizations (DSOs), the local authority in-house service providers.

The sample of authorities was selected according to representative and illustrative criteria. It was felt important to gain the sense of regional differences in England and Wales and to capture the variation in local government characteristics by type of authority and by political make-up. It was important to include enthusiastic 'enabling authorities' as well the more reluctant participants in the new market for local service delivery. Some seven colleges of further education were also included in this study as were six interviews with private contractors. In addition, ten key officials at national level from employers' organisations and trade unions were also interviewed in the research. The research was conducted in the year to March 1995.

5 Two Economic Discourses in the New Management of Local Governance: Public Trading and Public Business

Maureen Mackintosh

Introduction

> we are more limited I think by our imagination than by our resources at the present time. (Social Services Director talking about community care)

Are quasi-markets and the force-feeding of business and market concepts to public services staff generating in response new concepts of public economic behaviour? Sweeping shifts within local governance to decentralisation, externalisation and contractual working relationships (see the chapters by Lowndes, Pollitt *et al.* and Doogan in this volume) have challenged the economic imaginations of service managers and staff. Can the new organisational forms be bent to public interest ends?

Economic imagination necessarily operates through discourse. As experience of decentralised management and competitive bidding under fiscal stress lengthens, so shared and contested meanings of key terms in the markets and business vocabulary emerge. Public service managers and their counterparts in contracting organisations variously employ terms such as competition, market, price and profit as description, metaphor and ideal type. This chapter argues that by analysing shared and interrelated meanings of such terms we can see two economic discourses emerging within the new management of local governance. Labelled 'public trading' and 'public business', these competing discourses draw on distinct ethical bases and are experienced as increasingly external to individuals, though nevertheless open to individual influence and manipulation. This is therefore an essay on economic sense-making under pressure within local governance. The remaking of economic language is a key element in the remaking of economic behaviour. I assume, like Dryzek (1996, p. 103), that more than one discourse can operate in any particular setting, and that discourses are open to challenge and only partly incommensurable. People can and do move between these ways of seeing their world, and institutional redesign can be thought of as a 'conversation' among discursive perspectives. The extent of emergence of *dominant* economic discourses is a matter for empirical research, and a matter of concern for policy since thinking and behaviour interact. Increasingly, the economic literature on contracting registers the importance of the understandings of the participants in determining market and quasi-market decision-making (see Deakin and Michie 1997, and the special issue of the *Cambridge Journal of Economics*, vol. 21, no. 2 (1997), on contracts and competition). The economic culture of public service organisations, in the sense of economic ideas and behaviours and the feedback between them, is a strong determinant of public service outcomes.

This chapter proceeds by pulling some key discursive threads through several case studies. The threads are the concept of 'flexibility' and the complex counterpoint between notions of risk and control. The flexibility trope appeared frequently in the interviews, and offers an interesting angle on public economic discourse because of the key role it also plays in theories of state and economy (Jessop, 1994) and in the popular management literature. 'Flexibility' carries a complex mix of positive and negative associations: responsiveness, diversity and multi-skilling versus insecurity and ease of hiring and firing (Pinch, 1994).

A marked effect of quasi-markets is an increase in perceived personal, financial and professional risk. This is expressed throughout the interviews: in fears of being closed down for being 'too expensive'; in fears of losing tenders and hence jobs, or of losing jobs in order to win contracts; in complaints about increasing risk aversion among staff who stick to the rules because the personal consequences of mistakes have escalated; in worries about coping with tasks where the risks to *clients* of mistakes have escalated; in fears of overspending by mistake through poorly managed decentralisation; and in reiterated complaints about responsibility without control.

As organisation theory (and common sense) predict, people deal with these well-founded fears by seeking to reestablish control. They do this by a mixture of trying to making sense of their situation (discursive control), and trying to establish behaviour which 'works', which may include accepting more risk as well as shifting some of it. By following the threads of flexibility and risk, this chapter traces elements of the two economic discourses through five case studies: in catering, social care, financial services, interdepartmental trading and leisure services. The final section draws the evidence together and compares the two emergent discourses.

'Value added' in public business: a catering DSO

Public service debates now commonly understand the term 'value added' to mean not the financial value added to inputs at sale (the commercial meaning), but the public interest value of publicly financed activity. This usage has developed during the late 1980s and 1990s as a discursive claim by analogy, from within a business discourse, for the value of public services.

The concept appeared in reflections by a manager of a catering direct service organisation (DSO) on the problems of a retendering exercise. The manager worked under a twin-hatted director of Direct Services, the authority having retreated from an earlier hard split.

> I think that the way for organisations like ours to survive is to ingratiate themselves so deeply into the rest of the authority that first of all . . . they value us in terms of being inside the organisation . . . and secondly that they would definitely miss the added value that we give to services by being an inside provider . . . my job is to create that style of organisation, to very much try and differentiate us from a potential private sector supplier.

He contrasted this with a view of a DSO as a 'quasi-commercial business organisation reasonably discrete from the rest of the author-ity' with different goals and 'ethos' from mainstream local authority service departments. When pressed to define the added value, his examples were all about responding to the unexpected, from coping with a royal visit to supplying plates for a member's community centre tea: 'Just tell me what you want, we'll do it, because that's what local government officers do . . . we don't charge . . . it's trivial but it's regarded as important.'

The big example involved a major mid-contract rethink. The catering DSO, by improving school meals and working with schools, had pushed up take-up, in an authority where over 50 per cent of children were eligible for free school meals. Since the contract had been written in terms of a subsidy per meal, this threatened the Education Department's budget.

> it became a conflict of interest. It was very much in our interest to broaden our client base. There's also obviously a very strong social policy argument . . . you should feed as many kids entitled to free school meals as possible.

So for the final two years of the contract, the subsidy was capped, and the fixed subsidy transferred to the DSO, which then took on the objective of continuing to raise take-up by driving down unit costs. This, to the considerable pride of many people in the organisation, they had succeeded in doing. They saw it as the kind of risk only a DSO would take – and a risk a local authority could take only with a DSO – because of the perverse incentives inherent in a lump sum subsidy grant:

> it seems to be inconceivable that anybody [from the commercial sector] would bid on the basis of having to absorb the risk of increased take-up without unit per unit payments.

'Added value' therefore mixes risk acceptance, integration into the authority's social objectives and flexibility:

> the long term survival of organisations like ours and the only reason for being in the business is to entrench yourself in the public sector ethic . . . [to balance the books] while being flexible enough to address the concerns of politicians and senior officers, in terms of developing the service.

A contract manager for welfare meals in social services concurred:

> I still see it as an open-ended contract . . . you can get very comfortable when you've got an in-house contractor because they're usually very obliging . . . if it is a commercial contract [after

retendering] you've got to be much, much more explicit. We would have to tighten up our ordering procedures – we have great flexibility at the moment that we can add meals on, take meals off . . . tell the cook on the morning

– while a private contractor would charge for late notice.

Two meanings of 'flexibility' in care contracting

The DSO manager's meaning of 'flexibility' as responsiveness to unforeseen needs, and its association with cost control, runs right through the research. But it is in sharp contrast to another set of meanings around flexibility, control and risk, well-illustrated by commercial and in-house social care contractors. The DSO manager was arguing (though this was not his language) that private contractors were risk-averse and instrumental in motivation. Others – including the chief executive of this authority – questioned this, noting that commercial firms can take a long-term view and can offer a lead on quality. Nevertheless, the manager's view of private contractors' behaviour in low-paid manual services gains support in the care-contracting interviews.

The commercial contractors in domiciliary care expressed a risk-averse approach to contract specification. They all favoured clear specification and provision of a standard service, with competition on price, on an agency basis; staff were often self-employed. The for-profit contractors all rejected block contracts as 'inflexible', in part because they made it awkward for the contractor to decline difficult work. 'Flexibility' – a term of approval – meant standardised spot-contracting; even rate-per-hour contracts including transport were regarded as a 'risky calculation', the preferred payment system being time plus expenses. In-house care providers tended notably to share this approach: they resented their increased financial risk, and sought in response more 'business freedoms', especially more freedom to hire and fire, to weaken staff terms and conditions, and to sell services outside the authority.

Consistent with this approach to contracting, the commercial contractors interviewed rejected any notion of policy collaboration with the authority, preferring an arm's-length relationship. The contrast with the non-profit providers could not have been sharper. The non-profit contractors interviewed all sought a 'partnership' approach to contracting which explicitly implied assuming some financial risk and responsibility for resource allocation.

'Flexibility', in the non-profit managers' discourse, meant *both* delivering what clients needed *and* achieving a measure of financial control by the non-profit provider. No contradiction was seen between the two. The control envisaged included financial flexibility, to move resources as needs changed; hence block contracts in this discourse were regarded as *flexible*, because they passed responsibility for day-to-day delivery to the 'partner'. Thus, faced with fluctuating needs of residents in a housing-with-care project and with a capped local authority budget, one manager said, 'I would rather have a block contract which allows me to deal with it in a direct style', by moving a stable group of staff between residents as needed, and 'giving back' any spare staff time to the authority on a weekly basis for local domiciliary care outside the scheme.

The contrast in attitudes to block contracts was therefore sharp. To the commercial sector an 'alarming mishmash', to the non-profit sector they were a source of control, allowing flexible provision for residents' needs. In both discourses, 'flexibility' is deeply associated with control and risk management, but one approach implies risk-shifting case by case, and the other, internal risk management via financial control. The non-profit managers saw a strategic advantage in taking some risk from the local authority: this allowed them to seek a niche as high-quality providers, to provide more stable conditions for staff – and to charge authorities more in consequence. Local authority purchasers saw a need for an alternative to the predominant spot contracting:

> It's something about – can you, in terms of providing social care, or health care, work to certain levels of pre-defined efficiency which the market demands? Or must there be an area of flexibility and latitude, that caters for changes in the pattern of need, requirement, or changes in levels of risk?

Apportioning risk: selling financial services to schools

The problem of specifying services involving risk reappeared in a case study of competition in financial services. Under local management of schools (LMS), schools can choose their supplier of payroll services, and the economic culture shock in finance departments has been considerable, with jobs and economies of scale at risk if many schools depart.

In a case study of payroll services, the management of risk had become a marketing issue. The department had decided to offer three 'tiers' of payroll service: a minimal payments service matching that offered by small local bureaux, without calculation of pay or tax; a 'standard' service; and a 'full' service 'which includes . . . extra goodies . . . which they can also buy independently if they need to'. The marketing pitch mixed a stress on savings (the standard service was cheaper than the delegated budget), flexibility (add-ons) and risk:

> We tried to get across to them the problems they might have if they went to an external provider . . . the high schools have an appreciation of the complexities involved, because the things that tend to happen once in a blue moon, the high schools would come across, and, 'oh, we don't want to touch that'.

– while the primary schools were small and saw payroll as simple. The department had also given the schools 'more details about what their responsibilities are, if they decide not to buy the in-house service'.

This is the stick rather than the carrot?
Well, that's one way of looking at it!

Behind this marketing effort lay the risks of external competition. Private contractors used different labour organisation, with a few highly paid managers and cheaper processing staff. The department, tied to national terms and conditions, had responded by aiming to create 'flexible staff' who could tackle the full range of work including the new 'interface' with schools, providing payroll data direct to schools' information systems and answering direct queries:

> they are quite stressed . . . constantly having to perform better and better, and at the same time . . . being able to pick up the phone and know that the person on the other end of the line . . . could determine whether you have that service or not.

Pricing debates illuminate understandings of public business risk. Financial regulations sharply restrict local government's scope for competitive external pricing. Finance officers were therefore caught between two principles: the concept of full cost pricing embodied in

accounting rules, and the evident scope for apportionment of over-
heads to assist the competitive position of the authority (a dilemma
also familiar in the NHS; see Ellwood, 1996). As a finance officer put
it:

> local authorities traditionally have focused on costs and regurgitat-
> ing, reallocating costs. What we are moving to is thinking about
> price as a competitive tool and some [departmental chief officers] are
> closer to thinking about that than others.

The payroll manager had researched the competitors' prices, and his
finance director had decided to match the external 'bureau' prices,
opening up a small negative gap with internal calculated costs, a gap
covered by the much larger group of schools taking the 'standard
service'. The rules allow very little scope for such a calculation:

> We can't charge what we think the market will bear. I mean, we have
> to charge at least direct costs.

There was however some scope for taking on extra public sector work –
for example for colleges – at marginal direct cost:

> the rules are a bit grey but er, yes essentially you have to be able to
> do it within your capacity without taking on additional staff, and
> without impacting on the service that you're providing . . . you can't
> subsidise any external contracts.

Pricing rules are important in financial services because of the huge
fixed costs embodied in information technology (IT) systems, and
hence the large economies of scale. Several nearby authorities had
voluntarily externalised their payroll, implying that at least one large
local private contractor had the expertise and capacity to bid for new
contracts at marginal cost. The only potential public sector counter-
attack was a local authority consortium. This was possible in principle,
but had been stymied, in one manager's opinion, by differences in
political control. High fixed costs, especially buildings and (problematic) IT systems, the implied scale economies, and the pressure on
central services to keep down costs to DSOs, therefore formed a
threatening circle:

you either all stay in it or . . . once someone breaks out, that's it, the whole thing will fall apart I think.

Internal trading relations: the 'invoice' as metaphor

This image of 'things fall apart' once someone breaks the circle of internal charges is an image of corporate inflexibility and risk. A clear illustration is an argument about internal 'invoicing' for service-level agreements (SLAs) in one authority (for more detail see Mackintosh, 1997b). SLAs and the pressures of external competition on the client departments of central services had generated demands for 'pay as you go' systems in 'internal markets'; the latter phrase generally had audible quotation marks around it when used by finance officers, but not when employed by social services or housing managers.

As a housing manager put it, 'As a client I was assured that billing was available', while now she found it was not. Her aim was 'a pay-as-you-use service over which we have some control'. In meetings on internal 'trading', 'control' for client units had two key aspects: preventing unexplained changes to a budget, and forcing down central charges. A recurrent narrative in social services interviews was the 'vanishing budget': lower level managers complaining of unexplained debits (Mackintosh, 1997b). While recognising the danger of escalating bureaucracy by 'playing shops' (a recurrent metaphor in this whole study; see Mackintosh, 1997a), these managers saw 'billing' as the only way to find out what was being provided and to reduce its cost.

A social services manager put it this way:

> where there is a routine service that the departments have confidence in . . . then we would not wish to see the invoices . . . Where however the service . . . is subject to peaks and troughs . . . then it's very much more a pay-as-you-consume [situation] and more detail would be provided, and some sort of invoice, so we could see what was going through.

She contrasted payroll – routine, just wanted to see 'performance indicators' – with personnel, where services like job evaluations might be reduced to cut costs. Most intractable was finance: we 'take on trust what is needed' instead of being told who does what and why. Her opening bid – met with horror – was to demand time-sheet data for finance officers.

Finance managers recognised the 'invoice' demand as about a lack of trust from client departments and a desire for information and cost control. They fought it with estimates of the additional costs of 'an over-bureaucratic internal cheque and invoice-producing system' ('20 per cent impact' in IT services). But they implicitly recognised the force of the 'invoice' as a symbol, proposing:

> what I called semi-invoices, not a real invoice . . . but something that tried to bring . . . the roles and responsibilities of both the client and the contractor to the fore. And both sides didn't like it!

This 'semi-invoice' was a journal transfer with a default period for agreement by the client. Finance officers thought it 'added to the bureaucracy' since at present 'a pen doesn't touch the paper'. And the client departments said, 'when we do we get to see this?'

Note the use of 'real' to mean 'paper' above. Because of Finance control of internal financial transfers, 'real' invoicing meant a paper audit trail. Client departments also wanted an *itemised* invoice, stressing its information function and above all the ability of clients to refuse services once specified. Hence paper was 'real' because it potentially allowed cost savings not currently available to client units.

This was where the 'things fall apart' images reappeared. In internal exchange, one unit's saving is another's deficit. A housing officer sought to refuse to pay legal charges for property disposal that brought her department no income, arguing that SLAs meant 'no paperwork unless there is a benefit'. A finance officer countered with the example of closure of a unit with two staff: no reduction in payroll section costs, yet the overhead the unit carried had to go somewhere. Externally, a school had wanted IT services 'as and when with no baseline commitment'. In that case, interestingly, other head teachers had spotted the problem and urged the authority to refuse: 'it's like asking for an insurance policy after you've been broken into'.

All of these examples are about who carries the costs and risks of lumpy service capacity: 'you can increase or decrease the service but only in big chunks'. Social services purchasers, for example, wanted in-house residential homes to keep emergency beds but wanted to pay for them only when they were used, infuriating unit managers. A social services manager wanted finance pared down to a core 'routine' service, and other irregular provision from a pool of agency staff. A finance officer argued in reply that externalising central services through devolved budgets 'can mean less flexibility', even 'chaos':

if somebody buys a chunk of their own payroll somewhere else . . .
you don't need that bit of the mainframe . . . it's a huge pyramid of
things

– which is brittle, given the difficulty for local authority suppliers of
either abandoning the service entirely or diversifying clients.
Corporate policy officers focused on the impact of devolved budgets
and external contracts on the ability of the authority to handle risk:

One of the things that any administration will do, will be to look
corporately at its budget. And maybe it wants to change the
direction of its budget after its budget has been set. It may have a
problem on the horizon. Schools falling down, or something like
that. And [if] . . . we can't do a supplementary rate, if our reserves
are at their minimum, we can only find it from within.

If a council has 'real' devolved budgets, plus 'CCT-type contracts' and
the 'other degrees of ring fencing, housing revenue account and Care in
the Community' then:

the bit's contracting all the time to be able to deal with emergencies.
So this . . . does represent a loss of control, because that flexibility
will reduce.

So 'flexibility' here is scope for members' priority-setting: a corporate
response to perceived local need. 'Logically', as the finance interviewee
put it, this is squeezed into the area of SLAs, where 'if the politicians or
the administration wanted to they could say well I'm sorry but it's not a
legal agreement . . . they won't even say, 'I'm sorry!' That's what the
problem is.'

Centrifugal pressures: business units in leisure services

that fragmentation could actually just cause the whole thing to fall
apart. (Leisure Services Director)

Leisure services offered a rather different, social version of 'things fall
apart'. This leisure department, like others (A. Clarke, 1994), faced

conflicting pressures from members to generate income and to address rising deprivation and social exclusion. The department had been reorganised into 'business units', and the interviews were full of the language of boundaries, fragmentation and stress:

> I think we're all quite wrapped up in our own business units trying to survive. We have all become quite selfish in business units, focused inward.

The stress was closely associated with costing and trading relations:

> Everything that lives and breathes is now having to be costed . . . in old-fashioned local government you assumed someone did it, you chatted to a colleague and things got done.

In particular the hard split in the early period of the 'contract culture' had meant:

> where you have business units . . . don't look over the fence. If you look over the fence you're charged for it.

Fiscal stress and huge budget cuts meant that people placed great weight on their 'exchange relations' working effectively. When they did not, for example, deliver effective financial information, the response was to turn away and to buy services outside, officially or otherwise. Several managers, urged to run quasi-commercial operations, had begun frankly to operate parallel management systems, keeping their own accounts, buying their own inputs, doing deals to avoid using DSO services, and accepting the financial costs (for example, of double payment for a service or paying your own computer maintenance) as part of life.

The logic went: life is much more risky, overspending has much more serious consequences than before, so therefore I have the right to more 'freedom':

> We have all grown up haven't we? I mean I feel far more frustrated now than I did all those years ago . . . I would like to bypass a lot of the departments . . . I want the whole thing, I want to be able to do what I want to do.

And another manager:

> I can't be bothered justifying to an accountant why I'm spending
> more money advertising this . . . and it was kind of accepted that,
> just leave it alone.
> *You can vire between staff and advertising?*
> I mess around yeah . . . long as the bottom line's all right they're not
> bothered.

Many officers saw dangers in this style, including the effects on
relations with voluntary groups:

> the downside, it is about a negativism in the relationships . . .
> Everything has to have an exchange value rather than a helping
> each other atmosphere, and you have to try and balance that and say
> yes, we do have a new atmosphere, we've got to show what you give
> and what either party pays money for, but on the other hand we wish
> to sustain the old relationships of helping each other and working
> together.

This officer offered the example of a response to an emergency, a fire in
a block of flats at night:

> We had four community centres open within half an hour, and all
> the volunteers there . . . it was all almost easy and a response not
> only from paid staff but from voluntary people and the community
> networks . . . the local authority's well placed to do that and it would
> be very difficult to rebuild those traditional relationships from
> scratch for another body – a new quango set up to deal with
> emergency procedures.

The leisure department director's response was to aim for 'social
conscience': explicit shared social objectives. He wanted an 'internal
economy' based on explicit and accepted cross-subsidy among business
units:

> to create incentives for the units to act independently but at the same
> time rules about the terms of engagement, so whilst I have an
> internal economy, it's an internal economy that's based on certain

principles as to what is legitimate business and what isn't legitimate business.

The income-earning units, he said, needed to be constantly 'reined in', 'bringing them back towards a set of public service ideals' about developing 'citizenship' through ensuring participation of marginalised groups. One vehicle was to be a new 'leisure card': no longer merely providing discounts for disadvantaged groups, it was to become a 'marketing card', generating income from membership and commercial sponsorship to put back into improving facilities. He identified this mix of targeted support and income generation as representing the difference between the private leisure sector and local government:

> we have a role within local government not to simply provide for the fitness, health, quality of life, needs of the individual, but we have a responsibility to engender and encourage citizenship.

It is ironic therefore that the manager of the business unit managing the new card wanted to dissociate it from local government, to promote its financial viability:

> I don't want the council involved, it annoys me. I want to have my own business card with the branding but I have to have a corporate local authority card.

A hall manager similarly wanted nothing to do with the card: he thought it spoiled the image of a popular music venue. And from the opposite ideological pole, a community services manager imagined young people saying:

> If you think we come to this crummy youth club because it's a facility we want to pay for you've got another think coming . . . We help run it, we have our say in what happens, we help each other . . . If we want a night out . . . we then want a commercial deal . . . some decent style.

This was the circle the director was trying to square, but the logic of commercial sponsorship and business units with falling subsidies was pulling against him.

Business without exchange? Two economic discourses in local governance

In these five case studies, people are struggling to cope with the economic implications of decentralisation, contracting and 'business units'. Examining the competing meanings around flexibility, risk and control in context suggests the emergence of two distinct economic discourses.

The first can be called the 'public trading' discourse. Interviewees called it the 'contract culture', meaning provision of a specified service for a specified price. This set of meanings does *not* necessarily imply arm's length relationships, but is associated with a sense of individual vulnerability of business units: with pushing down risk on to their managers. The response of in-house managers is similar across all the case studies except finance and, strikingly, the catering DSO: demands for 'business freedoms', including weakening staff terms and conditions, buying inputs externally, dissociation from the authority. Internally, the perception of working relations being reduced to 'exchange values' is expressed in the demand for invoices and service cuts, and dissociation from corporate consequences, and the focus is on short-term decision-making within constraints.

This public trading discourse, though called 'selfish', has some ethical standing. Provider managers understood it as doing the best for clients on a fixed budget, and the purchasers as even-handedness towards competing providers. In driving economic behaviour, the trading ideas have had some successes in reducing costs, though their cumulative effect on transactions costs must be balanced against this. And finally, the discourse draws on the principal/agent contracting model which assigns to a single principal, the authority, the role of priority setter, construing therefore the main relationship of response to need as between the purchaser and the client.

A competing set of meanings is a discourse of incomplete specification and of adaptive response to need within organisations larger than a 'business unit'. I will call this the 'public business' discourse. This discourse sees the boundaries of 'business units' as permeable, and their budgets as non-contractual, subject to departmental and corporate priorities. Those concerned to limit internal trading reach for military metaphors such as 'terms of engagement'. A finance officer reversed this image in discussing the finance role in internal transfers:

> it's a bit like peace-keeping forces, isn't it? . . . It needs to withdraw, to enable the thing to get together.

These metaphors express a struggle to identify internal working relations as about something other than exchange: the leisure services director identified cross-subsidy in a 'family' of units; a finance officer specified information. The delegitimation of these alternative images in 'trading' contexts is illustrated by the leisure services officer who said, after admitting to unpaid advice from a finance officer, 'don't put that in the report!' The public business discourse legitimises an authority's own strategic aims and also allows a purchaser to pass over some control – and associated risk – to a contracting 'partner', such as a non-profit social care provider.

The ethical basis of this second discourse is, again, flexible response to need, but in this case the response involves the *provider*. Indeed a key element of the 'public business' discourse is to reclaim legitimacy for the provider's role in identifying need and for the provider/client relationship. The public business discourse can recognise multiple clients. The catering DSO had six categories: the Education Department, an 'operational client' in Direct Services, schools, parents, children, and the authority itself (the elected members). In practice, the authority's priorities had dominated DSO strategy, and driven a centralisation which had distanced catering staff from individual schools. The cook supervisors, much praised by management, felt monitored but not consulted.

The DSO management recognised this as a problem to be resolved. A 'public business' story only makes sense if some policy control can be 'given away' by the centre without wrecking economies of scale or destroying scope for response to emergencies. Furthermore, an ethical basis for this discourse which feels solid to participants must also involve incomplete and renegotiable working relations with outside bodies, which thereby acquire political legitimacy. Macneil (1980), in his discussion of contracting, suggests we need to recognise that we have a 'world without principals', and talk instead about 'agents and constituencies'. This is much less comfortable than the single-principal story, but more recognisable to many participants.

Table 5.1 sums up the differences between the two discourses.

There are also, however, clear overlaps between these discourses. For example, both are discourses of financial decentralisation, in which service managers claim more financial control. Although the public business discourse allows more long-term thinking, both discourses allow some space for strategy.

The conclusion of this chapter is not an even-handed one. The focus for economic imagination seems necessarily to rest with the public

TABLE 5.1 Two economic discourses

Public trading discourse	Public business discourse
Tight contract specification	Incomplete specification
Specified service for a price	Variable service on an agreed budget
Short-term focus	Longer-term focus
Even-handed choice between many contractors	Developing relationship with few contractors
Separation of priority setting and delivery	Association of priority-setting with delivery
Emphasis on purchaser/client link	Emphasis on provider/client link
Internal relations take 'exchange value' form	Internal relations take cross-subsidy form
Single principal	Many constituencies

business ideas. The trading discourse has behind it an internal coherence, an ethical basis, and years of government policy. The public business discourse has been generated in part by alarm at the logical consequences of institutional reconstruction on the trading basis. It too has an ethical basis, in local authority legitimacy and the observed need for adaptable and effective provider/client relationships. Its ethical problems lie in the accountability of funders and providers: *like* the 'trading' culture, arrangements of the 'public business' type tend to generate secrecy. Both discourses need an injection of ideas about open information.

About this study

This chapter draws on the project 'Economic Culture and Local Governance', forming part of the ESRC Local Governance Programme. The author would like to thank Madeleine Wahlberg, the research fellow on the project, for her intellectual input; to express particular gratitude for the generosity of the project's two host authorities; and to thank members of the Local Authorities Research

Consortium at the University of Warwick for their input to project design.

The case studies – which involved interviewing, observation and reading documents – were undertaken in two urban authorities, both with a historically high degree of administrative and financial centralisation, and both under high degrees of fiscal stress. The research focused on the interaction between economic discourse and economic behaviour, and case studies were chosen to raise issues of markets, trading, competition, and business strategy. Two of the case studies discussed here, of internal trading and social care contracting, draw on interviews in both authorities. Some minor editing of responses has been done to disguise an authority or respondent.

In addition to the references cited, this chapter draws on an unpublished paper on 'flexibility' in social care contracting. Each case study generated a report discussed with the relevant authority and department, and this chapter also draws upon these feedback discussions. The content of the chapter, including any errors of interpretation, is the sole responsibility of the author.

6 The New Management and Governance of Education

Stewart Ranson, Jane Martin,
Penny McKeown and Jon Nixon

Introduction

The research we undertook provided an opportunity to study the new public management of educational institutions in the context of differentiating governance. It was a study of how schools have accommodated the changes and chosen to develop their management practice over time in contexts of disadvantage. The schools were vulnerable to the pressures of market competition and formula funding based upon numbers rather than 'special' educational needs. The organising assumption of the government of the time was that placing public institutions under the pressure of competition would improve their performance. Moreover, institutions in the public sphere such as schools would flourish under this pressure if they developed models of management which, it was argued, had proved themselves in the private sector. Institutions were encouraged to develop the new public management – valuing the customer, strategic planning, targeting resources, delegation and quality assurance. Better performance depended upon better management: there was one model of management and it was private.

Our studies were located across the United Kingdom in some of the most disadvantaged areas which face the greatest levels of unemployment, poverty and social fragmentation. They are also areas which experience the richness and the opportunities of cultural diversity, but whose cultural traditions often experience exclusion and alienation. The research focused upon worlds of difference and otherness. In such stringent conditions schools would be likely to experience a more complex educational task, thus placing greater constraint upon staffing and resources, and requiring appropriate approaches to learning. Our assumption, however, was that management strategies that succeeded in such extraordinary conditions would work in schools generally. All schools can benefit from understanding what works against the odds.

To make sense of managing learning against the odds required us to explore how schools understand what disadvantage and difference mean for learning; how they are managing change in the curriculum, in teaching and learning and in relations with parents and the community. The research sought to understand the emerging institutional forms of managing change. At the same time the study of management processes – especially in teaching and learning and in home–school relations – explored conditions which enabled institutions to challenge as well as reproduce local cultural traditions. This has enabled the research to theorise the varying forms in which schools develop cultures of learning that value 'difference'.

The chapter will discuss: the neo-liberal reconstruction of education; the schools in their contexts of new publics; the emerging patterns and processes of the new management of schools; the influence of disadvantage, markets and nation upon the formation of management; and finally the implications of this analysis for emerging forms of education governance.

The neo-liberal restructuring of education

The radical reconstruction of education, by the Conservative Government, from the mid-1980s was designed not only to improve 'a service' but also to play a central role in the wider reform of the polity, in the realm of ideas as well as practice (Ranson, 1988, 1994, 1995; Ball, 1993; Deem *et al.*, 1995). The postwar world constituted a political order of social democracy based upon the principles of justice and equality of opportunity and designed to ameliorate class disadvantage and class division. Public goods were conceived as requiring collective choice and redistribution. Thus the significance of systems of administrative planning (the LEA) and institutional organisation (the comprehensive school).

These beliefs were called into question by the Conservatives. A new political order of neo-liberal consumer democracy was constituted, based upon different principles of rights and choice designed to enhance the agency of the individual. The public (as consumer) has been empowered at the expense of the (professional) provider. Public goods, to achieve equity rather than equality, have been conceived as aggregated private choices. Individual (negative) freedom will, it was purported, better deliver the goals of opportunity and social change.

This programme of reforms to restructure power and responsibility in education emphasised market formation, local management and national regulation of the curriculum. The central idea in the new system of governance was that of *market formation*, the objective of which was to increase public choice through two means:

- *empowering active consumer participation* by providing parents with information for accountability, the right to choose, appeal and register complaints, and the opportunity to play a leading role in initiating and running new grant-maintained schools (see Gewirtz *et al.*, 1995; Ball *et al.*, 1994, 1995).
- *differentiating the governance of education* by deregulating local government (for example, control of admissions) and fostering competition by increasing the diversity of institutional types within an internal educational market (see Fitz *et al.*, 1993; Power *et al.*, 1997; Glatter *et al.*, 1997; Halpin *et al.*, 1997).

This context was designed to constitute *the self-managing institution*. Schools, under new formula funding that eliminated traditions of privileged funding for schools in disadvantaged areas, became re-sourced according to numbers of pupils based upon principles of equity. This local management sought to encourage schools to use this autonomy and be flexible in the way they deployed resources and staff in the development of their distinctive identities (see Levačić, 1995, Deem *et al.*, 1995; Deem, 1997). The third strategy involved *national regulation* whereby schools would be subject to a planned curriculum that improved entitlement and standards for all by a better definition of what was taught and learnt (see Penny and Evans, 1997).

The agenda of the government was to reform the local governance of education by deconstructing its central organising principle: its commitment to planned, cohesive systems. The aim has been to change the relations of power, values and organisation between the individual and the system in the pursuit of a new social and political order.

This common political agenda was implemented with different emphases across the nations of the UK (Munn, 1993; Brown, 1997; Adler *et al.*, 1996). New forms of grant-aided school were created, but varied across the national regions: no City Technology colleges were established in Northern Ireland, but a new group of grant-maintained integrated schools was authorised there. In addition, while opting out to grant maintained status was available for governors and parents in England, Scotland and Wales, its uptake has been patchy in different areas. So, for example, almost no Scottish schools chose to opt out. Weaker school boards were created in Scotland compared with governing bodies elsewhere in the UK (Arnott *et al.*, 1997; McKeown *et al.*, 1997) while local management of finance varied between the regions (Bullock and Thomas, 1997). Education authorities, too, varied in their responses to the introduction of the market (Ranson, 1992; Cordingley and Kogan, 1993).

Cultural context thus mediated political intervention. Ideology confronted the boundaries of traditions. In Scotland the reforms were resisted by parents (against testing) and the profession which believed that an alternative model of community comprehensive education had increased social mix, reduced the attainment gap between pupils from different social backgrounds, and contributed to a rising standard of attainment among pupils from all social backgrounds' (McPherson and Raab, 1988). Research into the impact of parental choice revealed, by contrast, increasing institutional segregation and social polarisation (Adler *et al.*, 1989; Echols *et al.*, 1990). In Northern Ireland the reforms strove to increase the impact of parental choice while entrenching the deep structures of religious segregation and selective schooling which characterise the system (McKeown and Connolly, 1992; McKeown *et al.*, 1997).

New Publics

Our study of parents reveals a more assertive and aware parent public than schools have been accustomed to. Yet the data reveal distinctive differences between the 'parent body' associated with the most disadvantaged schools as against those of rather more advantaged schools. The two parent bodies have orientations which resemble Gouldner's (1957/8) distinction between locals, whose 'reference group' lies within immediate organisations or communities, and *cosmopolitans* who bring to their judgements networks of reference and communication which lie beyond the immediate community. The survey of parents suggests that these two groups bring different kinds of challenge to schools. Locals are more likely: to be assertive of their rights; to be actively involved in their child's learning; to value the educational role of parents and the home; to value the school as part of the community;

to have a closer understanding of and be more in agreement with the school and teachers.

The analysis of the survey suggests that 'locals' are more likely to be monocultural and to be associated with poor white schools which are in market decline. Cosmopolitans, however, are more likely: to be interested in the comparative performance of their school *and* other schools; to be more challenging about the school and what it is achieving; to be less in agreement with the teachers and professional judgement. The analysis suggests that 'cosmopolitans' are more likely to be multicultural and to be associated with schools which have capacity and are growing in the local market-place. Locals present a challenge about wanting to be more involved in the learning process *and* in decision-making about it. Cosmopolitans present a challenge to the institution and its performance and a willingness by implication to assert their choice and 'exit' from (Hirschman, 1970) a failing institution. Schools in contexts of disadvantage thus face more challenging, less compliant publics than they have been used to. They also face changing contexts of disadvantage.

New management and its formations

Our study has shown that despite facing adversity, some schools have transformed their management and have begun to grow, to succeed in that respect, against the odds. They have introduced the precepts and practices of the new management and this has provided their institutions with clearer educational purposes, greater coherence in curricular provision, more appropriate differentiation of the learning experience, sharper monitoring of student progress, and improved communication with parents. Some schools have sought to incorporate, but go beyond, the limits of this new professional management, believing that the motivation of pupils to achieve depends upon the school recognising and valuing cultural identity and thus upon reaching shared understanding and agreement with their parent publics. Through this new public management a school gains a double benefit: for the students commitment to the learning process is increased but also the authority of the school as an institution is enhanced.

Some schools with exemplary approaches to management, fulfilling most of what could be expected of them, remain vulnerable and face decline. How do we understand the complexity of the pressures upon institutions and their management in different cultural contexts across the UK? The survey suggests that there are associations between a schools context and particular characteristics of management:

(i) *Disadvantage* In this context all schools develop their support for pupils. In England, N. Ireland and Wales strategies on equal opportunities are strengthened. In Scotland and Wales, schools' orientation to pupil participation in assessment grows with increases in disadvantage. In our Welsh sample schools facing disadvantage are likely to increase support for their teachers with a programme of staff development. On the other hand, the management of schools in contexts of disadvantage in our sample appears to suffer from the constraints of adversity. They are less likely to have strategies for managing quality of teaching and learning, or to innovate in the curriculum. Their networks of support appear to decline, as does the orientation to involving parents in the life of the school. These characteristics appear to illustrate inertia in the face of complex pressures, and isolation from the support which appears to be a precondition for institutional well-being experiencing the greatest adversity.

(ii) *Market formation* Schools in market contexts develop a sharper focus upon their principal purposes and accountabilities, focusing their educational objectives and energies around serving particular children and their parents, detaching themselves from wider community links. Our analysis of local markets indicated growth and decline in school rolls. More than a third of schools with the highest levels of disadvantage are in a situation of declining rolls. Comparing schools which are under-subscribed, and with similar levels of disadvantage, those which are growing are associated with new strategic management of change while those in decline are not. But more than twice the percentage of schools with the highest levels of free school meals (FSM) (over 50 per cent entitlement) have spare capacity and are declining, compared with schools with less than 10 per cent FSM entitlement, and are more likely to be in local authority areas of higher market activity.

(iii) *Nation* There are influences which reflect distinctively different national cultures of school management. School management in the schools in our *English* sample are likely to emphasise new patterns of management, probably influenced by the movement towards local, self-governing institutions. In these schools, the governing body is likely to be integrated into the life of the school. The schools in our *Northern Ireland* sample reflect the Province's traditions of education; selection, formal curriculum and traditional pedagogy, and institutional management. Schools in our survey from *Scotland* are much more oriented to their local communities than our schools elsewhere in the UK: encouraging community use, the participation of parents and adult education. Our Scottish schools exhibit considerable collectivity and integration in decision-making: the teaching staff are likely to meet as a whole group for policy-making and pupil participation is encouraged. As is well-known, however, school boards are weakly developed. The schools in our survey from *Wales* express characteristics of management which emphasise a more professional tradition: professional development of teachers is likely to be a priority; staff are involved in school development and curriculum planning, focused upon the curriculum, on developing learning beyond the formal requirement of the National Curriculum, encouraging curriculum innovation. The new school management is emphasised.

Institutional management within social and political structures: choice and constraint

Schools can achieve against the odds of disadvantage and at times against the pressure of market competition. Nevertheless, it is clear from our research that some schools, in contexts of disadvantage, with exemplary styles of new public management, remain vulnerable and some are in decline in the face of market forces. How do markets work to defeat good institutions when the theory says they should flourish. The rivalry between schools leads to a search for relative advantage which emphasises distinction, social selection and thus the creation of hierarchies of esteem. By enabling parents and schools to make cultural capital the basis of choice, markets reinforce privilege for some and disadvantage for others. Markets in this way work to influence the distribution and inequality of opportunities and thus the interplay of social interests. In so doing they impact upon the social and political processes, the conflicts of interest, which typically underlie the structuring of schools. To understand the fortune of institutions requires analysis of the social and political structures in which they are located.

Regimes: social forces and public interest

Institutions are socially constructed 'regimes' – alliances of power and interest. The analysis of regimes evident in our case studies illustrate different patterns of domination reflecting an implicit struggle between social and public regimes, for example:

- *Traditional, social regimes* In some schools the dominant regimes express alliances between strong interests in the community and professionals. They are social regimes, reflecting the values and interests of particular groups in the community – a particular religious grouping or a particular social class faction. These regimes are traditional, reflecting the role of education in maintaining and reproducing a particular way of life that has become deeply sedimented in the community over years or generations. The schools reproduce the cultural boundaries and classifications which the powerful want to keep in the locality. In these schools the local authorities, the public authority, is invariably weak, unable or unwilling to resist – to take on – the regime which dominates an institution or a community. Or is in collusion with it. The clearest case of this is 'H' school where the most powerful local authority in Scotland – promoting comprehensive education in its public rhetoric – effectively abandoned this disadvantaged school to the power of local social forces, in so doing abdicating its broader public responsibility for the educational opportunities of all.
- *Progressive public regimes* Some of the schools in our study have sought, with the active support and involvement of the local authority, to reform their management structures and perspectives on teaching and learning. The role of the public authority has been key in ousting the old regime which served particular professional and local interests. The new regimes which came to lead these schools reached out to establish shared understanding between the schools and their local parent communities. The restructuring was worked out in partnership with these communities in formal discussion within newly created forums as well as, or alone within, the governing body as the legitimate public arena for a deliberating upon educational purposes and policies which different community traditions must agree to if the institution is to flourish or proceed at all. The role of the profession in these instances is to enable and support the unfolding public agreement about educational values and purposes. The key characteristic of progressive public regimes, then,

is that they are open, public, community-active regimes. The altered coalitions and alliances that these regimes denote involve a radical reappraisal of the key elements within the 'new' management of education.

Market pressure can operate to undermine the regimes of well-managed schools in contexts of disadvantage: not only the subordinate alliances in traditional regimes but also the dominant alliances in progressive regimes. But for different reasons. The subordinate regimes are defeated because they are weaker in a power struggle of social forces. Even well-led institutions are unlikely to succeed against the dominant local social powers. But even well-managed dominant, public regimes can be undermined when market formation characterises the public domain. This paradox requires analysis of the contradictions created within the governance of education by market formation which ensures that public choices lie beyond public control.

The public conditions for institutional management

The analysis of markets argues that there are constraints which schools cannot overcome because the conditions for doing so lie beyond their control. This paradox lies in grasping that the market is a public mechanism, which under the guise of the general interest – the principle of equity – actually works, as we have argued, to reinforce particular social interests against the public, collective choice. In so doing it alters the nature of public governance: institutions which enter into shared understanding and public agreements with their parent communities – for example to create a multi-ethnic institution which reflects that community – come to realise that they cannot be maintained against the unintended consequences of aggregated individual decisions to search for schools which are believed to possess greater social distinction. The effect of this can erode the confidence of local communities in those public judgements and agreements because they cannot be delivered and thus accelerates the drift from the public will.

The market as a result places collective welfare beyond the reach of public deliberation, choice and action: in other words, democracy. While some are empowered by the market to change their position ('exit'), individuals together are denied the possibility of 'voicing' their views to alter the collective distribution of educational welfare (see Hirschman, 1970). 'Exit' is used to hold 'voice' at bay, substituting the power of resources in exchange for the power of the better argument in public discourse. In principle, a community is denied the possibility of clarifying its educational needs and priorities as a whole through the processes of practical reason, in which judgements are formed about what is in the public good based on reasoned argument that leads towards practical collective choices that are monitored, revisable and accountable to the public. In particular, the disadvantaged are denied the possibility of deliberating upon and determining their life chances.

By removing the pattern of social relationships and the emergent structures of power and wealth from the possibility of critical scrutiny civil society is separated from the polity. The market entrenches the powerful beyond control. The market polity colludes in promoting the agency and choice of the public while actually extinguishing it. And while indicating radical change is actually entrenching a traditional order of authority and power.

Where the predicaments of a period are collective or public in nature – such as the educational opportunities of all young people – they cannot be resolved by individuals acting in isolation, nor by 'exit' because we cannot stand outside them: they require public institutions and public choices to resolve them. The case studies have provided illustrations of emergent forms of governance needed to support institutional development in contexts of disadvantage.

Towards new forms of governance

Any understanding of school management has to take account of its location in a distinctive system of governance which does much to shape the purposes, tasks and conditions of school management. Governance constitutes a system of rule about public policy and decision-making in relation to the diverse and competing social interests within society. Indeed, governance constitutes the principle of the public in relation to social interests: its task is to constitute the public rules which regulate social forces in society.

By defining how decisions are made and who should have access to them, governance shapes a society's dominant beliefs about who should have power and how that power should be exercised. These beliefs about the distribution of power themselves reflect dominant values about the form social and political relations should take: individual autonomy and public good, liberty and equality, active or passive participation and representation of interests.

Thus any system of governance, framing the public domain, forms a dominant order of values, interests and power. Such dominant systems constitute the relations of classification and difference in society. Cultures codify the essential boundaries of our deepest values and beliefs. To be placed in a different world is thus to experience the deepest codes of social classification: who, for example, is to be included as a member sets the boundaries of the social order. Systems of governance are systems of social classification which so embody the relations between communities that to be regarded as other or outside is to experience the greatest disadvantage – to be denied the dignity, and thus the sense of agency, that derive from being acknowledged as a fellow citizen with shared rights and responsibilities.

Because these classifications, of who we are and what we can become, can be recognised as social constructions we can also learn that they are amenable to revision. Systems of governance acquire authority if they are perceived as legitimate, that is, they have wide public support, and when legitimate they endure over time.

Some of the schools in our study have been responding to the neo-liberal system of market governance in different ways and in so doing have revealed emergent forms of governance of education which seek to constitute the relation of the public to social forces in different ways.

Governing with consent

The recognition that the motivation of young people to learn is enhanced with the support of parents has been accelerating across the country for some time and has led to a wide variety of practices that involve parents individually in the life of the school. But in the enclaves of exclusion which constitute many disadvantaged communities the fundamental issues of what an education is – what is to be taught and how – cannot be taken for granted. Emergent forms of governance began to emphasise a new orientation to the public. This took different forms of beginning to serve the public, and beginning to involve the public:

A new local governance of education began to emerge in some localities stressing strategic leadership rather than administration, institutional autonomy, partnership rather than control, orientation to public service, enabling and advising rather than providing services, contracting of services, formal rather than informal monitoring and evaluation of performance.

In other locations this new orientation, still driven by the professionals, was not enough. Parents and the community had to be involved. The school had to learn from its parent communities. The learning school grasps that if the dialogue about expectations and capacity is to be effective it cannot be enclosed by the profession alone. Only by listening to the community and its different traditions can a school begin to develop agreement about its most basic purposes and policies.

The school learns that it can only dissolve the boundaries of social classification which stifle the aspirations and agency of young people by reaching out to, and seeking agreement with, the traditions which it serves. An institution needs to constitute within itself the differences which live within the wider community so that by recognising and according them value a school celebrates the springs of identity and purpose of its young people. This approach to governing with consent 'seeks to increase the scope for collective community choice and to widen the local political process in order to meet the challenges of . . . uncertainty' (Stewart and Stoker, 1988).

For some schools the differences between traditions appear so significant that they are creating forums for parent groups to meet, and re-present their educational traditions, in a discussion of the key issues facing the school that can allow shared purposes and policies to emerge for governing body decision-making. A school cannot proceed without the agreement of its parent community and some institutions are learning that because this can no longer be taken for granted new forms of governance must be constituted to allow democratic participation, agreement and consent. By providing forums for participation the new polity can create the conditions for public discourse and for mutual accountability so that citizens can take each other's needs and claims into account and will learn to create the conditions for each other's development. Learning as discourse must underpin the civil society as the defining condition of the public domain.

The challenge is to create a governance for cirit society Intermediary institutions become an essential prerequisite for a participatory democracy (Keane, 1988; Hirst, 1994; Cohen and Rogers, 1995) forming an inclusive network in which all citizens may voluntarily associate. Such a network creates the domain in which private meets public: a public sphere where private interests are reconciled in the context of the public good. As such the civil society will not be just a space to be colonised (Kumar, 1993) but a process of mediation, as Kumar (p. 378) puts it: 'The "concrete person" of civil society differs from the isolated subject of the sphere of morality in that he gradually comes to recognise himself as a member of society and realises that to attain his ends he must work with and through others.' Institutional arrangements which recognise different interests and accommodate cultural diversity will strengthen the public sphere through an active democracy (Martin *et al.*, 1996).

The challenge for a new governance of education

Learning requires motivation, self-worth, confidence and a sense of purpose which generates the energy for endless hard work. These are qualities which society expects of young people in the most difficult of circumstances. In some of the communities we are visiting the scale of disadvantage is such that living itself is an arduous struggle. Many live in the shadow of enclaves of 'otherness'. Despite the scale of such corrosive disadvantage schools can succeed in motivating young people to realise their potential. What we learn from them is that to alter the way students think of themselves and what they are capable of, to transform hopelessness into purpose and kindle capacity, requires a sharing of vision, an energy and cohesiveness of purpose amongst teachers, parents and community traditions. Working together, schools with their communities will generate the sense of purpose that can dissolve the boundaries that emphasise place above horizons.

This is why a restrictive view of professionalism which recognises only pedagogical skill and subject-specific knowledge is inadequate. The recognition of disadvantage, and of the difference it makes to learning, is not an optional extra; nor is it, as so often portrayed, just the concern of a few 'politically motivated' or 'ideologically driven' teachers. An understanding of how disadvantage impacts upon learning, and of how culture both reinforces and resists that impact, is neither 'extra-professional' nor 'unprofessional'. It is an essential component of professional knowledge, without which teachers cannot hope to develop the shared understanding upon which integrative action is based.

Our central argument is that schools must, *as a matter of survival*, reach out to the local community in order to establish an alternative power base from which to reclaim their professional legitimacy and authority. This requires both institutional restructuring and professional reorientation – away from school-led change and towards community-based action that points to a new governance of education.

Structural conditions within the governance of education

To make sense of managing learning against the odds has required us to explore how schools understand what disadvantage and difference mean for learning; how they are managing change in the curriculum, in teaching and learning and in relations with parents and the community. The research has sought to understand the emerging institutional forms of managing change. At the same time the study of management processes – especially in teaching and learning and in home-school relations – has explored conditions which enable institutions to challenge as well as reproduce local cultural traditions. This has enabled the research to theorise the varying forms in which schools develop cultures of learning that value 'difference'.

Analysis clarified the following argument as central to the study. The conditions for young people taking themselves and thus their learning seriously depend upon the school establishing a vision of achievement and practices of learning which are shared by teachers, the different parent communities and the young themselves. Schools can transform the way young people think of themselves and what they are capable of achieving when shared values – of the highest expectations of potential, belief in capacity, and value of cultural difference – are invested in agreed practices of learning and teaching.

The institutional changes necessary, in contexts of difference, to reach agreements with parents and the community about the purposes and processes of learning are at the same time renewing the authority of the institution. Processes, thus, which are central to pedagogy are those which also deepen and reconstitute institutional legitimacy. A study of institutional change at the level of the school is forming understanding of the agreements which underlie not only the renewal of learning but also of governance of the civil society.

The analysis of this report, if it is in any way correct, has the most profound implications for public policy which at present is under the influence of a dominant ideology that schools can be improved merely by addressing internal issues of improvement. Institutional systems and contexts appear residual factors for these ideologists. The argument of this report is that while schools can transcend the constraints they face by internal restructuring, some schools with exemplary management remain vulnerable and are in decline because of constraints which are beyond their control. Structures matter. Many schools will only be able to sustain the strategic changes they make to their institutions when the appropriate conditions are established locally and indeed nationally.

Community-based restructuring offers the best possibility of institutional survival for schools, particularly those located in contexts of disadvantage. However, the structures that support the new community-active regimes remain 'fragile conquest[s] that need to be defended as well as deepened' (Mouffe, 1993, p. 6). They cannot be taken for granted. In particular, they require two conditions, neither of which is currently in place:

(a) *A system of local planning* Each of the schools committed to community-based restructuring is vulnerable to both local demographic change and competition from neighbouring schools. These two factors render the institutions highly vulnerable. The risk of merger or closure is chronic for the majority of schools we have studied and is a measure of the extent to which local planning remains market-led.

(b) *A national agenda that protects response to need* Even in those instances where systems of local planning are in place to support community-active regimes, the lack of a national agenda that favours (or even comprehends) planned response to need (as opposed to unplanned response to the outcomes of market forces) still renders these regimes vulnerable.

About this study

The purpose of the study on which this chapter draws was to investigate the diverse forms of management adopted by schools in contexts of increasingly market-like relations and social disadvantage. The work involved surveys of schools and parents and case study work based on interviews and documentary analysis in a range of schools. The study dealt with systems in operation throughout the UK. The work was conducted between October 1993 and September 1996.

7 The New Management of Community Care: User Groups, Citizenship and Co-Production

Marian Barnes, Steve Harrison, Maggie Mort, Polly Shardlow and Gerald Wistow

Introduction

One aspect of the changes taking place within the local governance of welfare is the way in which those who have been seen as passive recipients of services are taking part in their production. This has been enabled by changes within welfare systems which have separated the purchase from the production of services and by policies which have emphasised consumer responsiveness. But it has also been the result of self-organisation on the part of service users. It is this which formed the subject of our study: 'Consumerism and Citizenship amongst Users of Health and Social Care Services'.

In this chapter we focus on the way in which collective action amongst disabled people and users of mental health services can be seen as contributing to the citizenship of socially excluded groups. This perspective has substantial implications for the policy and practice of community care, as well as for the structures of local governance. The fieldwork was conducted during 1994/5, four years after the passage of the 1990 National Health Service and Community Care Act. Whilst all but one of the six groups we studied predated this legislation, the Act's definition of community care as well as the structural and procedural changes intended to ensure greater user responsiveness provides the context in which both users and officials were negotiating their relationships at the time of our study.

Community care policy: the context

The 1990 Act marked the cumulation of a series of reports and enquiries which had been set up to explore reasons for the slow and uneven implementation of community care policy. Whilst community care had been the declared policy of successive national governments (DHSS, 1971 and 1975), services at a local level were still highly dependent on institutional and hospital-based resources (Audit Commission, 1986). The Audit Commission recommended organisational, staffing and funding changes intended to provide an impetus to change. The content of the 1990 Act itself was presaged in the White Paper *Caring for People* (Secretaries of State for Health, Social Security, Wales and Scotland, 1989) which set out how the government proposed to improve community care over the next decade and into the twenty-first century. The White Paper defined community care as:

> providing the services and support which people who are affected by problems of ageing, mental illness, mental handicap or physical or sensory disability need to be able to live as independently as possible in their own homes, or in 'homely' settings in the community. (p. 3)

Political commitment to the policy derived from both ideological and resource considerations. The social security budget which paid for residential care in the burgeoning private sector care homes during the 1980s was getting out of control. Community care policy was intended to curtail the 'perverse incentives' which had led to a massive increase in this budget. Whilst warning voices were heard saying that community care should not be considered a cheap option, it was certainly viewed as a cost-effective one. Moreover, residential care and long-stay hospital care were collective solutions to welfare 'problems' which were inconsistent with the individualist ideology of the 1980s. An assertion that family care was both the best and the preferred option for those with social care needs fits neatly with an ideological position which emphasised personal responsibility for welfare. It also had the added advantage of saving the state a good deal of money. The Carers' National Association estimated in 1995 that the total value of in-kind contribution of family care was £30 billion.

Political preferences for community care were supported by a professional commitment based in an analysis of the detrimental impact of institutional care. Wolfensberger (1972) first developed the philosophy of 'normalisation' in relation to people with learning difficulties (then known as mentally handicapped people). The three basic principles of normalisation were later defined as:

(i)   Mentally handicapped people have the same human value as anyone else and also the same human rights.
(ii) Living like others within the community is both a right and a need.
(iii) Services must recognize the individuality of mentally handicapped people. (King's Fund, 1980, p. 14)

Normalisation was a response to the effects of institutional care which had served to separate 'abnormal' or 'subnormal' people from the 'normal' population. Breaking down institutional practices and the stigmatisation resulting from these was a key strand in the development of professional thinking about community care. Closing the institutions and supporting those who were being moved out was seen as the main task. Services were to be 're-provided' in the community to replace those which had been concentrated within long-stay hospitals. This meant not only finding accommodation for people whose 'home' had been a hospital, but also opportunities for activity, the provision of personal support and specialist therapeutic intervention where necessary.

Whilst broadly accepted as the philosophical underpinning of community care, normalisation attracted criticism of the objective of making individuals fit with dominant assumptions about what it is to be 'normal'. In response Wolfensberger (1983) later redefined the philosophy as 'social role valorization'. This was intended to emphasise the significance of the extent to which people are able to fill socially valued roles. Thus, it recognises that it is not enough for people to be 'in the community', their role within the community has to be experienced and recognised by others as a valued one. This is particularly important for the self-esteem of those with stigmatised identities – especially people with learning difficulties or those with mental health problems (Ramon, 1991).

Whilst the NHS and Community Care Act was centrally concerned with 'community care', any discussion of what 'community' might mean in this policy context is signally lacking. The unstated assumption underpinning the way in which the term community was used is that it is, quite simply, 'not hospital'. Community, in the terms of the Community Care White Paper (Secretaries of State, 1989) is living at home or 'in homely settings' in regular contact with family, friends and neighbours. Community is assumed to apply to locality: community services are 'locally based' in contrast to the 'remote mental hospitals' situated geographically separate from the original homes of most of their inmates.

The disputed nature of the concept, evident in much sociological literature exploring both empirical and theoretical aspects of community (for example, Bulmer, 1987), is ignored in official policy. In practice the objects of community care policy are individual disabled people, older people, people with mental health problems, and their families. Community is simply the unexplored context within which families are expected to provide care to their needy members. Community care policy has nothing to say about the needs of the communities into which those leaving institutional care were to be discharged.

As well as setting out the organisational and funding arrangements through which community care services were to be delivered, the Act sought to achieve a shift in favour of consumer rather than producer interests (Harrison, 1991). In the context of changes throughout the public sector with similar aims, this was to be achieved through:

- encouraging user and carer involvement in the process of assessment by which services were to be accessed;
- requiring that social services authorities consult with users, carers, voluntary organisations and others during the production of community care plans;
- the introduction of a complaints procedure containing an element of independent review;
- the establishment of 'arm's length' inspection units with input from lay members – who could be, but are not necessarily, users of services.

Before the passage of the Act, 'user involvement' had been something encouraged by the more innovative social services authorities (see Barnes and Wistow, 1994). By the early 1990s it had become a statutory requirement. But if there was now top-down encouragement to listen to what service users were saying, there was also a growing movement amongst service users who were dissatisfied not only with the nature of the services they were receiving, but also with their lack of control over them.

The British Council of Organisations of Disabled People had been formed in 1981, in response to dissatisfactions not only with statutory services, but also with able-bodied control of voluntary organisations. 'People First', an organisation promoting self-advocacy on the part of people with learning difficulties, was established in the UK in 1984, whilst the mid-1980s also saw the first mental health patients' councils being established in the UK. Both locally and nationally, user groups were articulating their own objectives which were not always consistent with those of officials who were starting to promote user involvement.

It is within this context that we consider action from within self-organised groups of disabled people and people with mental health problems, and the response that this has received from health and social care officials.

User groups and community care

Whilst the groups we studied all aimed to influence the way in which statutory agencies delivered community care services, they also had broader aims. They focused on the legacy of prejudice, discrimination and disempowerment experienced by disabled people and people with mental health problems resulting not only from exclusionary social policies, but also from public reactions to those considered 'different'.

The broad objectives of community care policy were welcomed in principle by most of those we interviewed. However, users were critical of the failure to resource the successful implementation of the policy. Some also recognised that it was more difficult for them to 'organise' those who were dispersed throughout the community rather than gathered together within an institutional location. Their methods of making contact with service users therefore had to adapt to changing patterns of service provision.

One interviewee reflected a concern that the changes in welfare provision were emphasising individualism rather than collectivism. He saw the campaign for anti-discrimination legislation with its emphasis on individual rights as an example of this. Nevertheless, there was a high level of commitment to the need for such legislation amongst the disabled people's groups. Involvement in campaigning on this subject was less evident amongst the mental health user groups. Similarly, disabled activists were more frequently committed to the objective of control over services through the ability to purchase them directly than were mental health activists. Legislation to enable social services authorities to make direct payments was introduced after this research had been completed.

It is important to distinguish two strands of thinking within the disability movement on such issues. One is the widespread commitment to the social model of disability which was expressed by one of our interviewees as follows:

> the common identity is the social model of disability. And that's been a difficult one to get over to disabled people who have been brought up in the old medical model and it is quite difficult to get people to see that we are not disabled by our bodies going wrong, we are disabled by society not working appropriately to enable us to participate in society.

The medical model results in services intended to alter the bodies of individual disabled people, or to enable them to make psychological adjustments to cope with their 'abnormality'. In contrast, the social model targets exclusionary practices within education, employment, environmental design and public attitudes which constitute barriers to participation. But the social model can have both an individualist and a collectivist emphasis. This is evident in the distinction between models of 'independent living' and 'integrated living' which have influenced the design of alternative services such as the Centre for Integrated Living which one of our study groups manages jointly with the local authority. The concept of 'independent living' is seen to emphasise both the aim of individual choice equivalent to choices available to the general population and the rights of individuals to have their needs met. 'Integrated' living is seen to emphasise the full participation of disabled people within the community. It emphasises the responsibilities as well as the rights of citizenship, and mutuality as well as independence. Amongst the activists we interviewed there was evidence of this difference of emphasis and of debate about what this meant in terms of the strategies that groups should be pursuing.

The other dimension of the social model is the 'rights' versus 'needs' approach to community care. Oliver (the first Professor of Disability Studies in the UK) argues against the notion that 'need' should have a central place in determining welfare policy and provision (1996). He claims that no professionalised service based on the assessment of need rather than on citizenship rights to welfare can redress the imbalance of power between disabled people and service providers, or ensure that the receipt of support is not dependent on budgetary constraints. This has been an important strand of thinking both in relation to anti-discrimination legislation, and in the campaign for direct payments.

Whilst the collectivist and individualist versions of the social model have different emphases, they both share a view that community care policy needs to focus outwards on the nature of the community in which people live and from which they have been excluded, rather than inwards on the impaired functioning of the individual.

Although the social model has not been as influential within thinking amongst mental health service users, there are important aspects to be found amongst the groups we studied and more broadly within mental health user movements. Some users accept mental health problems as an illness capable of being treated by the use of drug therapy. They seek acceptance of the 'normality' of mental illness as part of the experience of many people at some stage in their lives, and argue that being mentally ill should not result in stigmatisation or social exclusion. Others argue that mental health problems should be understood in a broader context:

> I think that widening out the ideas so that people can see their mental health as being about their emotional life, about their relationships, about their relationship to the environment and so on, and seeing so-called mental health problems as symptoms, or mental illness symptoms as being extreme versions of what every- body experiences – it seems to me is the way to break down stigma which people with mental health problems face. It's an aspect of re- integration of people with mental health problems and it's a different way of seeing re-evaluation of the quality of life which is very important for the Green movement and all sorts of political, social processes.

The mental health groups we studied sought to include amongst their members and their objectives action capable of responding to both views. Again, what they share is a belief that, in order to enable people to participate within communities, action is necessary within commu- nities as well as directed at individuals.

User groups and new management

The shift from producer to consumer interests represented by changes introduced by the 1990 Act were not experienced entirely positively in terms of the potential for increased influence by user groups. In spite of the statutory requirement to consult, the majority of interviewees felt that only limited user involvement in planning was allowed. One group believed that only 'passive' users were consulted. Another thought that their local authority had previously scored political points by involving users. Now that user involvement was an expected aspect of the way in which authorities should work, there was less commitment because there was less to be gained from it politically. The group regarded their relationship with the local authority as worse than it had been in the mid-1980s.

At one level, health authority, trust and local authority officials responded very positively to the existence, activity and new formal legitimacy accorded to user groups. Officials did not offer any principled objection to these developments, recognising a changing political and social climate in which the user voice ought to be heeded, both on the normative grounds that paternalism was now inappropriate and on more pragmatic ones which recognised that users had a level of knowledge and expertise not always possessed by professionals and service managers. This was not to say that user views were represented as being dominant in official thinking, rather, officials perceived themselves as effectively 'holding the ring' amongst a plurality of interest groups:

> The point that I'm trying to make is that our relationship with [user groups] is no different to others . . . They are just one of the players and they take their chance in the game like everyone else.

This professed role as umpire in a pluralistic game is a source of legitimacy for the official managerial role which frequently spilled over into micropolitical manipulation. A number of respondents referred to the 'user card' (Mort *et al.*, 1996), a resource to be employed in attempts to secure their own ends:

> The card that you have to play all the time is user need, user preference and user view on something, and whether I am negotiating with other people inside this building, arguing with the Trust, negotiating with the Social Services Department, arguing about how we ought to spend joint finance . . . you in effect play the user card.

Yet the same officials who had expressed positive views about user groups had simultaneous and serious reservations about them. The groups were variously held, with numerous examples, to be unrepresentative either of users or of the general public and to be 'chaotic', poorly organised and riven by internal politics. In summary, officials simultaneously held the user groups to be legitimate and illegitimate, practically useful and yet useless. This offers an obvious opportunity for what might be called strategic micro-politics: the ability to gain legitimacy from user group opinion when it is acceptable to officials, and yet grounds to disregard that opinion when it is inconvenient (Harrison *et al.*, 1997).

The dilemmas faced by groups seeking to find a place within the changing system of local governance can be summarised as follows:

- There is potential for their energies to be dissipated as a result of seeking to engage with an increasingly diverse set of bodies resulting from the fragmentation of systems of governance.
- There is an associated danger of becoming reactive to agendas set by others, rather than being able to determine their own priorities for action. As authorities increasingly look for feedback from users on their own performance, user groups are a readily accessible source of information. Responding to an increasing number of such requests presents user groups with the dilemma of refusing to do this and thus being accused of being uninterested in involvement, or responding to requests from authorities and thus being unable to pursue issues which their members or other users have identified as priorities for action.
- Dependence on statutory agencies for financial support and the potential inhibition on campaigning activities as a result.
- At an ideological level, having their agendas shaped by a consumerist philosophy. This may provide legitimacy for user involvement, but may also encourage a model of competing interest groups, or the pursuit of individual rights, rather than encouraging collective action to achieve social change which can benefit those who are not involved in user groups as well as those who are.

User groups and citizenship

Our analysis demonstrated ways in which user groups have adopted strategies which are intended to enable people to become more effective consumers of services (Barnes and Shardlow, 1996a). But this is insufficient as a way of understanding the significance of user self-organisation and we also need to consider ways in which collective action can contribute to citizenship.

The renewed interest in notions of citizenship within both academic and political discourse can be seen as evidence of crisis in the relationship between individuals, communities and government. The concepts of both citizenship and community are being reconstructed as a basis for understanding forces which include or exclude individuals and social groups, as well as changes taking place within systems of governance. They are thus highly pertinent to a consideration of ways in which excluded groups are seeking to influence policies intended to enable them to live ordinary lives within communities (Barnes, 1997).

Both concepts, citizenship and community, are being used to describe very different versions of the social changes taking place. Within the tradition of political liberalism, the 'citizen' of the Citizen's Charter is an individual consumer of state services, guaranteed procedural rights of proper treatment, but without substantive rights to receive services of which he or she stands in need, and with no suggestion that he or she should have a part in determining the nature of services in the first place. In contrast, critics on the left and operating from a feminist perspective have embraced the notion of community membership as a basis for citizenship, whilst emphasising difference within and between communities, and addressing the implications this can have for the roles citizens might play in the collective well-being of the community. Feminists emphasise the significance of private as well as public roles through which citizenship can be expressed (for example, Lister, 1995; Pateman, 1992), whilst others (for example, Roche, 1992) have emphasised citizenship obligation, or citizenship practice (Prior, Stewart and Walsh, 1995).

For communitarians, upholding the normative status of community within the moral order is the way of overcoming the assertive individualism of rights-bearing consumers and citizens (Etzioni, 1995). In reaction to this, the legitimacy of the moral sway of community has been questioned by those who see community as a force which can exclude difference (Friedman, 1989). Community itself has been reinterpreted both empirically and theoretically so that an equation between community and locality can no longer be assumed. Communities based in *shared identities* as, for example, women, black people, or disabled people, and communities of *interest* based in common commitment to a cause such as environmentalism, may be more important as a basis for community membership than locality, and may provide greater motivation for participation in action through which citizenship can be expressed (Phillips, 1993).

Locality nevertheless remains a significant factor in the bond between individuals and governments. State services which are managed,
provided and, in some instances, governed at a local level are often the
means through which the relationship between the individual and the
state is mediated. Administrative boundaries can determine the nature
of services to which individuals have access, as well as the political
ideology through which they are governed. The relationship between
the management and government of public services is another key
factor in the debate about the changing nature of citizenship.

In this context collective action amongst service users can be
considered to provide a means through which citizenship can be
expressed in three ways:

1. through enhancing the *accountability* of public services to their
    citizen users;
2. through pursuing objectives of achieving social rights associated
    with the *status* of citizenship;
3. through providing a forum from which excluded individuals can
    contribute to the *practice* of citizenship.

Accountability

Users can require service commissioners and providers to give account
of their actions, even though they are not in a position to hold them to
account.

> it is very easy for professionals to write a really glowing document
> saying this is what we are providing, but if the end result is that it is
> not what is really happening, then they have to be made accountable
> for that particular statement and so one of the roles I think we play is
> to actually challenge the quality assurance issues, for instance, laid
> down in the contract between the mental health unit and the
> purchasing group of the health authority. And if they don't meet
> that then we will actually raise it both with the purchaser and say,
> you know, what are you going to do about this? (Mental health
> activist)

User groups enable those who have been excluded from such forums
to develop skills and confidence to challenge those unused to being
required to account for their actions:

One of the major roles that we can play is actually to say, we are users, we can participate at this level, we can articulate, we can challenge, we can negotiate, we can write papers, we can do this, instead of [being] some bumbling idiot that doesn't know what they are doing. (Mental health activist)

Citizenship rights

Disabled people's groups are explicitly campaigning for 'civil rights' through the campaign for anti-discrimination legislation (passed after the fieldwork was completed). Both disabled people's groups and mental health service user groups challenge the exclusionary forces of discrimination and aim to achieve social justice in terms of access to services as well as to all aspects of community life:

We are all unanimous that we want to have people with mental health problems to have much more say in their life in general, where they live, what medication – it's just the right to do as other people that are sound in mind, limb and body want, we want the same for people, you know, all of us. (Mental health activist)

People with mental health problems can, in some circumstances, experience explicit constraints on their civil rights. Those assessed as being mentally disordered can be compelled to enter hospital and receive treatment; the management of their financial affairs may be taken out of their hands; they may effectively be prevented from exercising their right to vote. Advocacy by user groups can enable individuals to exercise their procedural rights in such circumstances, although there was no evidence of campaigning against compulsory powers *per se* amongst the groups we studied (Barnes and Shardlow, 1996a).

The practice of citizenship

User groups provide a forum in which people can 'practise' citizenship in three ways:

1. Participation in the group itself provides support and self-help to members and others who benefit from advocacy provided by the groups. This can be of particular importance to people who have experienced the stigma attached to mental illness:

> I think the majority of people who have been in [the group] . . .
> they've all got . . . similar experiences of having suffered not
> only from illness or trauma, but very often from the kind of
> negative attitude that's out in society towards illness to do with
> problems that affect you mentally . . . so the principles always
> seem to be the same, that you're trying to make things better for
> people. [mental health activist]

The groups comprise voluntary associations which contribute to
the overall vitality of civil society, as well as being an important
source of friendship and understanding to those they support
directly.

2. In some instances the support received from within the group can
    be a base from which participants can take on other roles within
    the community:

    > We've had about three or four young women that have started
    > and we've had one young man here, he was both physically and
    > mentally disabled and when I first met him, I thought never in
    > my life are you going to get fit to get a job. He's working for the
    > Council full time! [Mental health activist]

    For some groups achieving broader participation in public roles
    is an explicit part of their purpose:

    > More [disabled] women are having relationships . . . getting
    > married . . . having children. So it is obvious to anybody that
    > we need access to health care, we need access to schools, disabled
    > parents need to be able to go on to Boards of Governors and
    > things like that to have a say in their child's education . . . But
    > we still can't get the message over to everybody. [Disabled
    > activist]

3. Groups provide a means through which people who receive
    services can contribute to their production. There are many ways
    in which user groups are achieving this: including: through training
    professionals and managers, through participation in planning and

purchasing forums, or through the joint management of services. Collective organisation enables user participation in service decision-making to be more effective than would be possible without such organisation:

> I think the Patients' Council works well because it does work on the principle that it's not one or two service users . . . sitting on the edge of a meeting or a Trust Board or a management meeting or whatever, it is managers, senior managers coming to meetings of service users to be accountable and really they have to account on the spot. (Mental health activist).

The groups are making a direct contribution to determining the nature of community care services, and in some instances providing an alternative vision of what such services should comprise. They suggest that rather than thinking solely in terms of community 'care', policy should be emphasising community 'participation' (Barnes, 1997).

User groups offer a very different model of the 'active citizen' from that of the traditional volunteer. This model is one in which people who have been constructed as needy take action not only to support each other, but to contribute to the development of welfare services in which all may participate. They seek not only a choice of services more capable of meeting individual needs, but also to enable people to participate in collective purposes for what they see as the good of the community as a whole. They are concerned not only with enabling people to realise their citizenship rights, but to contribute to the practice of citizenship through determining the nature of welfare and playing their part in other social and public processes.

Participation in groups can be a source of valued roles for marginalised people as well as providing experience of the potential of collective action for social change. User groups contribute to action within civil society through which both welfare and government can be democratised. Nevertheless, activists recognise that only a minority of users will want to play an active part in groups. The pursuit of objectives which are intended to enable all mental health service users and all disabled people to have more influence over the services they receive, and which challenge a narrow welfarist view of community care, reflect a concern with the citizenship of those beyond movement activists.

Conclusion

The focus on user self-organisation in this project has made it possible to consider the implications of user activity for the relationship between excluded citizens, their communities and processes of governance. Interviews with officials indicated that, whilst there was broad commitment to the principle of user involvement, few readily associated this with notions of citizenship (Barnes *et al.*, 1996). When invited to reflect on this some did feel that citizenship provided one dimension of their relationship with users and some acknowledged that the role of citizen was one which they shared with those who used their services. However, there was also evidence of a reluctance to acknowledge organised user groups as being anything other than self-interested pressure groups, and to accord them a higher legitimacy than any other stakeholder group within the increasingly complex systems of local governance (Mort, Harrison and Wistow, 1996). This position fails to respond to the cultural significance of autonomous action on the part of those constructed as dependent, or even incompetent, and the impact of this on the nature of the discourse through which welfare is constructed.

Collective action on the part of mental health service users and disabled people has the capacity to challenge the assumptions of welfare professionals as well as lay attitudes towards 'needy' and stigmatised groups. There is evidence of collective action by user groups impacting on the nature of service provision, on decision-making processes, and on both national and local policy. Nevertheless, much of the rhetoric concerning the shift from producer to consumer interests which surrounded the 1990 Act has been seen to be empty as resource constraints have meant that accessing basic services via the assessment process is denied to many disabled people (Davis *et al.*, 1997). Within this context will user groups feel themselves forced into a position in which defending the individual interests of service users means they lose sight of broader campaigning issues? The introduction of legislation to enable local authorities to make direct payments to disabled people to buy care is one example of successful campaigning by the disability movement. But it can also be seen to be a triumph for exit models of influence, rather than those of voice. There is some evidence that user groups are increasingly entering the market as service providers. Such moves are being made reluctantly in some instances, in recognition of the way in which this can transform social movements into more formal organisations with less scope for creative thinking and action. Nevertheless, in an uncertain future, taking direct control of services may feel a better option than expending energy in seeking to influence defensive social care providers. Social movements always face the dilemma of incorporation as their ideas start to become accepted and transformed within the mainstream. Many of the activists we spoke to recognised ways in which they had changed and the tensions which were affecting future plans. User groups are not fixed in organisation, objectives or activities. They seek to respond to diverse needs amongst their members and changing circumstances in which those needs are experienced. Participation in the movement leads to changes in the participants. Thus we can expect to see further changes in the place they occupy within the new management of community care, and within systems of local governance more broadly.

About this study

We studied six groups: three mental health service user groups and three disabled people's groups. We also studied the responses to these groups of 'officials' in local health and social services agencies. The purposive sample was intended to include groups adopting different approaches to influence within statutory health and social service agencies. Thus we included groups which had roles in providing services, those which sought to work in partnership with statutory agencies in service planning and development, and groups which adopted campaigning tactics. Interviews were conducted with activists in the groups and with key officials with whom they were in contact. Interviews were taped, transcibed and analysed using the Ethnograph computer package for the analysis of qualitative data. Interview transcripts were sent to user activists for checking and case study reports were sent to each of the groups for respondent validation. Four of the six user groups met researchers to discuss the analysis before results were finalised.

In addition to listed publications arising from the project, detailed discussion of two case studies will be published in Barnes, M., Harrison, S., Mort, M. and Shardlow, P., *User Movements and the Local Governance of Welfare* (Bristol: The Policy Press).

8 Reframing the Delivery of Local Housing Services: Networks and the New Competition

Barbara Reid

Introduction

The creation of quasi-markets within the social housing sector has put more emphasis on local authorities' indirect regulatory, strategic and enabling roles, increased cost-consciousness and encouraged competition between a full range of providers of local housing services, and heralded in 'the new management' (Goodlad, 1993; Le Grand, 1990; Stoker, 1991). At the same time the emergence at local level of networks and coalitions of service-providing organisations and the growth of interorganisational approaches to housing and urban management projects has increased opportunities for collaboration and coordinated approaches. This development extends Ball *et al.*'s (1988) notion of 'structures of housing provision', with its focus on social agents and their interlinkages, to encapsulate generative causal mechanisms and the exercise of powers and liabilities within these mechanisms. This echoes the approach and focus proposed by Bhaskar (1975) and Sayer (1984).

Organisations which provide local housing services are, to refer to Mackintosh's argument in Chapter 5, caught between the discourses and practices of quasi-markets and networks, and of competition and collaboration. As Lowndes shows in Chapter 2, local authorities have been at the forefront of the public sector management and organisational change, though many of the issues she raises apply also to other organisations providing local housing services. The change for them has two basic dimensions. As the traditional local authority-led model of local housing service provision has been weakened, so the organisation and delivery of local housing services increasingly depends upon networks of organisations, linked together cross-organisationally, cross-functionally and cross-departmentally intervening in specific 'projects'. In short, there has been a fundamental alteration to the governance of local housing services as seen in the patterns emerging from the governing activities of the expanding range of actors involved in providing services (Kooiman, 1993).

This chapter considers the processes through which housing policy is implemented locally and their modification through the combined effect of changes in central government policy and changing local responses. It goes on to explore the organisational response at local level, focusing on the operation and management of the emerging interorganisational arrangements. It then considers the management change which is associated with these arrangements, making the point that the management practices which are developing in the sector are eclectic in nature, and tend not to conform to any type of 'standard model'. The chapter concludes by arguing that local housing service provision has not abandoned its public service orientation in favour of market principles, but has instead developed an intermediate position, using management and organisational techniques from across the whole scope of policy coordination to maintain a sustainable stake within the new competitive environment for the sector as a whole and for its component organisations.

The context: reframing housing policy

Since 1979, when the Conservatives took office, public sector intervention in the sphere of housing has been transformed. First, there has been a vastly diminished and constrained role for local authorities and other public sector housing operators. Second, there has been an emphasis on private sector solutions to housing 'problems', reinforced by policy measures such as privatisation through the right to buy, large-scale transfers of stock, the private finance initiative, and marketisation initiatives such as the attempt to introduce compulsory competitive tendering of local authority housing management services. Third, there has been a focus on housing associations as hybrid 'mixed economy' service providers, capable of working simultaneously in both public and private sector operating environments (Rao, 1990; Stewart, 1988).

An obvious result of these trends has been the fragmentation of local housing services, described by Hoggett (1991) as 'a crisis of the bureaucratic mode', and a subsequent emphasis on the need to reestablish local capacity and reintegrate services by drawing together service providers in joint projects, representing the statutory sectors, as well as from the private sector, the voluntary sector and from other interest groups. Given 'the complexity of joint action' (Pressman and Wildavsky, 1984), the joint working arrangements which have emerged are disparate and complex in their institutional, functional and managerial features.

Interorganisational initiatives have clustered around particular aspects of housing service provision, suggesting that certain policy areas have both driven and been capable of sustaining joint projects. These policy areas are not discrete, nor perhaps, are they surprising. They comprise:

- *Projects involving the use of or necessitating the access to private finance, usually centred on residential development projects.*
  Projects, for example, funded under the Business Expansion Scheme, or involving the use of housing association-raised private funding, have generated different forms of interorganisational arrangements, including the development of different approaches to agency arrangements, the use of brokering arrangements, mergers and partnership agreements;
- *Projects linked to local authorities developing their 'enabling' role.* In practice many of the joint projects in this category stem from local authorities changing their role. Large-scale voluntary transfers of council stock, voluntary and compulsory competitive tendering of housing management services, and Housing Action Trusts are all examples of cases where the redistribution of housing responsibilities and powers has generated interorganisational activity. Other service areas, such as homelessness advice and referrals, local social housing waiting lists and one-stop services have also provided a focus for joint planning and projects;
- *Area-based renewal initiatives.* City Challenge and the Single Regeneration Budget are examples of initiatives which have resulted in the growth of interorganisational projects, not only because they rely upon leveraged funds and public–private sector links, but also because of the integrated approach which they require, in terms of

crossovers between different functional service delivery areas, and between statutory organisations, the voluntary sector and local community groups;

- *Consumer involvement.* Tenant participation, resident involvement, customer care and Citizen's Charter initiatives have led to the development of joint arrangements which take account of service user and tenant organisations;
- *The joint service provision model: community care.* Because it is a requirement of community care that the key services of housing, social services and health collaborate at local level to provide care services, this has provided an obvious focus for joint arrangements;
- *Top-down and bottom-up models.* The majority of the pressures to develop joint arrangements have been 'top-down', linked to the promotion of government initiatives. However, at the same time, 'bottom-up' responses are significant, where local housing service providers themselves are active in developing new practices and projects in the context of the redistribution of powers and resources.

The reframing of housing policy at local level has partly been driven by central government policy on privatisation and reducing the size of the state sector through the formation of partnerships with the private sector. However, the local response to this has led to the growth of more broadly focused interorganisational networks which go beyond the public–private sector partnership model and incorporate a wider range of organisations, interests and competencies.

The organisational response

Much of the early discussion of the joint working arrangements which were developing as the result of national policy pressures assumed that the partnerships being established were, and would continue to be, primarily bilateral in character. Local authorities were the primary partner, seeing their enabling role in terms of the contract culture. The purpose of contracts was to reconstruct the implementation capacity which was in the process of being diminished. The subcontracting of areas of management responsibility, management agreements involving organised groups of tenants, the transfer and delegation of housing stock in transfer agreements, and the targeting of renovation grants on private landlords in return for the right to nominate homeless households as tenants are all examples of the way in which this kind of bilateral activity was understood.

Multilateral activity has now become more important as a local policy coordination and implementation mechanism. Multilateral initiatives, referred to as 'multi-actor implementation' by O'Toole (1986), because they involve an extensive range of different specialist areas and organisations, are able to cut across functional divisions of labour as well as bridge gaps between public and private organisations. They can also bring together organisations and interests which represent different territorial and geographical areas. Thus multilateral arrangements are seen as a means of tackling complex problems, by combining areas of expertise not normally available in a single organisation or pair of organisations.

Examples of multilaterally organised projects include development consortia comprising more than one local authority or groups of housing associations working together to innovate and secure economies of scale across several small-scale developments; projects based on individual local authorities and local housing associations working on new IT-based systems or locality planning approaches to aspects of services; 'housing-plus' initiatives, such as foyers, where local employers and housing organisations collaborate to cater for both the residential and employment training needs of young people; or strategy-building initiatives where local statutory organisations, private sector bodies, voluntary sector groups and community groups collaborate on an area of shared strategic interest. Multilateral approaches, though more complex organisationally and managerially, provide opportunities for integrated approaches, for maximising specialisms, and for innovation.

Bilateral and multilateral arrangements provide for different approaches to organising joint working. Harrigan and Newman (1990) refer to the forms of interorganisational cooperation which result from organisations' need to work together as 'coalition strategy alternatives'. The following patterns were found in the context of housing:

- A propensity to establish arm's-length agencies, where the aim is to create a 'neutral' vehicle through which to operate. The decision to establish an arm's-length agency can also be tactical: the aim may be, for example, to secure tax or other financial advantages, to control the distribution of power in a partnership, or to build cross-organisational links.

- A focus on building strategic alliances or coalitions of interest, where the longer-term interest may be, for example, to prepare joint strategy, to promote, safeguard and defend specific practices and interests, or to share expertise and knowledge.
- A focus on joint arrangements clustered around marketable 'products', capacities and expertise. Here, joint working arrangements are based on combinations of specialised expertise, which, once formed in relation to a particular joint project, are capable of being 'marketed' as contributions which individual or groups of organisations could offer to other potential joint ventures or projects. There is therefore a keen desire to standardise any organisational inputs capable of subsequent replication.
- A focus on joint arrangements which incorporate groups of users or tenants. While the majority of joint initiatives in this category result from 'good practice' obligations on housing service providers to involve tenants in particular initiatives, other 'bottom-up' organisational groupings do exist. A difficulty here is that once such arrangements are established, the fact that tenants' and user groups tend to be organised relatively informally means that they may not in effect be equal partners in a joint venture, and their participation may have been sought for cooption purposes only.
- The involvement of external consultants as intermediaries and coordinators of joint projects. Because of external consultants' substantial involvement in this area, they accumulate potentially marketable experience. There is a potential problem over the 'transfer out' of organisational and process knowledge and the potential limiting of organisational learning because of reliance upon commercial consultancy.

Management change

The management practice which is emerging in interorganisational local housing networks is difficult to categorise. The redistribution of powers and resources associated with the structural reframing of the housing policy 'system' has led to an explosion of interorganisational activity which has provided a number of challenges for the coordination of local housing services. First, the hierarchical implementation structures and patterns of policy decision-making with which the public sector, and particularly social housing, is associated are challenged by more emergent styles of policy design and implementation which favour negotiated forms of bargaining and exchange, both as a means of identifying the scope and goals of policy or projects, and managing the implementation process. Hyder (1984), Emery and Trist (1965), Barrett and Hill (1984) and also Pressman and Wildavsky (1984) have already reported on these processes in other contexts.

Second, the prevailing model of democratic accountability and control, once again traditionally associated with the public sector and with social housing in Britain, and justified in terms of the need for control over public money, is challenged by a growing emphasis on managerial accountability, as individuals take more personal responsibility for management and operational decisions. Third, the public sector management 'conventions' associated with defined roles, responsibilities and procedures in a hierarchical setting are challenged by the requirement for managers to employ new entrepreneurial and intrapreneurial skills, and to be responsive and innovative in a restructured environment characterised by change and uncertainty. Managerialist solutions have come to play an important role within the housing sector.

While the restructuring of the housing system constitutes in itself an important example of the way in which the coordination of public policy has changed, it also raises issues for the definition of the scope and organisation of 'housing practice' in Britain. In other words, the work of managers within the reframed housing service is in itself in the course of being reframed.

The new interorganisational approach to organising and delivering local housing services through joint working can be seen as based on policy networks based at local level, or 'local housing networks'. Local housing networks in turn comprise groups of different service-providing organisations, some of which are 'independent' in that they are not regulated directly by the state, or they are part of the voluntary or community sector or the private sector. Organisations in networks contract together in an interdependent relationship to provide a particular service package or carry out a defined 'project' (Reid, 1995). Their interdependence is mediated through interactive exchanges of resource power, which must occur if goals are to be achieved (Tjosvold, 1986).

Some of the advantages of networks are structural. Because networks can integrate their efforts to provide a product or a service, they can adjust more rapidly to changes in their external operating environment, such as, for example, changes in funding arrangements, in government policy, or in market conditions. They also have the flexibility to be able to develop new products, services and solutions within a relatively short time-frame (Alter and Hage, 1993). In terms of their operating arrangements, networks exhibit similar flexibility. They are neither organised on the basis of straightforward hierarchical systems of orders and administrative edict, nor based on market relationships where the principal actor searches for the least-cost supplier of goods or services and maintains only a short-term arm's length 'buyer–seller' relationship with its suppliers (Thompson, 1993).

In the context of local housing services, therefore, the formation of networks of service providers on the one hand leads to the establishment of a local service which is responsive to change and innovative in developing service 'solutions', while on the other, managerially and organisationally, they fall between hierarchy and market in terms of interorganisational and internal policy, practices and conventions. Indeed, local housing organisations working in networks may actively adopt different stances to different joint projects and initiatives, making a conscious choice over the coordinating mechanism they operate, depending upon the circumstances. Thus, as Williamson (1985) suggests, an organisation can be simultaneously be subject to and operating within the full range of coordinating mechanisms at any one time.

The reframing of local housing services is read by many to constitute a discernible shift towards market principles of organisation and the incorporation of 'the new management'. In practice however, it has led to an intermediary position, between hierarchy and market, where network forms of coordination are being employed to secure this position. Management practices derived from each of the dominant modes of policy coordination are in practice combined with techniques to create an specific approach to management which is coming to characterise housing services in particular, and may be present in other sectors. As Daft and Lewin (1993) argue, the management of organisations can be said to be undergoing a paradigm shift. The characteristic of the new paradigm in the housing sector is that individual housing organisations and their staff are freely adapting solutions to management 'problems' from a wide range of tactics and approaches which have not hitherto been deemed an important component of 'housing practice'. In developing new practices, there is little concern as to whether these are recognisable as 'public sector administration' or 'private sector management' techniques, and more of an emphasis upon 'making things happen'.

Management in local housing networks

Three themes emerged from the research as characterising the nature of management activity within local housing networks, the way in which housing services have positioned themselves between hierarchy and market, and the 'black box' or 'trial-and-error' qualities of management practice. These were *uncertainty and change, emergent strategy and implementation*, and *interorganisational and micro politics*.

Uncertainty and change

Uncertainty and change are the terms which are used most frequently in housing organisations to describe their operating environment. This is in turn expressed in terms of the disappearance of universally understood decision-making structures and procedures, and 'not knowing what's over the horizon'. There are three main aspects to the views of managers towards uncertainty and change.

In the first instance, managers refer to fashions for particular types of project and for creating high-profile initiatives. Thus, for example, consortium-based volume-build initiatives and common waiting-list initiatives are talked of in terms of 'solutions' or good-practice models which can be copied and adapted to fit local conditions. Though initiatives such as these require joint working arrangements, 'joint working', 'networking', 'partnerships' and so on are *in themselves* also regarded as a fashionable way of working. Uncertainty and change therefore are simultaneously about the changing nature of the projects which the housing service is expected to undertake and the changing organisational and managerial environment in which they operate.

Second, there is considerable pragmatism among managers about the reasons for interorganisational working, and the uncertainty and change which they associate with this way of working tend to be explained almost universally by reference to resource constraints and cuts in government funding, which have left organisations with little choice but to operate in this way. As a result, it now appears acceptable within local housing service-providing organisations for the issues of corporate survival and growth to be discussed openly in relation to organisational strategy. Interorganisational and network arrangements therefore provide organisations with a mechanism through which they can collaborate to secure efficiencies and economies of scale in service delivery. Thus for example, common waiting lists are seen as a means of reducing voids and increasing income streams.

In order to attempt to control for uncertainty a
corporate survival, it would appear that some local housin
build on relationships which are already tested and in place.
local authority policy officer put it:

> The five organisations and the council have worked together before.
> There was no difficulty in pulling them together, and that definitely
> did help the partnership.

Housing service providers also scrutinise the market for services
more carefully, to assess whether it is worth their while becoming
involved in particular projects. This scrutiny may address issues as far
apart as the publicity gains and the likelihood of sustaining financial
losses.

A third major issue for housing organisations is the extent to which
they can create a degree of certainty in their working environment and
minimise any risks to themselves of not being prepared for changes in
either the substantive focus of their work or the operational environment. On one level, interorganisational working is believed to produce
more information for potentially collaborating organisations about the
wider considerations around their project interests. However this wider
perspective is to an extent outweighed by a perceived loss of independence by some organisations, which is seen to develop out of the
interdependencies which become established after networks are formed
and projects are identified.

On another level, there are frustrations that aspects of the regulatory
and funding systems which are applied to local housing initiatives are
not yet sufficiently adapted to the operation of network arrangements,
with new procedures being worked out as new projects are followed
through. Financial and other resource commitments have also been
known to change during the lifetime of projects. As a result, housing
service providers suggest wariness in some quarters, for example
among local elected members, to support interorganisational approaches to projects, because the risks are seen to be too great. The
role of funding agencies in 'bringing comfort' to the project development process, particularly where projects are costly, is seen as important from all perspectives. As one policy officer from the Housing
Corporation put it:

> I think the Corporation's guarantee was very important. It is such a
> finely balanced local authority – politically and organisationally –

and to get everyone on board it needed the Corporation to be very positive about their collaboration. So we said here's our guarantee to support you.

The effort which goes into raising comfort levels around complex or expensive projects, however, appears to be outweighed by two further concerns. Housing organisations point to the fact that they are unable to benefit from longer-term efficiencies from innovative projects, because many of the interorganisational projects in which they are involved cannot be replicated, because of changes, for example, in funding arrangements or legal restrictions. The effort which goes into particular projects therefore brings with it particularly high levels of scrutiny both internally and externally. Finally, the quest for a little certainty in a time of changed funding patterns – most usually in the form of some guaranteed core funding – also carries risks, with organisations being tempted to set unrealistic outputs for projects, which at worst can place their corporate survival in jeopardy.

'Emergent' strategy and implementation

In an interorganisational setting, strategic decision-making and the process of implementation are emergent, in that they evolve, are the subject of continuous renegotiation, and are modified and adapted as a function of the interactions which form part of the interorganisational process. This 'non-linear' process creates tensions around the balance between control and flexibility, and the extent to which different approaches are judged appropriate to different types of network.

In the first instance, managers suggest that there are two tendencies in networks. Some networks are described as 'controlling'. This is linked usually with functions or initiatives which are seen as 'obligatory' or 'top-down', such as, for example, local authorities setting up homelessness forums, or housing advice and referral arrangements. In such cases, managers talk in terms of organisations resorting to old conventions, using hierarchical levers within the network, and building restrictions around the working pattern by using devices such as procedures or committee cycles. Other networks are described as 'task-focused', where participants are committed to a particular shared purpose. This focus is seen to be associated with organisations making voluntary commitments to work together, in a 'bottom-up' sense. Such networks are believed to be more flexible overall.

The tensions between flexibility and control are evident in both tendencies within networks and they produce different ways of working. On the 'control' side, it is clear that in some settings, networks are used as forms of control, where the aim is to achieve an element of standardisation in procedures across a range of organisations with a similar stake in a particular aspect of service delivery.

The means of securing control over the network go further than this however. At a very basic level, 'forum'-type arrangements, which may be led by different organisations, and are not tied in their initial stages to any particular project, can be instrumental in creating loyalty and trust relationships between organisations involved. At a further level, the shape and structure of a network can be controlled by influencing which organisations are invited – and not invited – to join the grouping. The practice of carefully selecting partners is well-understood and used by managers, though is often interpreted by organisations left out of networks as being a form of cartel-building. Structural constraints can also be imposed on networks using time targets or goals, while the collaborative or implementation process itself can be controlled through a structured division of labour, which may be supported by some form of contractual arrangement.

The willingness to be flexible and permit flexibility within networks is seen by many managers as the way to make progress in interorganisational projects. There is a general understanding that the need to be flexible in part stems from the fact that the reframing of local housing services has provided opportunities for housing organisations to have inputs into areas of local and corporate policy to which previously they had little access. Pragmatic managers once again take the view that 'moving with the times' in this context means making adjustments within their organisations which will allow them to produce the concrete outputs in interorganisational settings which they need to secure their organisation's future. Organisational change and changes in styles of working resulting from the experience of interorganisational projects are examples of how organisations create an internal culture of and support for flexibility. In practice, in the context of interorganisational projects, flexibility is seen to be about the ability to enter into, negotiate and sustain trade-offs during the implementation process. As one director put it: 'We all have to be flexible now; anything to get our hands on the money'.

However, a further stumbling block here relates to the pace of working within networks. 'Flexible' tendencies within networks are seen by organisations to have the advantages of helping participants become better-informed more quickly, and therefore be ready to act or become operational more quickly. They rely upon relatively rapid communication, limited need for reporting back arrangements and outputs, rather than staged processes. In contrast, 'controlling' tendencies tend to be seen as spending a great deal of time securing agreement and consensus, to the extent that the networks become slow and ponderous talking shops, which are unproductive and 'bogged down'.

Interorganisational and micro politics

In the context of concerns about uncertainty and change, and about emergent strategy and implementation processes, it is perhaps not surprising that current management practice is seen as being dominated by interorganisational and micro politics. Against the background of the traditional public sector values with which social housing is associated, this is seen as particularly problematic, and there are considerable differences between organisations in terms of their willingness to operate on this basis or to acknowledge the importance of the new practices for 'getting things done'.

The different attitudes of organisations towards this issue are indicative of the dilemma they face about the continuing nature of their social purpose in the first instance, and following on from this, about how they then position themselves between hierarchy and market. For example, while social purpose might be associated with an official stance towards networks in terms of coalition-building and alliance-forming, speaking with one voice and exploiting the supportive and collaborative qualities of networks, at the same time it is clear that organisations in practice both act in ways which constitute a departure from this stance and adopt different stances in different networks. Thus individual housing organisations can have relationships between each other which are simultaneously competitive and collaborative, though in relation to different networks. Organisations are also aware of the need to exploit opportunities for combined roles and this influences stances within a network. A financial specialist from an individual organisation, for example, also simultaneously displays the corporate face of that organisation.

Part of an organisation's stance in relation to networks may be determined by the extent to which they are willing to accept the implications of the new environment for their practice. The overall change in the environment in which local housing services are set is universally understood, but as yet there seems little genuine understanding of how this might be impacting on people's work, except at senior management level. The difficulty in deciphering the significance of 'pre-network formation foreplay' leaves organisations in a dilemma about which opportunities to pursue and which to disregard, the solution to which appears to be a form of 'presenteeism' which, in itself, is seen as time-consuming and often unproductive.

The organisations which are seen to be achievers in a network context are believed to be so by virtue of their size and financial status, and it is certainly the case that high-profile network-based projects favour more robust organisations, with, in some cases, the most robust of these 'leading' the network. It would appear that such organisations have concentrated on finding ways of 'achieving clout' in networks, over and above the basic advantages such as size and financial position. Having individuals with decision-making powers in their organisations actually involved in making decisions about the network project was cited as important, along with the need to be clear and creative about leadership, purpose, commitment and the ability to 'make things work'. A number of tactical considerations were also believed to be important. These included knowing when and on what issues to be willing to give up power and control, and when to abandon internal procedures in the interests of contributing to a more effective solution, understanding where the opportunities lay for strengthening particular competencies through network projects, and understanding the more medium-term gains from being involved in a particular network.

Clearly, any suggestion of a move away from management practices based on professionally regulated competencies and conventions and a veering towards management practices based more explicitly upon the interplay of power and 'generative structures' raises some issues for local housing services providers. First, there is a sense that it has become harder to be clear about 'where business is done'. In other words, the interactions between organisations within a network are concerned primarily with making the network function and being accountable to each other, rather than being accountable in an external sense. Second, some networks experience difficulties because of symbolic political struggles being fought out over minor issues, while in others, fear of creating tension or conflict can serve a similar political purpose. In both cases, however, the work of networks can either speed up or slow down as a result. Third, there are ongoing concerns expressed about the extent to which networks are seen as being inclusive and exclusive in the way that they are established and operate, with the dangers of the 'old-boy network' being frequently cited. There is also a discernible perception that tenant involvement may be seen as incompatible with networks. As the director of a voluntary sector group put it:

> The danger with networks is that they're just a modern version of the old boy network. I think you need to pay attention to who's in the network, who's excluded, who's not invited to participate. It really does depend on how the networks are used. They can be exclusive in their very formality.

Finally, there is a clear message about the personal resources and skills which individuals need to have at their disposal and the way in which they deploy these within networks. These were summed up by the director of a housing association:

> They need to communicate. They need to promote action. But the most important thing is that they need to get to know all the key people, intimately, so they know how to get what they want out of each of them. As individuals.

Conclusion: the new competition?

Within an environment of uncertainty and change, where there is increasing emphasis on emergent forms of policy-making and on the importance of micro-politics in this process, the management and delivery of local housing services has taken on something of a 'black box' quality, where inputs and outputs are recognisable and under-stood, but the processes by which these are achieved are becoming less visible. The need for housing organisations to be prepared for flex-ibility, for organisational learning, for responsiveness to change and for coordinated approaches to solving policy problems which are packaged as 'projects' has altered the way in which housing services are governed in the local context, particularly in relation to decision-making and organisational procedure. At the same time, the redistribution of housing 'powers' and resources across a wider range of service-provid-ing organisations has further fragmented the governing activities associated with housing services provision overall. Organisational restructuring, sectoral restructuring and the development of regulatory frameworks at local level have further altered the way in which housing services are governed, in that they are spread across a different range of providers, and coordinated differently as well as differentially.

Government has explicitly promoted the market model of policy coordination where housing services are concerned, and in the development of regulatory mechanisms this has been based substantially upon private sector models. However it has proved difficult to dislodge housing organisations from their public sector orientation and to embrace market principles. Instead, they appear to have positioned themselves in an intermediate policy coordination setting, where they can exploit the opportunities thrust upon them in relation to joint working and network arrangements, while employing operating arrangements and management tactics from across the board, and in such a way that, as far as possible, their best interests are safeguarded, their organisational survival supported, and their service providing capacities sustained. In this sense, housing organisations and their managers appear to have reached the realisation that they need to accept the drive for continuous innovation in their processes and service design, and engage proactively in sectoral and internal restructuring, in short, to work within the context of 'the new competition'.

Housing organisations have developed their ability to operate in this setting over a period of years where government policy has focused on rolling back the state, on privatisation and on reducing public expenditure. The local response has been to form networks and frame the new competitive environment as a function of the links needed to reintegrate local housing service provision. This has resulted in new finance, resources, competencies, organisations and knowledge being drawn into the local housing 'system'. The challenge now will be to develop network-based forms of policy implementation which are seen less in terms of financial necessity by managers in local housing services, and more in terms of a better way of working, grounded in local needs, interests and capacities.

About this study

This chapter is based on research carried out for the project 'Inter-organisational Relationships and the Delivery of Local Housing Services'. The project was coordinated by Barbara Reid, who now works in the School of Urban and Regional Studies at Sheffield Hallam University, and the research assistants were Barbara Iqbal and Nealam Tumber. The main part of the research was based in three large metropolitan local authority areas in the north of England, and on nine specific 'project'-linked networks, or 'local housing networks'. The purpose of these case studies was to analyse the management practices and organisational forms emerging in the context of the dual competitive–collaborative interorganisational environment surrounding local housing services. A secondary purpose was to gauge the extent to which these both constituted part of 'the new management' or whether they were a departure from this. Around 80 semi-structured interviews were carried out over 1994 and 1995 with policy-makers and project managers, on the changing nature of their practice in relation to interorganisational working and policy implementation, and project management. The research findings raise important issues for housing policy and practice, for the social orientation of local housing services, and for the construction of 'the housing profession' itself.

9 Community Governance of Crime Control

John Benyon and Adam Edwards

A paradoxical result of local government restructuring under the Conservatives was that although local authorities experienced a significant reduction in their traditional functions as direct providers of key services they acquired a leadership role in other policy areas. This has been attributed to a major shift in the perceived purpose of local authorities – away from their orthodox task of delivering services towards a broader mission of enhancing the 'well-being' of the localities for which they are responsible. The concept of 'community governance' encapsulates this developing role for local authorities (Stoker, 1997a).

The growth of the partnership approach to local crime prevention is a good example of the development of community governance, with local authorities playing a leading role. This chapter outlines the context in which crime prevention partnerships have arisen, and examines the advantages claimed for community governance of crime control, in particular its capacity to enhance governability and to generate increased citizen participation.

The chapter draws on two case studies of crime prevention partnerships on outer housing estates in two English cities. Findings from this research indicate that the potential of partnership arrangements to enhance both governability and local democracy has been frustrated by the institutional framework in which they have been expected to operate and the overbureaucratised organisational forms they have adopted. The research suggests that fundamental challenges confronting the development of community governance are the coherence and durability of partnerships, which are undermined by the short-term, competitive, funding arrangements.

TABLE 9.1 **Distinguishing local government and community governance: focus, orientation and technique**

	Focus	Orientation	Technique
Local government	Delivery of services addressing social problems regarded as separate and discrete	Unilateral interventions by single agencies	Rigid dependence on hierarchical/ bureaucratic or (quasi-) market mechanisms
Community governance	Managing the problems of citizens' 'well-being' regarded as multifaceted and inter-dependent	Multilateral interventions by public–private partnerships	Flexible deployment of bureaucratic, (quasi-) market and networking mechanisms

Community governance and crime prevention

At an abstract level, community governance can be distinguished from traditional local government in terms of its governing focus, orientation and technique, as set out in Table 9.1.

The shift in focus

The development of community governance reflects a 'growing realisation of the complex, dynamic and diverse nature of the world we live in' (Kooiman, 1993, p. 35). Governing problems are multifaceted and interdependent, rather than monistic and discrete, and this requires a shift in the focus of governing, from separate elements of citizens' 'well-being', such as their access to better education, housing and employment opportunities, and increased personal safety, towards the interdependencies between these elements in enhancing well-being. The focus on interdependency suggests an appreciation of the diversity of citizens' needs – policy responses to problems of well-being need to be tailored to meet particular needs and conditions.

Another important dimension is the increasingly dynamic character of governing problems. This complexity and diversity shape the rate and direction of the changes in the causes and effects of well-being, and so, for example, problems of educational attainment may be attenuated in certain localities whilst simultaneously deteriorating in others. This may be understood, according to governance theory, by appreciating the complex and diverse ways in which interdependencies between problems of education and other social and political problems are configured in different places (see Duclaud-Williams, 1993).

The shift in orientation

For theorists of governance, multi-faceted problems require multilateral responses:

> The shift seems to be away from 'one-way steering and control' to 'two- or multi-way designs' in which (dis)qualities of social–political systems and their governance are viewed from the perspective of the recognition of mutual needs and capacities. In these efforts the higher complexity, faster dynamics and greater diversity of (major) social–political problems we want to tackle comes to life. (Kooiman, 1993, pp. 35–6)

The growing appreciation of interdependencies accounts, in part, for the shifting orientation of local authorities towards other governmental and non-governmental agencies. Recognising the multifaceted composition of social–political problems implies an understanding of the limits to 'do-it-alone' governing – 'government' – and the need for cooperative arrangements – 'governance'. Given their increasingly complex, diverse and dynamic qualities, these problems are not amenable to unilateral interventions on behalf of functionally specific agencies or departments. It is in this context that the rise of public–private partnerships (PPPs) can be understood and acknowledged as a defining characteristic of community governance (Stoker, 1997a, 1998b).

The shift in technique

The concept of community governance can also be understood in terms of the technique it promotes and how this is distinguished from the technique of local government. The failures of local government can be explained in terms of reliance on either bureaucratic/hierarchical mechanisms, such as central planning, or quasi-market mechanisms, such as compulsory competitive tendering. The rigidity of these mechanisms means they are unable to respond effectively to the complex, diverse and dynamic qualities of social–political problems (see Levačić, 1991). Community governance involves a more flexible deployment of governing mechanisms, questioning the ways in which they can be combined and tailored to different local needs (see Frances *et al.*, 1991).

The concern with flexibility accounts, in part, for the interest in 'networking' as a feature of governance. The key characteristics of networking are the informality, trust and cooperation that it encourages between partners. Because they are less anonymous and rule-bound than relations in bureaucratic hierarchies or markets, networks enable protean forms of collaboration which are more responsive to diverse and interconnected social and political needs. However, the informality of networks raises significant issues of accountability, equity and propriety in the absence of objective rules regulating their operation (Stoker, 1997b, p. 17). There may, therefore, be a trade-off between the role of networks in enhancing the governability of social–political problems and their capacity to revitalise local democracy.

Claims for the community governance of crime prevention

The distinctions between local government and community governance enable a greater understanding of the dynamics behind the rise of local crime prevention partnerships and the advantages claimed for this approach to governing problems of crime and 'anti-social behaviour'. Crime control in England and Wales was long regarded as the preserve of local constabularies and, despite the substantial financial contribution by local government, police authorities have exercised very limited influence over the priorities and operation of police forces: 'the police authorities pay the piper (or more precisely share policing costs with central government) but do not call any tunes' (Reiner, 1992, p. 237). The 1964 Police Act confirmed this exceptional relationship of constabularies to the local populations they serve by arguing that chief constables should have 'operational independence' from both local authorities and central government as a means of ensuring their 'political impartiality' (Benyon, 1986, pp. 13–19).

However, the rise of the community governance of crime prevention has enabled local authorities to gain a growing influence over crime control policy. To understand this greater influence it is useful to

TABLE 9.2 Comparing the local (police) government and community governance of crime control: focus, orientation and technique

	Focus	Orientation	Technique
Local (police) government of crime control	Individual criminals and their crimes	Police operations independent of other crime control and prevention agencies	Law enforcement, including uniformed patrolling, rapid response to calls for assistance, and heavy investment in detection
Community governance of crime control	Problems of 'community safety', constituted by a range of crime events and forms of anti-social behaviour	Multi-agency partnerships including the police, local authorities, probation services and local populations	Strategic crime prevention, including networking between, and coordination of, partners' preventive efforts

compare the focus, orientation and technique of the local (police) government of crime prevention with the community governance approach, as shown in Table 9.2.

The shift in focus

The emergence of the community governance of crime control can be traced back to work by criminologists in the research wing of the Home Office. The 'new criminologies of everyday life' (Garland, 1996, pp. 450ff.) argued that conspicuous failures in crime control policy could be attributed to misconceptions about the character of crime. Instead of regarding crime as reducible to the actions of pathological or undersocialised individuals, crime was seen as a normal social fact shaped by the situational opportunities for its commission. Rather than focusing on the 'dispositions' of individual criminals, the 'new criminologies' highlighted the multifaceted dimensions of crime events including potential victims, vulnerable targets and the 'everyday routines of social and economic life which create criminal opportunities as an unintended by-product' (Garland, 1996, p. 451).

The shift in focus was also driven by Home Office research into the severe limits to orthodox police methods of crime control. Contrary to popular belief, analyses of police effectiveness revealed that the simple presence or absence of patrols had a negligible effect on crime patterns (Clarke and Hough, 1980). Moreover, police successes in detecting and clearing up crimes were overwhelmingly attributable to information provided by the public rather than police investigations.

The shift in orientation

On the basis of this research the new criminologists argued for a reorientation of the policy response to local crime away from unilateral interventions by agencies, such as the police, courts and prisons, towards multilateral strategies involving these agencies in partnership with individuals and organisations in 'the community'. A Home Office circular on crime prevention in 1984 expressed the new nostrum of crime control policy:

> A primary objective of the police has always been the prevention of crime. However, since some of the factors affecting crime lie outside the control or direct influence of the police, crime prevention can not be left to them alone. Every citizen and all those agencies whose policies and practices can influence the extent of crime should make their contribution. Preventing crime is a task for the whole community. (Home Office, 1984, p. 1)

This circular marked the first official recognition of the role which local authorities, as the institutions in command of many of the key policies and practices that can shape crime patterns, should play in crime prevention initiatives. Their increasing involvement was, however, the subject of some political controversy. The antagonistic relations between the Conservative government and Labour-dominated municipal authorities meant that the leadership role of local authorities in 'community safety' was resisted.

The shift in technique

With this reorientation, alternative techniques for combating crime were promoted. In contrast to the purported deterrent effects of intensive police patrols, punitive sentencing and tough prison regimes, the new criminologies of everyday life advocate prevention through increasing the risks of offenders being caught (through improved surveillance), increasing the effort of committing crimes (through 'target hardening') and reducing the rewards of offending (through 'target removal') (Clarke, 1995). A distinctive feature of these techniques is that they are located in the community and require the active participation of local citizens in their implementation.

Initially, these 'situational crime prevention techniques' predominated in the approaches of local partnerships, which tended to be led by the police in view of their expertise. However, as local authorities became increasingly involved, the agendas of local partnerships evolved to include more 'social crime prevention techniques', which embraced broader issues of 'community safety' affecting entire neighbourhoods.

The idea of community safety suggests that personal and collective insecurity is a product of the whole range of crimes in a neighbourhood combined with problems of public order and anti-social behaviour such as 'noise pollution', boisterous juvenile gangs and inter-neighbour disputes. The community safety approach was outlined in the highly influential 1991 report of the Home Office Standing Conference on Crime Prevention, *Safer Communities: The Local Delivery of Crime Prevention Through the Partnership Approach* (Home Office, 1991).

The Morgan Report, named after the chair of the group, James Morgan, outlined an agenda for community safety and this strongly linked effective local crime prevention with a more general programme of urban regeneration. A sample portfolio of community safety activities suggested in the Morgan Report is shown in Table 9.3. It illustrates the broad concern with citizen well-being that lies at the heart of the community governance concept. The report also underlined the claims made for community governance over local government in enhancing the governability of complex, diverse and dynamic problems. These claims can be summarised as follows:

1. The community governance of crime control focuses on the multifaceted character of community safety as it is constituted by a complex range of social and situational factors.
2. In recognising this complexity, community governance aspires toward a more holistic and strategic response to the threats to citizen well-being presented by crime and 'anti-social behaviour', avoiding partial interventions with only partial successes.

TABLE 9.3   A portfolio of community safety activities: some examples

Tackling the causes of crime

- Family support initiatives
- Youth programmes
- Community development programmes and neighbourhood initiatives
- Pre-school programmes
- Alcohol and drug misuse prevention schemes
- Education and school-based programmes
- Work with offenders and their families
- Employment and training programmes
- Debt counselling

Reducing the opportunities for crime to be committed

- Improved security in homes, public buildings and business premises
- Improved lighting in streets and public areas
- Improved security and design of residential areas, city centres, and car parks
- Security considerations in planning and managing public transport
- Safety considerations in the management of licensed premises
- Good management and delivery of local services
- Adequate levels of preventive patrolling

Tackling specific crime problems

- Domestic burglary
- Domestic violence
- Auto crime
- Racially-motivated crime
- Crimes against children
- Crimes against the elderly

Helping the victims of crime and reducing the fear of crime

- Victim support schemes
- Self-protection initiatives
- Securing positive publicity for successful initiatives

Source: Morgan Report (Home Office, 1991, p. 32).

3. In promoting a partnership approach to crime, community govern-
    ance increases the available resources for crime prevention work
    and enables the recruitment of crucial local expertise.
4. The recruitment of this local expertise enables the formulation and
    implementation of strategies which are tailored to locally-specific
    problems of community safety.

5. Informal networking between the agencies recruited into local crime prevention partnerships enables a more flexible response to the dynamic qualities of community safety, as certain problems of crime and anti-social behaviour are improved whilst others recede.

A final advantage claimed for the community governance of crime control is that it can enhance local democracy by empowering citizens through their active participation in the formulation and implementation of crime prevention strategies.

The remainder of this chapter is devoted to an examination of the research findings on the operation of two local crime prevention partnerships and the extent to which they appeared to have achieved the benefits claimed for the community governance of crime control.

Community governance of crime control in practice

Context

A noticeable feature of the partnership approach to crime prevention is that prior to the passage of the Crime and Disorder Act in 1998 local agencies were under no statutory obligation to work together. As a consequence, the establishment of local crime prevention strategies has been uneven, dependent on the response of agencies in particular localities to the exhortations and inducements of national organisations. These included interdepartmental circulars from Whitehall to all chief constables and local authority chief executives, in 1984 and 1990, advice on 'best practice' from the Home Office Crime Prevention Unit and the Home Office-sponsored charity, Crime Concern, and the need to demonstrate multi-agency cooperation as a prerequisite of competing for government grant aid through the City Challenge, Safer Cities and Single Regeneration Budget programmes.

The Morgan Report examined the progress made by local agencies in delivering crime prevention through the partnership approach and found that the lack of a clear statutory responsibility for local government had inhibited developments. Successful multi-agency approaches required the formulation of an overall crime reduction strategy and structure, within which agencies could cooperate.

The research we conducted examined developments in local crime prevention since the publication of the Morgan Report. The study had two dimensions. First, it examined the institutional framework in which local partnerships were asked to operate and how this shaped their access to resources. Second, we conducted case studies on the practice of partnerships on outer housing estates in two English cities, Leicester and Nottingham. Using these case studies to test the claims made for local crime prevention partnerships in enhancing the govern-ability of crime and empowering local populations in relation to crime control policy-making, we identified three interrelated problems con-fronting the accomplishment of the community governance concept in this area: coordination and coherence, accountability and durability.

Institutional framework

The Morgan Report's recommendation that local authorities should be provided with a statutory responsibility for supporting the partnership approach was premised on four main arguments. First, local autho-rities control a range of services and resources which need to be committed to crime prevention strategies and are thus best placed to coordinate the programme in their locality. Second, the active partici-pation of local authorities encourages a wider acceptance of responsi-bility amongst other partners. Third, a statutory competence would provide permanency, continuity and a clear focus for the involvement of business and voluntary organisations. Fourth, it would enable the legitimate and productive involvement of local elected members who could provide important political support to partnerships.

The Home Office Standing Conference on Crime Prevention has a quasi-independent status and in its formal response to the Morgan Report the Home Office rejected the proposal for a statutory respon-sibility, arguing that there was ample evidence of successful progress within the existing institutional framework and, consequently, there was no compelling argument for placing a further financial 'burden' on local authorities and local taxpayers (Home Office, 1992).

Subsequently, the Home Office Police Research Group argued that a statutory competence would place too much power in the hands of local authorities and would jeopardise the principles of corporate problem-solving and multi-agency 'ownership' of the crime and public order problems that are the basis of partnership working. Moreover, the record of local authorities in delivering other services did not suggest that crime prevention/community safety activities would be provided any more coherently or responsively in the wake of new legislation (Liddle and Gelsthorpe, 1994, pp. 26–7). It has also been argued that local authority leadership of crime prevention partnerships

TABLE 9.4 Government grant-aid programmes for crime prevention

Government department	Funding schemes
Home Office	Safer Cities; Crime Prevention Department (F10); Crime Prevention Centre
Education	Drug abuse/health education; difficult pupils; training for youth and community workers
Employment	Security of staff and property
Environment	Estate action; Urban regeneration (Urban Programme; Urban Development Corporations; City Action Teams; City Challenge)
Health	National Association for the Care and Resettlement of Offenders (NACRO); Intermediate Treatment; working with drug misusers; Alcohol Concern
Social Security	Security of offices; prevention of violence to staff
Transport	Unlawful interference with public transport
Welsh Office	Welsh Urban Programme

Source: Home Office Crime Prevention Department (F10).

was blocked by the Association of Chief Police Officers (ACPO) who were concerned about the threat to their operational independence and share of resources for local crime control (Jones *et al.*, 1994, p. 293).

Local crime prevention partnerships have been dependent on a broad range of government grant-aid programmes for funding their activities, as listed in Table 9.4. The total estimated government expenditure on crime prevention across these departments amounted to £168 million in 1991–92, £201 million the following year, and £250 million in 1993–94. The Safer Cities budget was the principal single source, contributing £7.2 million in 1991–92, £7.6 million in 1992–93, and £6.0 million in 1993–94. From April 1994, however, the Safer

Cities programme was subsumed into the Single Regeneration Budget (SRB), with 19 other urban regeneration funding programmes, administered by the government's regional offices. The SRB does not represent additional expenditure and, indeed, it is estimated that there was a 1.4 per cent reduction in resources for 1994–95 (Hogwood, 1995, p. 15).

An important characteristic of the Safer Cities and, latterly, SRB programmes is that the funding is provided on a competitive basis. Proposals from local partnerships are vetted by the relevant government regional office, with government ministers having the final decision. Local partnerships are also in competition for resources provided by charitable trusts and the National Lotteries Board.

The galvanising effect which this process can have on inter-agency relations was highlighted by a research respondent who played an important role in developing the partnership on the case study estate in Leicester:

> The partnership has been resource-driven, if you want my real opinion of it. I think it was the attraction of additional funding for crime prevention work which acted as the catalyst for co-operation.

A similar view was expressed by a councillor, who was at the forefront of developing the community safety partnership on the estate which was studied in Nottingham:

> I think having to bid for funds brings you together because you have got a common purpose . . . it is a common achievement which is condensed into a very short time-span so it is a perfect target around which partners can amalgamate.

However, this councillor pointed out that failure with the grants application could undermine a partnership: 'the problem is that if you are unsuccessful in the competition for funds it is extremely demoralising and this raises difficulties for sustaining the commitment of the different partners'. A Leicester respondent commented that common financial motives did not necessarily overcome other problems: 'Although people are beginning to realise the wider benefits of working in partnership, relations are still very difficult.'

Coordination and coherence

In the absence of a national strategy for coordinating crime prevention, progress in its local delivery has been uneven, as it has depended on the initiative shown by agencies in particular localities and their success in competing for grant aid. Furthermore, developments have been erratic, largely because grant aid provided on a fixed-term basis has left particular projects vulnerable to collapse when initial, 'pump-priming', investment has ended. A local activist in Nottingham stressed that the existing system did not promote durable partnerships:

> Ultimately, I think you won't resolve the problems without longer-term funding and longer-term strategies and some sense of permanence because the one thing people out there are suffering from, apart from poverty, is instability . . . It is not so much the level of funding which is the problem as the need for a 'standard flow' of resources.

A related problem is that the current institutional framework does not promote the coordination or coherence of local programmes. The provision of grant aid on a project-by-project basis, with continued funding dependent on the accomplishment of project-specific targets, means that individual projects (which together constitute a 'local strategy') frequently have different time-scales. Even when funding is secured for all the projects constituting the strategy, divergent time-scales may undermine synchronisation and, therefore, the beneficial effects of their integration, as envisaged in strategy 'action plans'.

The impact of the funding regime may be particularly damaging for the coordination of community crime prevention strategies aimed at the restoration of order and reductions in crime across whole neighbourhoods. A local government community safety officer in Leicester pointed out to the researchers that a key problem on the estate being studied was putting the crime prevention strategy into practice:

> What you get is people becoming preoccupied with the individual projects . . . Most of the time they are under extreme time constraints – they have just not got the time to think about what the links are between their project and somebody else's. If you are in a pressured situation and you have to achieve certain outputs within different time scales, then you don't always have the time to do the

linking work which sometimes, I feel, is more important than the contribution of specific projects.

These problems are compounded in longer-term, city-wide, community safety strategies aimed at managing the displacement of crime and victimisation from one neighbourhood to another. As the number of projects expands, and as the scope of the strategy's geographical and temporal applicability is broadened, inter-project coordination becomes ever harder to accomplish and management of the overall strategy is often dissipated into project-based interventions. In the current institutional framework, this dissipation occurs even at the neighbourhood level.

The coherence of local crime prevention strategies is also dependent on relations *within* the participating organisations. The 'peripheral' status of crime prevention in the major statutory agencies involved in partnerships – the police and local authorities – is exacerbated by externally imposed performance criteria.

In the case of the police, forces are assessed annually by Her Majesty's Inspectorate of Constabulary (HMIC), using performance indicators which emphasise reactive rather than preventive targets for crime control, such as arrest, detection and clear-up rates and response times. If such targets are not met, a force may be denied its 'certificate of efficiency', thus jeopardising its Exchequer grant, amounting to 51 per cent of all constabulary expenditure. HMIC also has the power to 'recommend' changes in a force's objectives and operational practices, in line with the Home Secretary's directions on police efficiency. Since the passage of the Police and Magistrates' Courts Act 1994, these directives have been issued on an annual basis. Whilst the national objectives have incorporated crime prevention through the partnership approach since 1994, the overwhelming emphasis remains on more easily measurable, quantitative, targets for police *reactions* to crime.

Thus, the police have strong incentives for subordinating their involvement in crime prevention partnerships to the unilateral pursuit of the crime control targets assigned to them. As a police–community liaison officer involved in the Nottingham partnership argued:

> We are being pushed in a certain way, as are other agencies, and it's not necessarily what the government are advocating in terms of the 'need for partnership', rather it is more to do with the performance criteria they are setting for ourselves, probation, social services etc. . . . police work is now even more about what might happen today

and tomorrow, not involvement in 'strategic' crime prevention. It is so a divisional commander can say: 'My burglary arrests are so and so, the number of burglaries are going down, car crime is staying level and we have had so many arrests', that is the consequence of current police reforms. So, I think everything that is happening at the moment seems to be working against partnership – it seems to be putting us back into compartments.

Local authorities have played a central role in developing strategic approaches to crime reduction and community safety. At the national level, the local authority associations have issued detailed policy statements (AMA, 1990; ADC, 1990; LARIA, 1994; ACC/ADC/ AMA, 1997) and the National Network (NatNet) of Community Safety Co-ordinators was established in May 1995. Many authorities have established specialist 'community safety' units and some have created community safety sub-committees. However, the non-statutory status of their role in crime prevention has meant that the operational commitment of those local authorities that prioritise community safety remained vulnerable to cuts in resources imposed through more general constraints on their standard spending assessment (SSA).

The active participation of local authorities in crime prevention projects is inevitably subordinated to the fulfilment of their statutory obligations. This point was emphasised by a community safety officer in Leicester, interviewed during the research:

It would be easier, internally, to argue that crime prevention and community safety should have more money because we have to do it . . . should we provide clean streets or should we have a community safety project? Well, you know, we have to provide a general level of cleanliness, we are obliged to do that. So it is harder for councillors to allocate resources to things that we don't have to do, however much they understand that it's something that we should be doing.

The coordination and coherence of local crime prevention strategies may also be constrained by the internal organisation of partnerships. A common format for partnerships, advocated by the Home Office and Crime Concern, is a four-tiered structure involving a steering group of representatives from all participating agencies; a planning group, including the strategy coordinator and leaders of the individual pro- jects in the strategy; thematic subgroups, into which the individual projects are placed, such as 'education', 'family' and 'community'; and project groups of all those involved in a specific intervention. As the scope of a partnership's strategy expands to encompass a broader range of crime-related problems and a wider geographical area, there may be problems of managing the increased work load. Partnerships may become increasingly fragmented into particular problem areas of intervention, which enables inter-agency coordination on specific projects but frustrates overall, strategic, coordination. Bureaucratisation often leads to a proliferation of meetings, additional demands on the time and resources of participating agencies, and the consequent collapse of certain projects or even thematic sub-areas of a strategy through lack of support.

A police officer seconded to the Leicester Safer Cities Programme, and involved in monitoring the performance of the case study estate's strategy, argued that the organisation of the partnership was a particular problem:

> The problem, as I see it, is the way in which crime prevention partnerships are organised. The project groups tend to work in isolation and don't tend to know what the other groups are actually involved in and where they are at in relation to their particular work and responsibilities.

This respondent accepted the need for the steering group and project groups, but was concerned about the role of the planning group:

> The planning group was set up to improve the management of relations between the projects, but in practice it has ended up replicating the work of the steering group . . . the planning group has become an additional, unnecessary, tier which has increased bureaucracy without addressing the coherence of the overall strategy for crime prevention on the estate.

Accountability

One of the principal arguments for partnerships, and for community governance more generally, is that they facilitate more responsive policy-making, geared towards the needs of local conditions. However, the shift of decision-making responsibilities from elected councillors to multi-agency partnerships has attracted criticism for undermining accountability. Conversely, advocates of the partnership approach argue that it empowers local populations through the opportunities for direct participation in decision-making. Further, they argue that local authorities have not been particularly successful in responding to the competing demands of different neighbourhoods and groups in their populations.

It is useful to distinguish between different modes and types of accountability of crime prevention partnerships. Discussions of local governance have identified two basic *modes* of accountability – the 'top-up' mode, in which service providers privilege the interests of elite policy-makers and funding bodies, and the 'bottom-down' mode in which providers focus on the interests of individual users, groups and communities (Burns *et al.*, 1994, p. 277). It is also possible to distinguish two basic *types* of accountability – 'political' accountability, which involves conventional concern with the definition and prioritisation of competing policy goals, and 'financial' accountability, which refers to contractual arrangements between funding bodies and service providers, typical of the 'new public management'. The 'value for money' of services provided by local agencies is assessed according to performance criteria set by the funding bodies. Subsequent financial support is conditional on fulfilling the contractual terms (Weatheritt, 1993; McLaughlin and Murji, 1995).

The accountability of local crime prevention partnerships is better understood in terms of these modes and types of accountability than in terms of the institutional location of decision-making in elected local authorities, constabularies or partnerships. Given the reliance of partnerships on non-local sources of funding, their capacity to develop strategies around the interests of local populations is severely constrained. The contractual criteria set by non-local funders imposes a strongly 'top-up' mode of accountability on local partnerships.

The political accountability of partnerships is also strongly 'top-up' as the definitions and goals of 'strategic' crime prevention are effectively driven by the performance criteria attached to grant aid by non-local funders. Where such criteria permit a degree of local discretion in deciding strategic goals, partnerships have the capacity to cultivate a more 'bottom-down' mode of accountability. However, the capacity to sustain this mode beyond the involvement of local citizens in defining the initial priorities depends on the coincidence of local citizens' priorities with those of the funding agencies. Where the priorities do not coincide, the credibility of a partnership's commitment to involving local people as equal partners can be jeopardised.

A youth worker involved in the Leicester estate partnership which was studied identified this problem as a key reason for the difficulties encountered by the partnership in addressing the priorities of local residents. At the outset of the partnership, the city council commissioned a survey of local people to ascertain the principal crime problems and suggestions about what should be done. One of the most favoured suggestions, confirmed at a number of public meetings, was to establish a motor project to work with youths who were involved in car crime and 'joyriding' them round the estate.

> At this stage there was a lot of interest and good-will from the residents, but when the council officers presented the draft action plan the motor project was left out. Apparently, the Safer Cities people had rejected this recommendation because it was too expensive and because its outputs were insufficiently clear. So, we had gone through this elaborate rigmarole of consulting the local community only to turn round and tell them they couldn't have what they really wanted. Of course, the goodwill evaporated – I don't think we have recovered from that.

Partnerships have struggled to develop the 'bottom-down' mode of accountability, particularly amongst the heterogeneous populations and cultures which characterise 'high-crime' neighbourhoods, preferring, instead, to 'imagine' such populations as a morally homogenous community of interest. This can be explained to a large extent by the participation of certain kinds of community-based organisations in estate partnerships and the absence of others. In both of the estates studied, tenants' associations, composed typically of elderly residents, were the principal 'community representatives' on the partnerships, whilst young people were conspicuous by their absence. A school teacher involved with the Leicester partnership commented:

> Amongst the teenagers, I suspect their view is that they wouldn't be taken seriously by the partnership and so 'what's the point of getting involved?'

Local government officers were aware of the effects of the lack of young people's views, for example, in the priority accorded to the concerns of the tenants' associations with the 'incivilities' associated with 'boisterous' youth gangs and noisy neighbours.

Durability

The difficulties with the 'bottom-down' accountability of partnerships have significant implications for the durability of community governance of crime prevention. A defining feature of governance is the enhancement of governability through the long-term capacity of service providers to 'self-organise' and 'self-reproduce'. The active participation of local 'communities' is vital for the viability of crime prevention partnerships, particularly in view of the constraints on public expenditure. However, this is undeniably the weakest dimension of progress on the partnership approach.

Members of the case study partnerships gave four principal reasons for the limited participation of local communities.

1. 'Lethargy'

It was argued that populations in high-crime neighbourhoods suffered from a culture of dependency on statutory agencies and were impervious to their own responsibilities for accomplishing reductions in crime and 'community insecurity'. A member of the Nottingham partnership felt it had not been sufficiently successful in reaching ordinary people on the estate:

> I don't think many of them know it exists – I don't think they give a toss whether it exists. We do need to start involving a lot more local people, but I am convinced that apart from half a dozen local people, who are prepared to commit themselves, all local people want to do is dip in and out when something affects them personally.

2. 'Alienation'

The low participation was thought to be a historical legacy of tensions between local residents and the police. A youth worker on the Leicester estate commented that the absence of young people participating in the work of the partnership was unsurprising:

> As an outreach worker I have difficulties trying to establish trust and credibility with the kids on the estate because they still see me as, you know, part of 'the state'. I mean, yes, there are benefits to the idea of working in partnership, but inevitably we get associated with the police and the housing department who, because of the jobs they

have to do, are not exactly popular amongst some groups on the estate who have had 'run-ins' with them before. I think the issue of trust is behind the difficulties we have had in connecting with young people on the estate.

Partnerships also encounter problems of credibility given the failures of former urban policy interventions – they often suffer from scepticism amongst local residents, whose expectations have been raised and then dashed by previous, unsuccessful, attempts at regeneration. A local government officer involved with the Nottingham partnership explained that when she began work on the estate 'people said, "well, yet again, another person is parachuting in"':

> I understand why they thought that . . . you've got to do more than simply express your commitment: you have to demonstrate, to do things, to build confidence and trust and that is very hard work. They've had enough experience of agencies coming into the area with a great fanfare and then leaving with little impact.

3. 'Intimidation'

Given the close residential proximity of victims and offenders in high-crime neighbourhoods, it was said that some people decline active participation in crime prevention strategies for fear of retaliation. This was identified as the principal reason for the absence of Asian and African-Caribbean participants by a member of the Leicester partnership, who was the head of one of the schools on the estate:

> With the African-Caribbean and Asian members of the community there is an isolation that hasn't been broken down yet . . . I feel there is a fear of coming out, certainly after dark, which has prevented their involvement. There is a fear of making oneself known, which comes down to just a basic fear of personal safety and security . . . You must remember that the National Front had their headquarters on this estate, so you have got an almost endemic racism at times in certain areas of the estate.

4. 'Poor training and support'

Low participation was also attributed to the lack of confidence, knowledge and skills of local residents and the absence of training and support to prepare them for such active participation. A community safety officer involved in the Leicester partnership argued that:

> You can't just expect community groups to lock into your way of thinking. You don't just empower them by saying 'come to a meeting'. You have got to give them the skills and the knowledge to participate fully and as equally as possible at the meeting.

Having emphasised the importance of training local citizens in the practice of governance, this same officer acknowledged that control over resources was the ultimate factor in the durability of partnerships and the empowerment of local citizens:

> Ultimately the quality and equality of participation is a question of who controls the resources. It is a hard thing to say, but it's true. Local residents can be part of the decision-making process, but come the end of the day, if we say, 'no, we just don't feel that we can employ three youth workers for your estate', they can't say, 'well, we will then'. So, in truth it is not an equal partnership in that sense.

Prospects for the community governance of crime control

The Labour government came into office on 1 May 1997 pledged to implement the Morgan Report's recommendation for a statutory role to be given local authorities. This should help to attenuate some of the problems of coordination and durability associated with the institutional framework for crime prevention partnerships. Of itself, however, this is unlikely to solve the problems of coordination and coherence resulting from pressures on partners to adhere to performance criteria which undermine, rather than encourage, cooperation. Taking community governance seriously requires a systemic restructuring of the way statutory agencies' performances are assessed and how they are consequently enabled to participate in public–private partnerships.

The fragile funding structures and foundations of statutory sector involvement mean that the prospects for the long-term durability of local community safety partnerships seem to be highly dependent on enhancing voluntary and active citizen participation in the community governance of crime prevention. Hence, a major challenge is how to increase local involvement and sustain it. This is related to the profound problems of involving, and catering for, the disparate social groups in partnership neighbourhoods.

A key question for the development of community governance is whether certain social–political problems are amenable to being resolved to the satisfaction of an expanding range of different groups, and the problems of crime and community safety exemplify this challenge. They illustrate the difficulties of coordination, accountability and durability in a particularly stark form, given the acute intergenerational and inter-ethnic social conflicts they are capable of provoking amongst residents in the same neighbourhoods.

Community governance is concerned with enhancing the well-being of local citizens, by involving different agencies and citizens themselves. The diversity of cultures, lifestyles and needs within localities makes consensus difficult to achieve, but more secure funding for projects would assist in fostering a greater faith in the partnership approach amongst the disparate groups. The Morgan Report set out a wide-ranging agenda for local community safety and many of these ideas, supplemented by calls for legislation, were included in the local authority associations' manifesto entitled *Crime – The Local Solution* (ACC/ADC/AMA, 1997). The problems of crime and its control are key issues on the local political agenda and, without doubt, they provide one of the most fertile fields for local community governance, but also one of the most testing.

About this study

The research project upon which this chapter is based was entitled '*Local Strategies for Crime Prevention: Coordination and Accountability*'. The study set out to investigate the claim that local crime prevention strategies and the partnerships which implement them enhance the capacity of local agencies to respond to problems of crime and public order at the neighbourhood level, and also to discover the ways in which such arrangements affect local accountability. The researchers examined the national context and the institutional framework in which crime prevention partnerships have developed. They then undertook two case studies of crime prevention partnerships in Leicester and Nottingham, looking in particular at the central issues of coordination, accountability and durability.

The study employed a number of different methods, including documentary analysis of official publications, reports and policy statements. Interviews were conducted with a number of key decision-makers in Leicester and Nottingham, drawn from the local authorities, the police, and pressure groups. An important method was observation of the two partnerships in action, and informal interviews and discussions with participants.

10 Networks in Post-16 Education and Training

Kathryn Riley

Introduction

The issue of networks has received little attention in education but has been well-worked in many areas of social policy. Social studies has traditionally concerned itself with issues of linkage and relationship, and the study of organisations has always involved issues of network character. The contemporary surge of interest in networks, and the basis of the research reported in this chapter, stems from changes in the pattern of management of public sector organisations. The interest is particularly important because it challenges the boundaries between disciplines and requires us to think about the ways in which sociology, economics and political science relate to each other.

This chapter looks at the nature and complexity of these networks and interrelationships within one locality, South-East London. The study focuses on post-16 provision and broadly includes all those agencies, organisations and institutions which had an interest in, or responsibility for, the organisation, delivery or support of post-16 provision in the area. Those organisations were linked together by a web of resource transactions, project and service funding and student transfers. Within that broad post-16 network, a number of formal and informal forums and consortia (labelled as sub-networks) had been set up with differing, although sometimes overlapping, purposes. The emergence of the different sub-networks reflected the changing power relations and new organisational arrangements which had left the local education authority, along with the Training and Enterprise Councils (TECs), colleges, funding agencies and other organisations to forge new relationships and develop new practices.

In carrying out any network study, the initial problem is the starting point. When Alter and Hage (1993) undertook their study on networks in the USA, they were able to draw on a manual which listed all the major agencies involved in a particular network. No such manual exists in education. The starting point for this case study was, therefore, a broad locality and South-East London was chosen, given the knowledge that the author had of the area. Apart from an initial definition of locality, the boundaries for the network were established through interview data.

Networks and Networkers

South-East London TEC (SELTEC)

When the main part of the fieldwork was carried out for the project, the TEC (South-East London TEC) covered four local authority areas. During the course of the research, however, the TEC went into liquidation, with major consequences for the local funding of training (as is discussed later), and the TEC boundaries were also later redrawn because of the collapse. It could be argued that because of this, the case study was a special case in that to date, no other TECs have gone into liquidation. However, it could equally be argued that the extreme turn of events in South London served to highlight the fragility of networks in the current system of local governance.

The TEC network was largely – although not entirely – based on exchange relationships and the purchasing power of the TEC. From the TEC's perspective there were three types of networks: those to which they made an input; those they utilised; and those which they coordinated, including the Special Needs Forum, the Education Business Partnership and the Strategic Education Forum. The Education Business Partnership was described by a number of its members and by TEC staff as a helpful and successful network, providing links between education institutions and local businesses. The Strategic Education Forum brought together the interests of local business, local authorities, colleges and universities within South-East London. TEC respondents saw it as a major vehicle for establishing a 'bank' of good relationships between participants which could be drawn on at a later stage. Members of the Forum, such as this FE college principal, were somewhat sceptical about its purposes:

The image that I have of the Forum is all these 'barons' . . . powerful people who have broken away from local authorities and are having to find their place in the market place and are jostling with each other . . . It doesn't work because the TEC does not have enough authority to make it work.

The composition of the Strategic Education Forum reflected the geographical parameters of the TEC's responsibilities, South-East London, but this in itself was problematic. Whilst South-East London may exist as a London Transport concept (defined by the river and the lack of a tube service) it is essentially an artificial construct which the TEC itself endeavoured to promote as an entity through musical and sporting events. Although some coordination took place across borough boundaries, partly in response to the considerable amount of cross-borough traffic of students, growing fragmentation and increased complexity have created a refocusing on immediate localities, mainly local authority areas, which were known and understood. This wish for coordination within the local authority boundaries was exemplified by the establishment of post-16 forums in all four boroughs.

Local authority area

A number of sub-networks with a post-16 brief existed in the local authority area studied, such as the 'Linkways' consortium of head teachers and deputies from four schools and the FE college; the Chairs' Forum (of all chairs of governors in the borough); the Forum of Chairs and Headteachers of secondary schools; and the 14–19 management group (a formal but collaborative network of local authority providers which looked at borough-wide issues, such as the curriculum). Key individuals were also drawn together by existing funding arrangements such as City Challenge, as well as by new funding bids.

A particular focus of empirical enquiry was the Post-16 Forum, a strong formal network which was set up in 1994, following a local authority-initiated conference which brought together representatives from the range of agencies involved in the provision of education and training. Membership included the Principals and chairs of governors, of the FE and VI Form Colleges; a senior member of staff from the TEC; two secondary headteachers and their chairs of governors; and representatives of special needs, higher education and of the local authority (the 14-19 adviser, the Director and Chair of Education). All of the main participants in the Post-16 Forum were interviewed.

At its inception, it was envisaged that the Post-16 Forum would be a strategic rather than operational grouping which would set a common framework for otherwise diverse and competing agencies. Whilst the local authority had taken a leadership role in establishing the Forum, its legitimacy to continue in that leadership role was not uncontested. Perceptions about the Forum and the LEA's role within it varied, to some extent reflecting institutional concerns, from FE to retain autonomy, from schools to reduce competition, and from the local authority to create coherence in the pattern of provision.

> The issue here in [x] is to create a plurality of provision which builds on the strengths of different organisations . . . The LEA has to make sure that it doesn't hi-jack that agenda and the distinct visions of education that the different organisations have. (Governor, FE college)

> We need to rationalise provision locally and provide a common curriculum entitlement for young people. (Community Education officer)

> We're trying to find our way through a maze. It is appropriate for [the] Council to set up this Forum. We are the only body that represents the whole community . . . the ideal group to convene that organisation and to enable relationships to happen . . . We all have information about 16+ and we need to share that. What we have to be careful about is that we're not going back to the old planning arrangements because the system is a market . . . What we are trying to do is articulate the issues for [the area]. The LEA can play a very important role. (Chair of Education Committee)

> There are some real tensions. The College could eat us up at post-16. What we need is some cooperation. (Head teacher)

London and national networks

April 1991 saw the abolition of the ILEA, a large single-purpose authority which had responsibility for education in inner London, and the transfer of education to the thirteen inner London boroughs. All this took place at the same time as the incorporation of the sixth form and FE colleges and had significant impact on both the organisation and delivery of education services in London and on the relationships between providers and users of services (Riley, 1993).

April 1994 saw the birth of ten new integrated regional offices (IROs) for England headed by senior civil servants who act as regional directors for the Departments of Employment, Environment, Transport, and Trade and Industry. The IROs were part of the post-Maastricht shift designed to strengthen regions; promote urban regeneration; create stronger links between the private and public sectors; and provide the basis for a more integrated approach to funding. Twenty existing funding regimes were to be subsumed into the 1.4b Single Regeneration Budget (SRB) pot to be administered by the regional offices (Johnson and Riley, 1995).

Whilst the Government Office for London was not a Phoenix rising from the ashes of the ILEA, or the Greater London Council, its London-wide focus was designed to meet some of the gaps created when the two authorities disappeared. The Government Office for London (GOL) set out to build on existing London networks (such as London First and London Pride) and to create new pan-London networks, in response to funding changes and pressures from the business sector.

Most of the senior figures in the different organisations and institutions in the South-East London post-16 network were also linked into a range of national networks and organisations. Central to the colleges was the Further Education Funding Council. Other networks, linked to specific organisations (such as the Forum for Catholic VI Form Colleges, the Association of FE Colleges and the Association of Metropolitan Authorities) provided differing degrees of support, information and advice. There were also a number of informal networks with differing purposes and organisational arrangements. These included special needs, Technical Vocational and Educational Initiative (TVEI) and student awards. The latter network, although bounded by legislation, thrived, according to a member, because it increased significantly their capacity to deal with fraud.

The development of networks

There is evidence of undoubted growth in a range of overlapping sub-networks. Relationships were constantly reforming: a veritable kaleidoscope which shifted in response to changing organisational responsibilities, or new funding arrangements. During the course of the fieldwork, for example, the careers service was put out for tender which had a destabilising effect on staff. By their very nature, networks are transient beasts and those who are involved in them have to move with the beast, and adapt to new tasks and ways of working. One local authority officer described those changes in the following terms:

> The whole way that we work has to change. There are so many funding arrangements and schemes that are creating work of themselves . . . The network which LEAs have to try and manage is now enormous.

Involvement in networks was not, however, consistent across organisations. There was an increase in largely formal networks for those at the top of their organisations but a reduction in both formal and informal external networks, (particularly professional networks, for middle managers in schools, colleges and local authorities). There were less informal networks than in the past for head teachers; few formal networks for educational issues (such as the curriculum); and no informal networks which attempted to disseminate good practice and promote the cross-fertilisation of ideas. This falling away of informal networks for those involved in the delivery of services was seen as a product of the new competitive climate in education, and a result of the abolition of the ILEA.

> Schools are increasingly atomising rather than working together. Headteachers treat each other with suspicion because of the competition between schools. There are less informal networks and no informal networks which attempt to disseminate good practice. There is little informal professional collaboration. At one time there would have been a sense that we are in a tough job together . . . that's gone. League tables reflect the nature of the problem. It has become a zero sum game. If your school is doing better then you don't need to collaborate. If its doing worse, then other schools don't want to collaborate with you . . . Schools don't collaborate because there is no prospect of new markets. (LEA officer)

Network leadership

The nature, form and purposes of the post-16 sub-networks varied considerably. Networks were more easily established and maintained where there was parity of status between members. The roots of conflict were generally historical and based on uncertainties about funding, for example, between the TEC and the FE college.

Tensions emerged where new structural arrangements created direct competition between organisations and where network leadership could not automatically be assumed by one organisation. The Post-16 Forum was a case in point. Networking was helped in a sensitive area because the interlinkages between its members were strong and created the dynamics and seed bed for collaboration. For example, a governor from the sixth form college was also a governor of the FE college and of a local secondary school. Staff from the TEC were on the governing bodies of the FE and sixth form colleges. Membership of the TEC board included staff from the major organisations. As a consequence of these complex interrelationships, most of the members of the Post-16 Forum were co-members of other boards, committees or agencies. Despite this, the combination of market forces and institutional interests created tensions within the group about network aims and leadership.

There was evidence that networks for policy and for administration tended to be separate and that the latter were easier to establish. Administrative networks such as 'Linkways' worked well because participants felt that they were solving common problems. Cooperation undoubtedly increased if network members had worked together previously in the same or linked organisations, or within the same geographical area. Such cooperation depended on trust, a common language and shared values. Network effectiveness in general was enhanced where key players were members of overlapping groupings.

Whilst personal relationships, common values and objectives (rather than cultural ties) were often more important than formal links, formal links could have greater financial consequences. A quest for joint funding, for example, could provide the basis for a strong short-term collaborative relationship but such networks were unlikely to be sustained once the funding imperative had disappeared, as in the case of partnership bidding for SRB money. Whether and how organisations cooperated did not seem to be dependent on their age but on either formal (largely statutory) factors, and on particular individuals.

The issue of network leadership raised a number of questions. 'Do particular individuals take a leadership role in the network because of their own personal strengths, style and characteristics?' 'Is network leadership dependent on their relative strength and bargaining position of individual organisations?' Leadership was required within the general life-cycle of a network and at specific critical points, such as for the bidding process for the SRB. Findings from the case study suggest that network leadership was largely about the capacities of individuals but was also inevitably dependent on relative organisational strength. Leadership was usually taken by a representative of one of the major organisations but successful network leadership derived from personal qualities and the ability to put aside parochial interests in favour of a wider vision. One head teacher described successful network leadership as being more about style and personal authority than status and hierarchy:

> There are a lot of issues about networking that are to do with style . . . There are issues about delegation . . . about creating opportunities but also taking risks . . . It may be a hackneyed word but she [the Director] has created a partnership – a philosophy of openness and sharing. She has established a clear educational leadership role and an authority which isn't about hierarchy. She could have sat in her ivory tower and tried to hold on to the last vestiges of power . . . all that is reflected back in the schools.

Leadership was also about the organisational legitimacy to take a lead where a range of institutions and organisations are in competition. The extent to which different organisations within a network assume leadership and the basis on which such leadership is presumed (moral, historical, or as part of an exchange relationship) also shapes the capacity of the individuals and organisations in the networks to collaborate effectively. Issues about organisational legitimacy emerged in both the TEC Strategic Education Forum and the Post-16 Forum. Had the TEC the 'authority' to take a lead in the Strategic Forum? What were the areas in which the LEA had a legitimacy to lead in the Post-16 Forum? The establishment of the Post-16 Forum was a recognition that a borough-wide vehicle was needed to articulate local interests and the council was best placed to convene such a forum. However, this did not solve the problem of the scope and extent of the legitimate leadership role of the LEA.

The costs and benefits of networks

There has been a movement away from a system in which the organisation and delivery of services were in the hands of major providers, to one in which power is now shared by a range of agencies and players and mediated through a range of networks. The implications of these changes for the governance of the system are far-reaching. They include issues about the nature of the task of public sector management and issues about equity, accountability and transparency.

Promoting, developing and participating in a complex web of networks has now become a major task for those who lead and manage organisations. There are costs in terms of loss of power and control and in the commitment of time and energy to sustain networks when, as one sanguine head reflected, 'there is so much else to do in education'. Whilst interviewees accepted that in the fragmented climate networking was something that had to be done and was frequently stimulating, nevertheless some, such as the Director of Education quoted here, also questioned whether more could be achieved by a different distribution of resources and decision-making powers:

> In reflecting on my job, networking has become an increasingly important part of it . . . I'm less running a service . . . Its about saying the right things at the right time at the right level . . . it's difficult . . . I sometimes have a picture of myself having all of these meeting but trying to get service managers to understand that it is relevant to them . . . And I reflect that I spend so much of my time and energy supporting the networks rather than delivering services . . .
>
> I do find it personally stimulating and challenging, particularly, working with some very good business people on the TEC, and in City Challenge . . . Breaking down the public/private sector divide has a lot of merit. I can see that the Government has done a lot in bringing business into the local partnerships.
>
> I sometimes feel quite bitter and twisted when I think about the level of mainstream local authority high quality provision that there was, say for after school care and the cuts that have taken place and then you've got some pathetic scheme which has half a million to spread over four boroughs . . . Government Ministers coming down to support it . . . I don't disagree with what has happened to the colleges, but now we're all having to struggle to talk to one another.

For others, the new system of local governance in which networks played their part was healthy. From the perspective of GOL, a relative newcomer, the pan-London networks had created a clear framework in which colleges and TECs could work together effectively. For others, such as this head teacher, it had helped remove organisational blinkers and resulted in the creation of new alliances and access to a range of opportunities.

> If I look at other heads, many of them don't network. It very much depends on your perception of the leadership of your organisation . . . Too many heads still see their life as being within the school . . . There are direct financial gains to be made from networking and there is also the opportunity to develop thinking, create opportunities . . . It's also important to get others to be part of the various networks, my deputies are key . . . they are important players in a range of networks . . .
>
> When I first started as head, we weren't part of anything and I was faced with a dilemma about how much time to spend. I want to encourage others to do it. Networking takes a lot of time . . . I've also reflected on whether this is something that women are more likely to do than men . . . is it a women's mafia?

There was also a recognition, however, of the inherent tensions created by competition across the system.

Successful networking can create financial gains for organisations or institutions. Equally of course, there are significant consequences for those who are not successful in bidding, or simply do not get to the starting gate. In a market-driven system resources are allocated on the basis of competition, and are dependent on the skills and capacities of individuals to access a network and bid effectively. This raises questions about who are the winners and who the losers in such a framework.

Dilemmas of accountability and transparency

By their very nature it is difficult for networks to be directly accountable for their activities, although individuals within the network consider themselves to be accountable to certain constituent elements. An FE college governor, for example, saw the college as being accountable to the students of that college for the services it provided, with the 'Students' Charter' acting as a strong accountability mechanism: 'I feel strongly about the issue of accountability. Local politicians can mouth it. I do worry about the fact that we are a self-perpetuating group but what matters is the reality, how we make ourselves accountable.'

However, overall decision-making processes and accountability structures – who is responsible for what – were frequently unclear to many within the system, particularly those with operational responsibilities and to those using services and affected by network outputs. The shift from a system of local government to one of local governance has created a complexity of decision-making which many middle managers find difficult to untangle. If accountability is not clear to those working within the system, it is unlikely to be clear to users and beneficiaries of services.

Most networks have little contact with the public. In networks which are linked to major bidding processes, such as the SRB, only a selected number of players understand the ground rules. The speed and complexity of the bidding process has wrested decision-making from the local democratic arena, distancing it from those most affected by it, and transferring it to the realm of interpretation by a national officer core accountable to central government.

The development of networks within the framework of local governance inevitably raises issues about how staff use their time, as well as the skills required to operate effectively in the new governance framework. It also raises broader issues about the control and distribution of resources. The demise of SELTEC which went into liquidation during the course of the study brought this issue into sharp relief. When the financial oversight of a complex organisation is shared by a number of parties and agencies (as with the board of South-East London TEC) it is difficult to achieve financial control. The TEC overstretched itself and ultimately the GOL refused to offer indemnity. The collapse had major consequences throughout the post-16 network, creating funding losses for schools, colleges and training organisations. Inevitably, there has also been a loss of trust between remaining organisations and a significant loss of belief in the capacity of a fragmented market-orientated system to manage the delivery of services in an equitable manner.

Concluding thoughts

There are a number of paradoxes and uncertainties about the growth and development of networks. Networks are pioneering new forms of governance, as well as new modes of service delivery. Networks also recast the elected member as one voice among many 'partners', each drawing its legitimacy from a different source, but members find it hard to play their traditional roles in inter-agency contexts (see Lowndes and Riley, 1998). In the new context of local governance, members' roles are being squeezed at both ends: direct consultation with users is challenging members' representative role, whilst managers' dominance in inter-agency working (including contracting) is challenging their strategic role. At one level, network arrangements could be seen as symptomatic of a political malaise, where appointed bodies and self-selected 'representatives' fill the 'democratic deficit' in local politics. At another level, networks could be seen as complementary to formal democratic processes, providing a means for different stakeholders to apply influence in policy-making and assume new roles in service position.

The evidence from the case study is that the development of networks is driven by the need of many involved in local governance to reintegrate ideas, expertise and resources within a system which has become fragmented. It is this search for coherence which drives those individuals and organisations to commit energy and resources into networking, despite conflicting views about whether the benefits outweigh the costs.

The evidence also suggests that networks will continue to develop – a finding supported by other policy analysts (Rhodes and Marsh, 1992a, Rhodes, 1996; Finlay, Holmes and Kydd, 1997). Undoubtedly, however, the national framework has worked against the development of systemic networks based on the achievement of common goals and directed towards an effective and interrelated network for the delivery of local services.

The boundaries for the post-16 network are competitive and market-orientated, driving individual institutions towards autonomy in order to retain their position in the market. Locally, the collapse of the TEC created a breakdown in trust and reinforced the notion that provision in post-16 services is no longer a public service. In general, collaboration was either through exchange networks in which mutual dependency was established through purchasing; or promotional networks which involved all the competitors in the field, such as the Post-16 Forum. Collaboration aimed at achieving common goals did, however, exist within a small number of informal networks which had been set up for mutual support and problem-solving. Whether the change of government will enable networks to be more collaborative and less competitive in the future remains to be seen.

About this study

This chapter draws substantially on Riley, K. A. (1997) 'Changes in Local Governance – Collaboration Through Networks: A Post-16 Case Study', *Educational Management and Administration*, vol. 25, no. 2, pp. 155–67.

The chapter draws on a broader research study described in chapter 2. The fieldwork for the particular case study took place in three interlocking phases. In phase I, interviews were conducted with senior representatives from a number of organisations involved in education in South-East London to help define the boundaries and focus for the study. Interviewees included: a vice-principal of a university, a principal of a further education college, a head teacher, a director of education from one authority and a senior officer from another, the chief executive of the TEC and a local authority chief executive.

In phase II, the focus switched to the micro level, the post-16 provision in one specific local authority area. Interviewees in phase II included heads of the various institutions, governors and senior officers, the chair of education from the local authority and members of the newly established Post-16 Forum who identified other individuals who were important 'players', such as the head of the 'Linkways' consortium, who were also interviewed.

In phase III, the analysis moved to a more macro, London-wide level. Interviewees included staff from the Government Office for London, the DFE (now the DFEE) and the Further Education Funding Council.

In total, some 32 semi-structured, taped interviews were conducted. Interviewees also completed an administered questionnaire aimed at eliciting the strength of the relationship between different organisations; the frequency and formality of the relationship; the degree of conflict or cooperation between the different organisations; and the importance of the relationships to the effectiveness of the interviewee's own organisation.

11 Networking for Local Economic Development

Kevin Morgan, Gareth Rees and Shari Garmise

Introduction

The twin themes of 'globalisation' and 'localisation' have been prominent features in the debate about economic development since the
mid-1980s. Paradoxically, as the economy becomes more and more
globalised the local dimension of economic development has attracted
more and more interest from both scholars and policy-makers. One of
the reasons for this apparent paradox is that localities and regions are
the day-to-day arenas in which the pressures of economic change have
to be negotiated, no matter how global these pressures may be in
origin. This process of negotiation takes many forms, but increasingly
it assumes the form of private and public actors orchestrating their
activities through networks with a view to sharing information, pooling
resources and designing joint solutions to common problems. We shall
refer to this process as networking, which in very simple terms means
the disposition to collaborate to achieve mutually beneficial ends. In
the theoretical literature networks are deemed to be an alternative
mode of governance to markets and hierarchies. In the network mode
of resource allocation, transactions occur neither through arm's-length
exchanges (markets) nor administrative fiat (hierarchies), but through
networks of individuals or organisations engaged in reciprocal, pre-
ferential and mutually supportive actions, where the basic assumption
is that one party is dependent on the resources controlled by another
(Powell, 1990; Cooke and Morgan, 1993; Sabel, 1993).

Deceptively simple in principle, networking is profoundly demanding in practice because, to be effective, it involves trust, goodwill and a
capacity to forgo opportunistic behaviour. Even so, the new rhetoric of
the economic development community in the UK is replete with
references to networking, so much so that the term is in danger of

going the same way as 'flexibility', a term that conceals as much as it reveals. Despite this danger several factors have conspired to put networking on the local economic development policy agenda in the UK:

- The shift from a system of local government to a system of local governance means that a wide array of services is now performed by a complex set of public and private organisations and this has led to a 'new governance' system, which is largely composed of self-managed interorganisational networks (Rhodes, 1991a, 1996).
- The localisation of training and business support services, to Training and Enterprise Councils (TECs), Business Links and Trade Associations, has forced public and private organisations to collaborate much more than hitherto in the design and delivery of these services (Cabinet Office, 1996).
- To access the EU's Structural Funds eligible areas must satisfy the Commission that they have created genuine 'regional partnerships' between their public, private and voluntary sectors (Wulf-Mathies, 1995).
- Similarly, area-based partnerships are required to access UK government funds, like the Single Regeneration Budget (SRB) in England and a similar one in Wales (Garmise *et al.*, 1996).
- More generally, public agencies are coming round to the view that the most effective business services are those which have been designed with, rather than for, the corporate sector and this has given a new impetus to networking between the public and private sectors (Morgan, 1996).

The main objective of our research was to investigate the extent to which local economic development networks had developed in two subregions of the UK South-East Wales and the West of England – with respect to the provision of business services and vocational education and training. The subregions were chosen because, in microcosm, they reflected the different political, cultural and institutional environments of Wales and England and this afforded an opportunity to examine whether the apparatus of a 'regional state' in Wales actually made a difference. The two policy areas were chosen not just because they lie at the heart of local economic development policy but also because they are widely perceived to be weak in the UK relative to other OECD countries (Bennett *et al.*, 1994; Cooke and Morgan, 1998).

In this chapter we propose to examine each subregion in turn by focusing on (1) the new system of local economic governance, (2) the reorganisation of business services and (3) the reform of vocational education and training. In the final section we draw some general conclusions about the scope and limits of local economic development networks.

Networks and networking in South-East Wales

South-East Wales (the former counties of Gwent, Mid Glamorgan and South Glamorgan) embraces some of the most prosperous and most deprived parts of Wales, the latter heavily concentrated in the Valleys, where the decline of the coal industry has left a legacy of acute deprivation. Districts in Gwent and South Glamorgan, by contrast, have received the bulk of the new jobs created in the 1990s, and these are the areas favoured by foreign inward investment. To address the problems of economic development these and other areas in Wales look to the 'regional state', particularly the Welsh Office and the Welsh Development Agency (WDA), to provide a lead. Although these two institutions are perceived to have given Wales an advantage over the English regions, we shall argue that their effects can sometimes be counter-productive from a networking standpoint, especially if they disempower their local partners.

The new system of local economic governance

The Welsh Office and the WDA are the only institutions to have a Wales-wide brief for economic development. They sit at the apex of a system which has changed considerably since the late 1980s: the reorganisation of local government spawned 22 new unitary authorities in Wales; seven TECs are responsible for training and enterprise support; a Business Connect network has been created to provide easier access to business services; further education colleges have become independent actors in the wake of incorporation; and, following complaints from the European Commission, the regional partnership in South Wales has been transformed from a plaything of the Welsh Office into an independent executive composed of all the regional stakeholders. We shall explore some of these changes in more detail later, but here we want to establish some of the key power relationships.

Most economic development initiatives in Wales tend to originate from the Welsh Office or the WDA, with local players brought in as partners. While this top-down model makes it possible to develop Wales-wide initiatives, it tends to provoke hostility from below, not least because the other players feel themselves to be junior partners. This is apparent in the approach to foreign inward investment, where Team Wales, ostensibly a partnership of all public sector bodies in Wales, is actually dominated by the Welsh Office and the WDA. It was also apparent, until recently, in the way the South Wales regional partnership was organised to manage EU Structural Funds. A European Commission review of these partnership arrangements concluded by saying:

Many of the partners see partnership in a horizontal sense in which equal partners work towards common ends. Central government has tended to see partnership in vertical terms in which the Welsh Office plays the decisive role with any alternative model viewed as unacceptable. Working relationships in industrial South Wales, although reasonably good, are limited in scope. (European Commission, 1991)

This verdict could equally well be used to summarise the entire economic development scene in South Wales. While administrative devolution creates the potential for close working relations between the Welsh Office and local authorities, the latter feel that the Welsh Office has neither the will nor the resources to initiate its own policies and that it is loath to delegate responsibilities other than to its network of unelected quangos, where appointees now outnumber elected local authority members (WLGA, 1996). The fact that quangos are not locally accountable to the communities in which they operate has been one of the biggest barriers to networking, a problem which was particularly acute when the Welsh Office was controlled by the Conservatives, a minority political party in Wales (Morgan and Roberts, 1993). This interpretation was reinforced by a parliamentary inquiry, which was 'disappointed to discover that so much mistrust exists between the regional partners, especially local authorities and the Welsh Office' (Welsh Affairs Committee, 1995). This situation may change with the advent of a Labour government which is committed to reforming the quangos to render them more publicly accountable.

The reorganisation of business services

In 1992 the government signalled its desire to overhaul the provision of business support because the proliferation of agencies and services had resulted in 'unproductive rivalry and variable quality standards' (DTI, 1992). The outcome of this initiative was a network of one-stop shops, subsequently called Business Links in England and Business Connect in Wales. An alternative model emerged in Wales for two reasons: first, the business support system in Wales was different, not least because of the presence of the WDA and, second, John Redwood, the then Secretary of State for Wales, was ideologically averse to copying Heseltine's more interventionist approach to Business Links.

The system of business support in Wales differs from England not just because of the WDA but also because private sector organisations, like chambers of commerce, are very thin on the ground, with the result that public sector agencies dominate the field. While local enterprise agencies, TECs and local authorities offer a wide array of business services, the most innovative services have traditionally been designed and delivered by the WDA (Morgan, 1997b). The aim of Business Connect was to offer a single point of entry to these services, all of which were supposed to be integrated into a seamless whole. In practice, however, Business Connect has proved to be a weak and ineffective model compared to Business Link.

Whereas Business Link partners were encouraged by the DTI to forge strong networking relationships, Business Connect received virtually no strategic guidance from the Welsh Office, with the result that Business Connect networks are both loose and anaemic in each of the former counties of South-East Wales. In the absence of a strong chamber the TEC is the lead body in all three Business Connects and the WDA is viewed with deep suspicion, not least because it is widely perceived to be uninterested in, and therefore uncommitted to, the network. Further tensions exist between local authorities and the TECs, in part because the latter are seen as unaccountable quangos. Not surprisingly, the response from local businesses has been poor, judging by the number of inquiries generated to date.

The Business Connect experience raises something of a paradox: the Welsh Office is generally perceived to be obsessed with control and loath to delegate while, in this case, it is accused of relinquishing control of the exercise. Local partners feel that Business Connect was a case of 'devolution gone mad' in the sense that the Welsh Office abdicated responsibility for providing a firm lead from above. One possible explanation for this paradox is that, in the Redwood era, the Welsh Office wanted minimal changes so as to reduce the costs of the exercise, one reason perhaps why the Business Link in Rochdale received the same level of start-up funds as the whole of Wales received through Business Connect (Fortune, 1995).

Business Connect in South-East Wales is generally seen to have been a wasted opportunity: providers have failed to weave their services into a seamless whole and local firms seem no less bewildered than they were before. Significantly, Business Connect has worked best in Mid-Wales, where it built on a local tradition of inter-agency cooperation. In other words it has not significantly improved networking in areas where robust business support networks did not already exist. While it clearly had the power, the Welsh Office recoiled from exercising it to force through a more radical overhaul, like the co-location of service providers, and this refusal was partly due to the cost implications. To this extent we can say that the 'regional state' in Wales did make a difference to the way in which a central government policy was implemented at the local level.

The reform of vocational education and training

The 'regional state' is perhaps even more of an influence in the field of vocational education and training (VET). In addition to the Welsh Office, which is responsible for all education, training and economic development policy, there are the Welsh Funding Councils for Higher and Further Education (HEFCW and FEFCW), which have a strategic influence through their funding regimes. In this field the Welsh Office has played a very proactive role, not least by launching a Wales-wide strategy for VET, highlighting its potential for stimulating the Welsh economy (Welsh Office, 1995).

The FEFCW appears to be more deeply embedded in the local economic governance system than its counterpart in England. For example, it was responsible for organising Fforwm, a highly effective network of FE college principals and senior managers, which deals with post-incorporation governance issues as well as acting as the voice of FE in the economic and political worlds.

If incorporation provided an internal stimulus for new VET networks an external stimulus has been the need to respond to inward investing companies, which are imposing ever more exacting demands on the regional VET system. This has led to the formation of loose networks between the WDA, TECs, local authorities and FE colleges (Rees and Thomas, 1994). For the larger inward-investment projects this frequently involves the creation of special task forces, the development of tailor-made training programmes and even the construction of specialised training centres, as occurred with BA's maintenance facility at Cardiff airport and as is underway now with the massive LG project at Newport. The main problem to date has been in sustaining these networks after the initial burst of enthusiasm, indeed it is noticeable that the longer-established plants in South-East Wales, plants which no longer qualify for special assistance, increasingly complain of recruitment difficulties (Morgan and Rees, 1994).

But by far the biggest problem from a networking perspective is that VET institutions are struggling to manage the consequences of the new, more competitive environment (Welsh Affairs Committee, 1997). The incorporation of FE colleges and the marketisation of the funding regime have radically altered the context in which the colleges interact. In many cases the outcome was a straightforward reduction in co-operation. As one college interlocutor put it:

> Whereas before in a county, the principals would have sat down on a regular basis and had meetings – county meetings of colleges from the same area – you rarely see that any more

However, our research suggests a more complex picture than pure competition. In Gwent, for example, the competitive threat inherent in incorporation was preempted by the merging of all the county's colleges into a multi-campus tertiary college, with courses being coordinated through a central academic board. Elsewhere, colleges find themselves collaborating in some areas, like regional economic development projects, but competing vigorously in other areas, for students for example. Many interviewees believed that managing these fluid relationships was most effective when personal and professional trust had already been established. In this respect, the development of trust-based relationships through joint involvement in regional economic development projects had been extremely useful.

In South-East Wales, therefore, there is substantial evidence of new VET networks emerging, many of them triggered by and focused on local economic development initiatives in this subregion, a trend which is actively encouraged by the FEFCW, the WDA and the Welsh Office (Andrews, 1997). Paradoxically, while the 'regional state' is having a positive influence in this regard, the competitive thrust of central government policy since the late 1980s has made this networking task that much more difficult.

Networks and networking in the West of England

Throughout the 1980s the West of England (Avon, Gloucestershire and Wiltshire) was deemed to be a model of economic prosperity. Although it always contained some severely deprived areas the strength of the defence, aerospace, electronics and financial service industries combined to provide high levels of employment and growth. The bubble burst in the 1990s as the cyclical UK recession converged with structural regional problems, like lower defence spending following the fall of the Berlin Wall. Of the 12 regions singled out by the EU as being especially vulnerable to defence cuts these three counties were the only UK 'region' to be identified. Accustomed to relative prosperity, localities in the West of England suddenly felt compelled to devise strategies and structures to promote economic development.

The West of England is the most developed part of the South-West, the largest standard region in England, stretching over 250 miles from Penzance in the far south-west to Tewkesbury in the north. This geographical structure helps to explain the absence of a distinct regional identity, a problem further compounded by the fact that Devon and Cornwall see themselves as a separate subregion with little in common with the more urbanised parts of the near south-west. Such is the strength of these subregional divisions that the Government Office for the South West, which opened in April 1994, felt obliged to open two offices, one based in Bristol for the five counties, the other in Plymouth to serve Devon and Cornwall (GO-SW, 1995). Although the Government Office was a top-down initiative from central government, it emerged during a period of unprecedented institutional innovation in the West of England, most of which sprang from bottom-up initiatives to create new governance structures in and beyond the local level.

The new system of local economic governance

The system of local economic governance in the West of England differs from South-East Wales in two important respects: there is no overarching 'regional state' other than the new Government Office and chambers of commerce are much more important players, especially in

Bristol. Other than that the West of England has experienced the same changes as Wales, with respect to the reorganisation of local government, business services and VET. The fact that the Government Office lacks the power and resources of the Welsh Office means that it is more conscious of its dependence on local partners, and this tempers the vertical networks which tend to form around the Welsh Office. Even so, the Government Office primarily sees itself as 'central government in the region' rather than the voice of the region in London, and this helps to explain why there are real concerns about its lack of local accountability. Aside from this problem of democratic oversight, another problem with which the Office has had to contend is its lack of resources, which inclines some players to believe that it is not a worthy interlocutor, though this is very much a minority view.

Modest as it is the Government Office is generally seen as a step in the right direction, particularly by the regional Confederation of British Industries (CBI) and the Bristol Chamber of Commerce and Initiative (BCCI), both of which support some form of elected regional governance structure to spearhead and coordinate economic development partnerships (Adburgham, 1995). A new partnership approach was deemed to be essential throughout the West of England, and nowhere more so than in Bristol. During the 1980s elements in the city council subscribed to the 'new municipal socialism', from which point relations with the local private sector slumped to an all-time low, and the council thereafter acquired an 'anti-business' reputation (Bassett, 1996). Chastened by the economic crisis, the city council was also forced to rethink its position when it failed to secure two City Challenge bids because its public/private links were judged too weak to form effective partnerships (Malpass, 1994). The city's new pro-partnership approach in the 1990s coincided with, and was in part facilitated by, a new generation of local business leaders, notably John Savage, a self-confessed 'Christian socialist' who has turned the BCCI into one of the most effective and proactive chambers in the UK.

Aside from Bristol new economic governance structures are beginning to emerge at the subregional scale, stimulated by the belief that a single local authority district is too small to practice a strategic approach to economic regeneration. Three examples deserve to be mentioned here:

- The Western Development Partnership (WDP) was formed in 1993 to act as an umbrella organisation for a wide array of public and private sector organisations. Although largely Avon-based it adopted the 'Western' name to signal the need for a subregional approach and to this end it has launched a number of task forces in key sectors – like aerospace, high technology and financial services – to promote better networking (WDP, 1994).

- The West of England Initiative (WEI) was also launched in 1993 to promote inter-urban networking between local authorities in Bristol, Swindon and Gloucester. This subregional alliance aims to encourage cross-border cooperation so as to create a stronger subregional forum for planning, development and EU funds (WEI, 1995).

- In 1995 the West of England Development Agency (WEDA) was created to give the subregion a stronger mechanism for attracting inward investment (GO-SW, 1996).

With so much institutional innovation in the West of England in the 1990s the key problem is how to coordinate all these different initiatives. With the exception of the WEI, there is also the problem of public accountability, a problem which may be alleviated by the Labour government's proposals for democratising the Government Offices in England.

The reorganisation of business services

The formation of Business Links has been the most important change in business services in the West of England, with the main aim of forging new partnerships between chambers, TECs, enterprise agencies and local authorities so as to offer a single point of access to a wide array of services. Although Business Links now exist in all three counties of the West of England, this was no easy matter: the Links in Avon and Wiltshire were delayed because of internal conflicts between the chamber and the TEC in the former and between the chamber and the enterprise agency in the latter. These tensions were finally resolved in Avon when BCCI and WESTEC agreed to offer their services jointly through Business Link West, while in Wiltshire the chamber and the enterprise agency actually merged and now function as one of the partners in Business Link Wiltshire.

Of the three Business Links the most successful appears to be Business Link West (BLW), covering the former country of Avon. This view was endorsed by an independent evaluation conducted on behalf of the Department of Trade and Industry, which has since awarded BLW a 1.7 million contract, under the Competitiveness White

Paper 2, to promote interfirm networks across the whole South-West region. This regional networking initiative is one of the most innovative business service programmes in the UK, and it has been well-received by firms in the region's key sectors, especially in the crisis-ridden defence sector. BLW's successful start can be attributed to two factors in particular: first, the high calibre of personal business advisers and network brokers, all of whom have extensive management experience and, second, BCCI's imprimatur gives firms a greater sense of 'own-ership' than would ever be possible in a TEC-dominated Business Link.

Given the inauspicious tradition in Avon, BLW demonstrates that local cultures are not set in aspic; indeed, Bristol is beginning to be seen as an exemplar of locally generated public–private partnerships (Western Daily Press, 1997). These are early days, however, and time alone will tell whether this promising start will achieve real economic benefits.

The reform of vocational education and training

The VET sector in the West of England has been struggling to cope with the key changes in this sector, like the incorporation of FE colleges, the creation of the TECs, the privatisation of the Careers Services and funding regimes which, to a considerable extent, tie resource levels to student/trainee numbers. As we have seen, these changes have produced a wholly new environment in which institutions have to interact and manage their affairs.

Most of the networking in the West's VET has been confined to the county level, hence there is little or no cross-border activity of the kind we saw in the business services sector. In fact only in Avon was there any evidence of formal networking at all, with the establishment of the Western Education and Training Partnership (WEATP). The latter merges the Careers Services, the Education Business Partnership and the TEC's Education Department in a new partnership to integrate vocational education, employer training and careers guidance, and to develop more effective networking arrangements in the VET sector.

Although WEATP represents the only formal networking venture in the West, each of the three counties has a collaborative forum for FE college principals, albeit as a legacy of the pre-incorporation regimes of the local education authorities (LEAs). Nevertheless, they meet reg-ularly and, at times, they have a mediating influence on competition between colleges, over student recruitment and marketing for example.

But they have no real power or control, and certainly do not function to shape skills provision in line with any local economic development strategy. Indeed, the evidence suggests that relations within each forum are no longer as open as they once were, especially regarding the type and amount of information exchanged. Since these networks hinge – at least in part – on personal ties which had been built up under the auspices of the LEA, some doubt was expressed as to how long they would survive once the individual principals leave or retire.

A similar situation existed in the Careers Services. At one time there was a strong South-West network among the Careers and Guidance Services but, since privatisation, the level of cooperation had diminished appreciably. As one respondent conceded: 'it's not such a free exchange of ideas any more. In the background there is always this issue of competition'. Although networks of this kind can still furnish important sources of information, they manifestly lack the capacity to make decisions or organise comprehensive collective strategies.

FE colleges have also found it difficult to establish useful links with business because employers are inadequately organised. One Gloucestershire college principal explained:

Trying to have a simple relationship with your commercial community is very difficult because they themselves in this area have not got a very well established system of organisations with which you can relate. Relating to something like Chamber of Commerce is but it only represents a relatively small community.

In Wiltshire, attempts to regularise college–employer relationships led colleges to sponsor the amalgamation of a number of small Chambers of Commerce into the West Wiltshire Association Chamber. It is perhaps no coincidence, perhaps, that it is in Avon, where BCCI runs an active education committee, that networking has progressed the furthest.

Despite the growing priority attached to skills development nationally, there is little evidence, apart from the Avon area, that VET provision is networked into a coherent economic development strategy. Indeed, it appears that the new environment has even weakened past collaborative mechanisms. Although there have been real attempts to maintain those structures of collective action, the imperatives set by national funding regimes have stymied the growth of networks which seek to move beyond information exchange.

The nature, scope and limits of local economic development networks

Both our case study areas – South-East Wales and the West of England – have witnessed a substantial growth of institutional networks, often under the guise of public–private partnerships. However, in terms of the associational model of the 'networked region' (Amin and Thrift, 1995; Cooke and Morgan, 1998), these developments remain extremely partial. In both areas the growth of networks is uneven and their structures remain fragmented, focused on restricted geographical areas or on the achievement of limited, often short-term goals. Many of the networking initiatives were, in fact, reactive responses to external pressures rather than proactive attempts to change the trajectory of economic development in a more thoroughgoing way. While the growth of these networks has consequences which are real enough, they remain circumscribed, not least because of the national environment in which they operated. In this final section we propose to elaborate on this argument by drawing six key conclusions about the nature, scope and limits of local economic development networks in these areas, relating these findings to the theoretical literature on networking.

First, in both areas the evidence suggests that informal links often seem to be the backbone on which successful networks develop. This reinforces a more general point, namely that the 'invisible factors' which constitute social capital (like the norms and networks of trust and reciprocity) are deemed to play an increasingly important role in economic development (Doeringer *et al.*, 1987; Putnam, 1993b; Morgan, 1997a). The majority of respondents stressed the role of personalities as an important factor in determining the success or failure of specific networks. Even so, while informal links may be a critical input, much depends on the extent to which these links are institutionalised so as to meet clear goals and governance structures. Just as formal structures are supported by informal means, informal relations require formal structures to provide a sustainable context.

Second, far from being powerless victims of circumstance, local institutions can and do make a difference by helping to shape their local environment. The differences in network development and institution-building between counties were often as great as differences between the two subregions. More significantly, as actors found themselves in different roles, often as a result of central government policy, their preferences, expectations and transactional modes were transformed through the process of interaction itself (Sabel, 1993). In other words, these changes provided the opportunity for actors to redefine themselves and the networks in which they participated: perhaps the best example of this point was Bristol, which proved that the adversarial local culture was not set in aspic.

Third, there is some evidence that networks do matter in terms of the framing of strategies and in achieving development objectives. One insider in Wales observed: 'We have learned from experience. Less successful examples of urban regeneration in Wales are in those areas which were unable to establish these networks.' Similarly, the formalisation of a partnership such as the WEATP allowed for a more comprehensive integration of both knowledge and strategies between two formally separate but functionally interdependent sectors.

Fourth, in both case study areas there was a growing realisation that the local authority jurisdiction was too restrictive a spatial scale to permit of a strategic approach to economic development, hence the priority attached to 'region-building' (Garmise, 1997b). Because South-East Wales is already part of a well-defined 'regional state' system, this tendency was most pronounced in the West of England, which feels 'piqued about a system which consigns this region eternally to come second to Wales, to Scotland, to the North' (Western Daily Press, 1996). Because the South-West standard region is so incoherent, geographically and politically, 'region-building' exercises have been largely confined to the West of England, where the WDP and the WEI have both sought to create a subregional identity around the M4 corridor. These efforts were predicated on the belief that the West of England could achieve more by acting in concert than by acting alone, especially in the battle to attract foreign inward investment and EU funding. In the absence of formal regional governance structures, however, these efforts have produced few tangible benefits to date and further progress may have to wait on the Labour government's proposals for regional devolution in England.

Fifth, contrary to our original ideas, the presence of regional institutions in Wales presents us with an uncomfortable paradox, namely that the Welsh Office, by virtue of its power and resources, tends to foster *vertical* networks which have the effect of disempowering local actors from building effective *horizontal* networks. The former tend to impede bottom-up collective action because:

A vertical network, no matter how dense and no matter how important to its participants, cannot sustain social trust and cooperation. Vertical flows of information are often less reliable than horizontal flows, in part because the subordinate husbands information as a hedge against exploitation. More important, sanctions that support norms of reciprocity against the threat of opportunism are less likely to be imposed upwards and less likely to be acceded to if imposed. (Putnam, 1993a)

In Wales the objectives and rules of network participation tend to be established in a hierarchical manner, rather than negotiated between equal participants. The hierarchical nature of network relationships in South-East Wales is accentuated by key features of the social and economic environment, in particular the muted role of the private sector, which makes for a heavy dependence on state initiatives. Partly for this reason a number of our respondents in the business services sector in South-East Wales bemoaned the fact that the Welsh Office had not played an even more directive role in the formation of Business Connect networks.

Conversely, the very absence of a central authority in the West of England meant that networks and networking tended to be of a horizontal character and, in the Avon area, these networks were largely self-generated, thereby encouraging self-reliance rather than dependence on a powerful regional institution. In the longer run this may provide a better basis for stronger networks because, as the strength-of-weak-ties thesis suggests, loosely coupled networks can often be the most robust (Granovetter, 1973).

Our final point concerns two aspects of 'the new governance' system, with its corollary of 'governing without government' (Rhodes, 1996). First, in highlighting the growth of 'self-organizing, inter-organizational networks', Rhodes argues that this trend raises new problems of democratic accountability, a point amply reinforced by our case studies. Far from being a luxury we can ill afford, democratic accountability would seem to be essential for *effective* networking because, without it, these networks cannot be sustained politically nor can they elicit sufficient trust and cooperation, as we can see from the experience of quangos in Wales and the initial reaction to the Government Offices in England (Morgan, 1997b; Mawson and Spencer, 1997; House of Lords, 1996).

However, the second aspect of Rhodes's thesis is more problematical. The suggestion that 'the new governance' constitutes a form of 'governing without government' carries the implication that central government is less important than hitherto. Yet the evidence from our case studies strongly suggests that while central government may no longer be so directly involved in the local economic development arena, it continues to exert an extremely powerful influence, not least in structuring the environment and in defining the rules under which local institutions interact. Perhaps the best example here is the way in which the VET sector in both subregions was struggling to devise cooperative local arrangements, only to find that the national policy regime was undermining these efforts (Garmise and Rees, 1997).

Perhaps the main point on which to conclude is this: while local economic development networks can indeed make a difference, especially when they have invested in social capital, their scope remains heavily circumscribed by non-local factors, so much so that the 'governing without government' thesis is a fatal conceit.

About this study

Based on a comparative study of new structures of local economic governance, the research for this chapter focused on two subregions (South-East Wales and the West of England), covering two policy fields (business services and vocational education and training). The principal vehicle of data collection was semi-structured interviews with 52 senior representatives from key institutions in local economic development. Most of these interviews were conducted in the early part of 1995, when very substantial changes were taking place in the local governance system, like the reorganisation of local government and the creation of Business Link in England and Business Connect in Wales. We would like to thank all our respondents for their time, particularly Richard Harris, formerly of the European Unit at Thames-down Borough Council.

12 Networking in Europe

John Benington and Janet Harvey

Introduction

The focus of this chapter is on the significance of UK local authority involvement in transnational (particularly European) networks, for policy-making and management. We are concerned not just with networks as institutions, but also with networking as a process.

Within the European Union, transnational networks are now a key part of the policy development process, and increasingly UK local authorities are getting actively involved, alongside their local and regional authority counterparts in other EU countries. In many cases the networks are not exclusive to local authorities but also involve a wide range of other organisations. They therefore provide a good opportunity to study both the vertical and lateral dimensions of governance – that is, governance of the interrelationships between both tiers (local, regional, national and supranational governments) and spheres (public, private, voluntary and community sectors).

There is a growing body of academic analysis of the emerging institutions within the European Union, and debate as to how far they are intergovernmental or supranational in form, and how far neo-realist, neo-functional or neo-rational theories provide helpful explanations (Schmitter 1996; Liebfried and Pierson, 1995; Marks, Hooghe and Blank, 1996). However, generalisation from political theory has provided more insight into institutional roles and structures than into the dynamic processes of policy-making within the EU. Case studies and longitudinal research can be highly productive methods through which to study innovations in public policy-making and to illuminate the complex patterns and fluctuating processes of innovation through networks (Hartley, 1994; Yin, 1994). The relative openness and fluidity of the emerging state-like institutions and processes around the EU makes this an ideal moment to carry out such a study.

Our study covers transnational local authority networks in three categories:

- *Sectoral networks* of local authorities concerned with the impact on their regional and local economies of the global and European restructuring of key industrial sectors: the Coalfields Communities Campaign and European Action for Mining Communities (CCC/EURACOM); the Motor Industry Local Authority Network (MILAN); the Aerospace Industry Regional and Local Authority Network (AIRLINE); and the Fashion Industry Network (FINE).
- *Spatial/territorial networks* representing the interests of cities and communities in different European member states, with common interests based upon place/space: EuroCities; Middle Sized Cities; Atlantic Arc.
- *Thematic networks* organised around particular policy issues, often in the field of social welfare: the European Anti-Poverty Network and Quartiers en Crise concerned with poverty; ELAINE concerned with race.

To provide the institutional context we have also monitored the work of the key supranational and intergovernmental organisations within the local government policy community, for example, the Council for European Municipalities and Regions (CEMR) and, particularly, the Committee of the Regions (COR).

Although it is possible to describe ideal-typical networks, or perhaps even ideal-typical features of networking, transnational networks are not an homogenous category. The form and content of a particular network is shaped within a particular historical, ideological and political economic and social context (Benson, 1982; Smith, 1993).

We therefore begin this chapter with our analysis of the specific political economic and social context within which UK local authorities and European networks operate. We will then summarise the development of the network concept in both the academic and policy communities, before moving on to analyse the opportunities and problems posed for local governance in the UK as a result of European economic and political integration, and the nature, processes and outcomes of transnational networking by local authorities. Finally, we conclude by arguing that new models of multilevel, multinodal and multinational governance are emerging.

The political, economic, technological and social context for local government in the European Union

The UK's postwar consensus in support of a Keynesian welfare state has been challenged over the 1980s and 1990s, and displaced by a neo-liberal preference for provision through the private market and the nuclear family. However, neo-liberal private market solutions have also been found incapable of tackling the increasing range of complex communal problems (for example, unemployment, social exclusion, crime and community safety and the environment) which confront British (and Western) society, and which cut across traditional divisions of responsibility between the state and the market and different levels and departments of government. Local governance is increasingly seen as the responsibility not of elected local authorities alone, but of partnerships between public, private, voluntary and community organisations and, increasingly, between different levels of government. This creates the preconditions for a proliferation of interorganisational networks.

There have been particularly far-reaching and fundamental long-term changes in the European context of UK local government (Benington, 1994).

The economic context for many UK local authorities has been sharply affected by the restructuring of key industrial sectors which is accompanying the moves towards a more integrated and competitive European market. This sectoral concentration is also leading to a spatial restructuring of investment, technology and jobs, in which some regions and localities prosper, while others suffer decline and others remain in protracted uncertainty. European integration is contributing, alongside other processes of globalisation, to the economic, social and technological restructuring of many UK regional and local economies, with far-reaching dislocation and considerable challenges and uncertainties for local government. Many local authorities are responding by developing economic regeneration strategies in conjunction with local, regional and European partners.

The technological context. The emergence of new microelectronic and computer-based information technologies and systems is having a major impact not only on the processes and relations of productions, but also upon social processes and spatial patterns. Castells argues that the information revolution has profound implications for the economy, society and culture, and is resulting in the reorganisation of most of the major social institutions in network form (Castells, 1996). According to

Castells, the new spatial order is a 'space of flows' quite different from our traditional 'space of places'. People still cluster in specific localities but their clusterings take their shape from involvement in global as well as local networks. These developments create contradictory pulls and pressures. On the one hand, some of the technological changes (for example, the Internet) open up opportunities for extending democracy and control over information and ideas. On the other hand, they may reinforce existing divisions between the information-rich and the information-poor, with the risk that whole sections of the population may be switched off or excluded from the emerging global networks.

The social policy context for UK local authorities is changing rapidly as a result of demographic and socioeconomic changes, and the EU's growing involvement and intervention in this field. In spite of the EU's very limited legal competence in social policy, UK local authorities are increasingly feeling the impact of the spate of new European legislation (on issues like trading standards, environmental regulation and transfer of undertakings) and of the European regional and social funds, community initiatives and pilot programmes (on issues like urban regeneration, anti-poverty strategies, and programmes for women, older people, the unemployed and disabled people). The Commission is now gearing up for a new phase of more active intervention in social policy, acting as a catalyst in promoting joint discussion, exchange of experience, and concerted action on a transnational basis in responding to complex common problems (such as unemployment and racism). Local and regional authorities are central to all these plans, and are increasingly being drawn into partnership with the EU in developing and implementing these policy initiatives, and into networks with other actors in the public, private, voluntary and community sectors.

The political context for UK local government has been influenced by the gradual strengthening and integration of the European policy-making process. The creation of the Committee of the Regions (COR) has given regional and local authorities a formal channel of representation and consultation within the EU. Its real significance for local politics and policy-making, however, perhaps lies less in the Committee's formal status and role (only advisory at this stage), than in the fact that it brings together elected councillors from the different regions and localities in all the EU member states, and puts them into direct contact with the European policy process and policy community. This exposes councillors (many for the first time) to the wide range of EU ideas and initiatives, and reveals the very different traditions and cultures from which their local government counterparts in other member states come, even within the same European political groupings. It has particularly strengthened UK local authority awareness of the regional dimension of government in other European countries, and of the possibility of regional and local contributions to the national and EU democratic process, at a time when the UK is considering greater devolution to Scotland, Wales and the English regions. The political context for local government is also influenced by the democratic deficit in the EU, where the non-elected European Commission seeks to legitimate many of its actions and interventions by actively consulting and involving regional and local authorities in its policy formulation processes.

Networks with and between other organisations are therefore seen as an important part of the EU's strategy for grappling with the profound changes in the political, economic, social and technological structure of Europe, and to formulate a distinctive European model of development which attempts to reconcile economic growth with social cohesion and inclusion. Networks and partnerships symbolise the kind of collaborative relationships which the EU is trying to develop both with different levels of government and also with many different organisations in the public, private, voluntary and community sectors, during a period of structural change and uncertainty.

Networking and the European Union

'Networks' and 'networking' have emerged as vogue words for the 1990s in popular discussion, in public policy debates and also, simultaneously, in academic discussion in a number of diverse disciplines, for example, management and organisation theory, sociology, anthropology, molecular biology, quantum physics, industrial economics, social and public policy, international politics, and information systems. It is striking that the definitions given to networks are not very precise in any of these fields. The language of networks often seems to be used as a metaphor rather than as an analytical category (for example, a web, lattice, grid, honeycomb, polymer chain, constellation, kaleidoscope). However, there are considerable differences between these various images of organisation, which suggests that the networks concept can mask some very different kinds of interrelationships. In general terms, however, the network metaphor is usually used to convey ideas of lateral rather than hierarchical structures; horizontal rather than vertical processes; collaborative rather than competitive relationships; flexible rather than routinised responses.

Policy network theory has been particularly influential within political science (Rhodes, 1981; Rhodes, 1988; Rhodes and Marsh, 1992a). Rhodes has called for an emphasis on 'networks of organisations as the most revealing unit of analysis' for sub-central government (Rhodes, 1988, p. 4), rather than the previous concentration on the local political system and institutions. The policy network approach has provoked considerable academic debate, and a large number of studies have followed, using and seeking to modify this perspective (for example, Grant, 1989, 1992, 1993; Mills, 1992; Stones, 1992). The policy network approach has, however, largely left the area of transnational networking unaddressed, although there have been some cross-national studies in this area (Van Waarden, 1992; Grant, 1992), and more recently Rhodes and others have turned their attention to policy networks in the European Union (Rhodes, Bache and George, 1996; Marks, Hooghe and Blank, 1996).

Our interviews with EU officials and analysis of EU documents have identified three main phases in the development of the idea and practice of networking within the EU policy community (Benington and Geddes, 1996). In the first phase, networks are conceived narrowly and in terms of formal constitutional or institutional relationships between representative bodies, primarily at supranational level. This phase is typified by the 'social partnership' between the EU and the employers, trade unions and certain socio-professional organisations, in a corporatist model of policy dialogue.

In the second phase (from the mid-1980s to the mid-1990s), the partnership and network concepts were broadened and deepened, to become a key feature of the EU's mainstream policy processes and programmes over a very wide field. This involved the extension of the principle to embrace other tiers of government, to include the national, regional and local authorities in new forms of cooperation, and to incorporate a wide range of bodies outside government, from the public, private and voluntary sectors and from civil society.

The third and current phase in the development of the network concept in the mid-1990s is one in which the EU is now wanting to promote a more active set of networks with other bodies to accelerate the rapid development of a more extensive, interventionist and innovative European social policy and employment strategy. Such a development would imply an important role for transnational networks as methods for exchange of experience, policy transfer and cross-national learning.

The overall conclusion from our research is that European integration presents local areas and local authorities with a range of fundamental political, economic and social changes, and associated challenges, opportunities and problems. These are opening up a number of new policy arenas for UK local government, and contributing to the development of some distinctive new forms of local, translocal, trans-regional and transnational governance. European integration is clearly not the only stimulus for these changes in governance, of course; there are many other influencing factors, at both local and global levels. However, European integration does precipitate UK local authorities very visibly into a new cross-national context and requires new patterns of leadership and management.

Many UK local authorities are responding to European integration and to global and domestic industrial restructuring by developing strategies for local economic and social development, and (in the climate of continuing constraints on public expenditure in the UK) turning to the European Union both for European Regional Development and Social Funds and also for special programmes and community initiatives.

This can generate substantial additional capital and revenue funding for a local area, but can also run the risk of skewing local authority priorities towards the particular funding programmes available at that time from the EU. The EU's financial regimes (often based upon retrospective and delayed payments of grants) makes it difficult for local authorities to link EU funding into their corporate strategic priorities.

The plethora of new EU regulations and policy initiatives is also having direct impacts upon local authority policy and practice. In some cases, these have the force of directives imposed from above. In other cases, they take the form of invitations to local authorities to bid for collaboration in European pilot programmes or community initiatives. An increasing number of these require local authority participation in transnational networks.

Many local authorities are responding to these opportunities by establishing European officers or units within their organisation, or outpost offices (often shared with other authorities) in Brussels, to monitor new policy developments and to act as antennae to give early warning of new legislation, policy initiatives, pilot programmes and funding opportunities. This can bring both material and symbolic benefits to the local authority. However, again there is a danger of opportunism and distortion in responding to the latest grants or projects on offer, rather than linking EU matters into the central policy-making mechanisms and processes of the local authority.

In addition to chasing EU grants and seeking early warning of EU initiatives, some UK local authorities have also seized the opportunity to try to influence EU policy-making in particular fields in which they have a specific or general interest (for example, economic and industrial development, poverty and social exclusion, ageing of the population). A still small, but rapidly growing, number of UK local authorities is involved in attempts to lobby the EU in regional combinations and associations, or in transnational networks.

The European Commission is still a relatively young organisation (Mazey and Richardson (1993a) have called it an 'adolescent bureaucracy'), with a relatively small staff, working in a very large and wide field of policy development with many different national actors and other interests to accommodate. The Commission's divisional structure is in some ways not so complex as UK national government, and the hierarchy is flatter. This may mean that its procedures and cultural practices are less entrenched than longer-established governmental bureaucracies. It is therefore potentially more open to influence from pressure groups and other forms of lobbying than longer-established governmental organisations. (It will be interesting to discover to what extent this relative openness is maintained as the EU develops and gains greater accountability through formal representative political bodies, for example, the Parliament).

As an unelected body, the European Commission is also very conscious of the need to legitimate its activities and interventions not just through the Council of Ministers and the European Parliament but also through the regional and local authorities who carry many of the economic costs and social consequences of the restructuring of the European market. EU officials are therefore keen to promote webs of relationships with regional and local authorities.

One finding which emerges very clearly from our interviews with Commission officials is the EU's increasing preference for dealing with local authorities, first, in regional groupings, and second, on a multilateral and cross-national basis, rather than responding to bids and pressures from single local authorities or single member states. This is one of the factors which has stimulated local authority involvement in transnational local authority networks.

Transnational networks nature, processes and outcomes

Our research suggests that local authority involvement in transnational (European) networks varies along a number of dimensions, including:

- the political economic, technological and social context surrounding the local authorities involved;
- the nature, range and complexity of the issues being addressed by the network;
- the relative autonomy of the authorities and/or network in relation to the Commission;
- the extent of its dependence upon EU funding or programmes;
- the values, vision, ideology and leadership style of the political leaders and top managers;
- the ratio of benefits, costs and risks at stake for the local authority in both economic and political terms.

The above dimensions are illustrated in the following analyses of our research findings. In addition we learned a good deal about the processes of networking as they develop and fluctuate over time, through what one respondent described as successive phases of 'forming, norming, storming and performing'.

The formation of transnational networks

In some cases, the initiative for setting up some of the transnational networks has come mainly from below, from local authorities and other organisations keen to influence European policy in some way (for example, the Coalfields Communities Campaign and EuroCities). In other cases (for example, the European Programmes to Combat Poverty), the initiative has come mainly from above, from the European Commission's attempt to 'ground' and legitimate its policy development in the regions and localities as well as in the nation states. In other cases (for example, the European Anti-Poverty Network), the initiative has come from local authorities and/or voluntary organisations, but then been fostered and funded by the Commission. The relationships between networks and the Commission are therefore interactive, interdependent and in some cases symbiotic.

The EU's interest in encouraging or responding to transnational networks arises from several factors. The EU wants to promote a sense of integration and cohesion within the Union at a time of potential disintegration and division. Several EU programmes and community initiatives thus support cross-national networks which establish links between the more prosperous and the less developed regions within Europe. Commission officials also want to get informal feedback and advice from the regional and local authorities which will be involved in implementing many of their programmes, before the formal responses from the member states and the Council of Ministers. Briefings from and discussions with experts from different countries, local authorities, and interest groups are a potentially valuable source of intelligence and advice to the Commission (whose bureaucracy is relatively very small), particularly during this developmental phase in the EU, when many complex policy problems have to be addressed, cross-national policies have to be formulated and experimental solutions piloted.

The Commission in some cases actively fosters the formation of transnational networks to match or mirror its policy concerns. For example, high-ranking officials in DGV stimulated and supported the formation of the European Anti-Poverty Network (EAPN), effectively encouraging it to represent the voice of the voluntary and community sectors more coherently at European level, to lobby for more comprehensive action against poverty, and to enter into a consultative relationship with the Commission, offering policy advice at the very highest levels, up to the President himself. Networks thus provide the Commission with an important source of information and ideas on how to respond to complex cross-national policy problems, where there are few precedents to follow. Networks act as laboratories for the research, development and testing of new policy ideas and initiatives, in a new transnational environment.

Local authorities and transnational networks

Our interviews and observations suggest a multiplicity of motives for joining and belonging to a transnational local authority network at European level, including variously a desire to raise the profile of the city or authority in the European policy arena; the ambition of a particular politician or officer to promote their personal image and reputation on the European stage; to get access to EU officials, grants and funding programmes; a strategy for lobbying the Commission or Parliament by establishing a coalition of similar interests across different countries to try to influence EU policies; to try to bypass Westminster and/or Whitehall in achieving policy objectives; an attempt to encourage policy borrowing and policy learning from and between other local authorities and actors in other countries, on emerging or fashionable issues; a wish to contact partners in other European Union countries, in order to fulfil the Commission's requirements for funding for cross-national programmes; an attempt to share and spread the costs and risks of experimental or pilot programmes to tackle complex policy problems; a more general desire to be in the right place at the right time to get to know and be known, in the hope of enhancing the authority's probability of gaining European funding and influence; a wish to be (and be seen to be) good Europeans, and in some authorities to show solidarity with other cities or countries with particular histories and experiences (for example, Berlin, Bosnia); and finally, but not insignificantly, an opportunity to spice up local authority routines by adding the glamour of overseas travel and meetings in attractive cities, with the buzz of international contacts and discussions with counterparts from several countries.

Our research thus suggests that transnational networks present UK local authorities with a wide range of material and instrumental opportunities in relation to the European Union (for example, to gain EU grants, to get early warning of EU policy developments, to have an input into aspects of the EU policy-making process). In addition to these potential benefits of vertical integration within the governmental system (linking local authorities into the emerging supranational tiers and arenas of government within the European Union), transnational local authority networks also open up an additional set of opportunities arising from horizontal integration (linking local authorities into lateral and often overlapping spheres and webs of rapid information exchange, policy borrowing, technology transfer, and learning about both successful and unsuccessful innovations in policy and practice).

Holding transnational networks together

Transnational networking often cuts across four sets of boundaries – between countries, between different levels of government, between political parties, and between public, private, voluntary and community sectors. Networks therefore have to actively build and sustain a common interest or a coalition of interests between organisations with great diversities in their membership and contexts, which may start from very different or even conflicting positions, and which may encompass actors and organisations which traditionally have negotiated separately or even in opposition to each other.

Developing a core of common values was found to be particularly helpful in holding the transnational coalition together. European Action for Mining Communities has built its cross-regional and transnational coalitions not simply upon their immediate common interest in winning compensation for declining coalfields areas, but also upon their much deeper-rooted solidarity as miners and ex-miners, with historic links to the trade unions and working-class organisations. It reinforced this by uniting in opposition against both the employers and the British government, and enlisting the European Commission as an ally. The European Anti-Poverty Network has also mobilised a strong sense of value-based solidarity. The Motor Industry Local Authorities Network found it harder to develop common values to counterbalance the competition between different motor industry regions.

A clear analysis and a collaborative strategy were also found to be necessary. The Motor Industry Local Authority Network (MILAN) and the Aerospace Industry Regional and Local Authority Network (AIRLINE) both found it hard to identify, negotiate and to sustain a unifying common interest or joint strategy across the different auto and aerospace regions of Europe. The restructuring of these two industries is very different from the coal industry – some areas are prospering, some are retrenching, others are in uncertainty. Different localities are often set in direct competition with each other for investment by their multinational firms. MILAN and AIRLINE have found it much harder than EURACOM to analyse and identify a common cause for their members to fight for at the European level. These examples of variation between sectors also show the importance of situating any organisational analysis of networking in its political and economic context.

A concern with, and understanding of, how to mobilise positive interorganisational processes was found to be important in sustaining transnational networks as they moved through different stages in their life cycle. These processual skills were found to be very different from those traditionally associated with political leadership or strategic management. New kinds of leadership and management skills were found to be crucial in sustaining common purpose and cohesion in networks.

Developing a sense of vision and common values clearly has been an important ingredient in the effective mobilisation of several transnational networks. The process of translating values into strategy is not easy or automatic. All the networks required hours of discussion and the deployment of some distinctive political, analytical and organisational skills. Crucial leadership roles were played not just by the formally elected chairs or committees, but also by elected politicians, paid officials, researchers, advisers (often working in combination) who were capable of thinking analytically, working strategically, moving beyond opposition into proposition, and building coalitions between competing interests. This was particularly apparent in Euro-Cities where their agenda (European urban policy) was very broad, the problems complex, and the policy context crowded and confused. Different kinds of leadership skills were deployed by different people at different stages of the building of the organisation and its policy agenda. One of the most necessary leadership skills was how to sustain active involvement in the network by all its members (especially peripheral authorities and back-bench members), and to prevent the emergence of an elite inner circle and a marginalised outer circle of members, especially during times of high-level negotiation with the European Commission, Parliament, or Committee of the Regions. Developing a range of different levels of involvement and types of contribution was found to be helpful.

The development of network policies

The successful networks put a lot of care into research, policy analysis and policy development work. Sometimes this work was carried out by members and officers of the local authorities in the network, in small cross-national working groups and policy commissions. In other cases, it was also generated by the network's paid secretariat, several of whom are highly regarded experts coming from academic or research backgrounds. The role and contribution of this new breed of 'organic intellectual' within transnational networks would repay further research.

Our research suggests that while European policies in some local authorities are becoming more corporate (for example, EuroCities meetings often involve the leader, the chief executive and/or other senior councillors and chief officers acting on behalf of the authority), they are not necessarily very strategic. Much local authority involvement in the European policy arena, and in transnational networks, still appears to be opportunistic and *ad hoc*. For example, part of our interpretation of the failure of the Motor Industry Local Authority Network (MILAN) to establish an effective transnational European network is that they allowed themselves to be diverted into responding to short-term opportunities to attract EU funding or to influence policy, to the detriment of longer-term strategic thinking and positioning, based upon a hard-edged analysis of the global and European restructuring of the industry.

How does policy learning take place within transnational networks? Much exchange of experience took place at transnational meetings and by visiting each other's areas and authorities for network meetings, conferences and workshops over a long period of time. Wining and dining and social activities also played an important part in building up relationships of trust and friendship within the networks. These collaborative and social relationships form the basis for continuing regular contacts by phone, fax and e-mail between network meetings, and in some cases the development of personal friendships between members of the network in different countries. However, two problems were repeatedly found in spreading policy learning. First, how to avoid the emergence of exclusive clubs and self-perpetuating cliques within the overall network membership; and second, how to transfer learning from the individual participants in the network back to their local authorities. Detachment and disconnection of the network from its parent authorities was a recurrent danger, with a continual challenge to the delegates involved in the network not only to report back formally, but also to engage the interest and understanding of leading members and officers in their own organisations.

The main tensions in transnational networks

We found a strong Northern European/Southern European tension in some networks. Apart from the material differences in their political and economic contexts, and in their relative states of development/ underdevelopment, cultural differences in language, patterns of thought and speech, and attitudes towards time also caused tension and sometimes division. (A late start after a long lunch at a transnational meeting in Spain frustrated the UK delegates and contributed to the break-up of Euro-MILAN!)

Size and the extent of inclusion was another source of tension within some of the transnational networks we studied, mirroring those of the European Union itself. The expansion of EU membership to 15 countries (and eventually more) was feared to increase the diversity and complexity of interests to a point where it became too hard to negotiate and sustain a common purpose, or to actively involve members from so many countries.

Tensions between member authorities and their elected executive committees were often focused around transparency, democracy, clientalism and so on, with very different styles of decision-making and management apparent between representatives from different countries.

Conflicts sometimes arose when members used information from network negotiations in independent bids for funding with other parties outside the network. This has led to a recognition of the importance (and difficulty) not only of building an initial coalition of interest to give the network a common purpose, but also of nurturing and sustaining relationships of trust within the network over time.

Tensions also arose between economic and social goals and priorities. Social policy is still subordinate to economic policy within the EU, and local authority networks tended to reflect these relative priorities (for example, the EuroCities social welfare committee found it hard not to become the poor relation of their much stronger economic committee).

The main source of tension for many transnational local authority networks however, has been with their national governments. Many UK local authorities (of all political persuasions) used transnational networks as a way of bypassing the Conservative UK government in order to gain access to EU resources or programmes. In obtaining RECHAR funding from the EU, on two occasions EURACOM was able to pursue and achieve a policy opposed by the then Tory UK central government. However, the CCC and the British government can be seen as engaged in an even more sophisticated cat and mouse game, with the Commission as a barking dog in the background – a complex pattern of continuously shifting alliances between the UK local authorities, the transnational network, the UK government and the European Commission (Bache, George, and Rhodes, 1996).

The main benefits and costs of networks

Transnational networks provided useful 'economies of scale' in the resources which their members could access (for example, pooling of information, intelligence and expertise; sharing the costs of research, consultancy and lobbying; access to a shared secretariat and office facilities, often in Brussels; gaining 'on the ground' EU knowledge, and early warning of new policy initiatives). A Brussels office also provided network members with practical administrative support, social contacts and grapevine news about developments in and around the European Commission and Parliament. Some local authorities referred to the networks as their shared intelligence system in the European Union.

Lobbying via a transnational network gave local authorities political clout and added value. It ensured that the EU was aware that the representation was not confined to a single local authority or national perspective, or special pleading by one area in competition with another. The more widely representative a network could demonstrate itself to be, the greater their potential credibility and purchase within the EU policy-making process. For example, EURACOM's leverage partly derived from its comprehensive membership (covering 450 local authorities representing the majority of coal-mining or former coal-mining areas in Europe) and being a cross-party organisation.

Our interviews with Commission officials showed that several networks had made some identifiable impact upon EU thinking, policy or funding programmes. However, whilst several networks had considerable success in the formulation stage of new policy and funding regimes within the Commission, there proved to be real limits in their ability to sustain these achievements through the Council of Ministers, and in the implementation stage of the new policies. Examples include the EAPN's inability to overcome the German government's opposition to their proposals for a fourth European Anti-Poverty Programme, in spite of the Commission's full support at the highest levels; and EURACOM's battle with the British government over the additionality of RECHAR funding.

Several local authorities were able to quantify the benefits of their involvement in transnational networks in terms of grants gained or access to prestigious or lucrative EU programmes and projects. We also observed a chain reaction effect, in which local authorities which had gained knowledge and trust of each other through a particular transnational network sometimes formed successful partnership bids for other programmes.

In addition to generating other bilateral partnerships and joint ventures, cross-national networks also frequently spawned joint ventures and other networks, usually of a more specialised character. We found a high degree of intersecting and overlapping membership between various transnational networks. Paradoxically this included the fostering of closer links between some of the British cities involved. We found a high degree of intersecting and overlapping membership between various transnational networks, and of cross-cutting links between different cross-national networks and networkers.

Transnational network members also saw real benefits in learning from each other, exchanging policy ideas and innovations between their members in different countries. Involvement was seen as giving them opportunities for rapid cross-national learning and policy innovation. This was regarded as particularly valuable in a context of rapid economic, social and technological change and loss of confidence in the flexibility and responsiveness of traditional 'vertical' channels of communication within the governmental system. Cross-national transfers of knowledge are well-established in the field of technology, but much less well understood in the field of social policy.

In summary, transnational networks were found to provide local authorities with opportunities, variously, to gain structural funding from the EU, to get involved in EU community initiatives or cross-national action programmes, to gain early warning of new policy developments and funding opportunities, to influence certain areas of policy at an early stage of their development through cross-national lobbying, to exchange ideas and experiences with their counterparts in other EU countries, to share in piloting innovative projects, and to gain rapid access to a pool of learning about how to deal with complex policy problems which cut across the boundaries between different levels of government, and between different departments, disciplines, and sectors. Transnational networks provide local authorities with opportunities to share the costs of policy research and development with others, and to spread the risks and uncertainties of change, during a period of rapid restructuring. Like all speculative ventures there is also always the possibility of getting little or no return on this investment.

New models of multi-level, multi-nodal and multinational governance

There is much theoretical debate about the nature of the emerging European institutions and policy arenas. Competing explanations are offered based upon neo-corporatist or neo-pluralist perspectives (Streeck, 1995), or neo-realist, neo-functional or neo-rational theories (Schmitter, 1996).

Others have distinguished between functionalist interpretations (whereby supranational institutions challenge national interests and incorporate lower tiers of government through their use of legislation and resource allocation) and intergovernmental theories (which argue on the contrary that nation states will continue to dominate decision-making).

Gary Marks argues that these contending accounts are too polarised around the relative roles and influence of supranational versus national institutions, and that we need a theory of multi-level governance within Europe:

> a system of continuous negotiation among nested governments at several territorial tiers – supranational, national, regional, and local – as the result of a broad process of institutional creation and decisional reallocation that has pulled some previously centralised functions of the state up to supranational level and some down to the local/regional level. (Marks, 1993, p. 392)

Our research supports Marks's general argument about the emergence of multilevel governance, in terms of the vertical axis stretching from local, regional, national and European levels of government. However, this model is too one-dimensional and unidirectional. Our research suggests the additional importance of other cross-cutting axes and arenas of governance, in which there is a kaleidoscopic pattern of constantly changing patterns of interrelationships between local and regional authorities, and with

(a) other tiers and levels of government;
(b) other spheres and sectors (public, private, voluntary and grass-roots); and
(c) other counterparts in different countries.

Our research suggest that the European polity is better characterised as *multilevel, multinodal, and multinational governance*, in which complex networks and lattices cross-cut both vertical tiers and horizontal spheres.

Policy networks are also often characterised in terms of interdependence, resource exchange and trust. Our research suggests that each of these three concepts must be modified in the case of transnational policy networks. Interdependence within transnational networks has to take account of three cross-cutting dimensions – intragovernmental, intersectoral and international, that is:

- between different tiers of government;
- between overlapping and interlapping spheres of state, market and civil society;
- between different national cultures and regimes.

This requires a notion of interdependence which takes account of the very complex different kinds of 'dependencies' and 'interdependencies' which operate in each of these three dimensions. Policy network theory has analysed the nature of interdependencies between different tiers of government, particularly at the meso level between national and local levels. Our research suggests that interdependencies between different nation states (at the local and regional levels), and between different spheres and sectors (state, market and civil society) need further analysis and theorisation. We found that the first of these sets of inter-dependencies (between different national representatives within transnational local authority networks) proved to be particularly volatile. The strongest and most cohesive transnational networks appeared to be those which were built up as federations of national groupings of local authorities and other bodies. Those networks in which there was direct representation from the local to the transnational body (without the building block of national groupings) seemed to be vulnerable to the intrusion of national (or perhaps ethnic and cultural) differences, as destabilising or divisive forces within the transnational coalition. The direct connection between the local and the European arenas of governance produced many sparks of creativity, but also seemed to act as a lightening conductor for other unresolved prejudices and cultural stereotypes about national differences. Interdependencies between local authorities appeared to be more manageable at a transnational level if first mediated through national groupings.

Our research suggests that interdependencies between different spheres and sectors also need more analysis. We have been struck by the many ways in which public, private, voluntary and community organisations differ from each other, and by the tensions and misunderstandings which this can generate within networks. This is nothing to do with personal relationships but with structural differences between different types of organisation. Hirschman's work may be helpful in explaining some of the variations in attitude and behaviour between representatives from public, private, voluntary and community sectors, within networks, and therefore some of the complex interdependencies between them (Hirschman, 1970). Adapting

Hirschman for our purposes, it can be argued that where the state sector is governed primarily through the mechanism of voice (voting and pressure group activity), the market is regulated through exit (consumer choice to take business to another supplier), and civil society through loyalty (associational ties). These (and other) differences between the sectors result in quite different patterns of representation and accountability, which need to be taken into account in any theorisation of interdependencies within networks.

Resource exchange, and resource dependency, within our networks, included not just material resources (such as money or information) but less easily measurable resources (such as knowledge, intelligence, values, vision, judgement). In fact, in many cases the networks were not so much involved in resource exchange as in resource production. Local authorities often combine in networks in order to collaborate in the search for solutions to the complex intractable problems which confront them, and to generate new concepts, new ideas, new strategies and new innovative projects. Because it is not easy to put a price on leading-edge knowledge, imaginative ideas or innovative experience before they are produced and tested, they are not easily susceptible to trading or exchange. It is in the interests of individual actors and organisations to pool their experimental efforts and their resources in order to share in the search for solutions, both in order to spread the costs and the risks involved, and in order to get the most rapid access to the experimental results. Collaboration of this kind depends upon negotiated trust. Transnational networks can be seen as part of the research and development process in the production of the knowledge and innovation necessary for the governance of a global, complex and uncertain environment. This requires a reconceptualisation of the political economy of networking in terms of the relationships of production (of knowledge and innovation) as well as the relationships of distribution and exchange (of resources of power and money).

Trust, on the basis of our research, needs to be seen not (as in much of the literature) as an inherent characteristic of networks, but as the by-product of a continuous process of negotiation and proactive coalition-building to generate and constantly recreate the common interest and common purpose between a number of different interests and organisations. Common interests, common purposes and coalitions of these kinds have to take into account not just interpersonal and interorganisational relationships, but also differences in the structure and in the political economic context surrounding those relationships. In order to do justice to these observations, we would want to

introduce into network theory a more dynamic and dialectical conception of trust, as a fluctuating and fluid set of inter-relationships
between partners, which takes account of shifting power relations
and social relations, and changes through time. Trust, like networking,
is a relational concept, where the focus must be on the interrelationships and interactions between parties and partners.

Conclusions

Our research suggests that the European Union is not only opening up
several new policy arenas within and around the vertical tiers of
representative government (for example, the European Commission
at supranational level, the Council of Ministers as an intergovernmental arena between the nation states, and the Committee of the
Regions as a multilateral body at the meso level), but also new kinds of
policy-making processes which cut across the tiers of government
(local, regional, national and European) and often involve overlapping
spheres of participation (from and between the public, private, voluntary and informal community sectors).

Involvement in transnational local authority networking brings
about not only the benefits and risks of vertical integration within
the governmental system (linking local authorities into the emerging
supranational tiers and arenas of government within the European
Union, and into new patterns of multilevel governance), but also an
additional set of opportunities and challenges arising from horizontal
integration (linking local authorities into lateral webs of interrelationships with organisations and actors in other sectors and other countries).

We found evidence of a new paradigm of multilevel, multinodal and
multinational governance emerging among the local authorities in our
research. This involved complex lattices of cross-cutting interrelationships with Brussels and Strasbourg, with their local authority counterparts in other countries, and with other organisations and actors in the
public, private, voluntary and community sectors. A new pattern of
networked governance (cross-national, cross-sectoral, and often cross-
party) seemed to be developing for leading local authorities within this
European policy arena. However, there are two important qualifica-
tions to this finding, which are noted below.

First, it became clear from our research that only a relatively small proportion of local authorities, and only a very small number of councillors and officers within those authorities, are involved in transnational networking. Active involvement is limited to a small interlocking 'cosmopolitan elite' of members and officers who meet each other in a succession of overlapping European networks and events. A larger number of members and officers is drawn into these activities for annual conferences and other special occasions, but the practice of transnational networked politics is limited to a very small inner circle within UK local government. The core is made up of a small number of social entrepreneurs with skills in para-diplomacy and the new politics of networking and coalition-building, in addition to the older political traditions of representation and confrontation. There is some evidence from our research that involvement by councillors in the Committee of the Regions is expanding the European awareness and personal contacts of a larger number of UK local authority policy-makers and managers, and gradually stimulating further transnational working.

Second, our research shows clearly that the new network politics may complement, but certainly does not replace, the traditional pattern of vertical tiers of representation, which is still the main spine of policy-making and implementation for UK local government. The transnational networks sometimes appear to involve a bypassing of Westminster and Whitehall, particularly at the stage of policy formulation. However, our research shows that national government continues to be a very powerful player within these policy arenas, particularly during the stage of policy implementation and resource distribution. This was particularly apparent from our case study of European Action for Coal Mining Communities and the RECHAR programme. (See also Bache, 1992; Rhodes, Bache and George, 1996.)

The transnational network, mobilising support not only from several hundred regional and local authorities around Europe, but also from many other stakeholders in the mining industry (for example, trade unions, employers and academics) was able to influence the European Commission decisively in the arguments for a new EU programme to compensate declining mining areas and to support programmes of retraining and job creation. However the British government of the time was able effectively to block (or to freeze) this initiative when it came to the allocation and distribution of the grant to mining localities, because of their primary role in the distribution of EU structural funds. The local authority network was undoubtedly influential in the policy formulation process, but the national government retained its control over resource distribution and policy implementation.

One of the key questions for the future is whether European networking will remain the prerogative of a small elite, or whether it will spread to a larger number and wider spectrum of councillors and officers, and emerge as a new paradigm for local governance. Our observation from this research is that British politicians and officers often seem to experience particular difficulties in these new modes of networking, compared with their counterparts in mainland Europe. Effective transnational networking requires councillors and officers to move beyond their national stereotypes of other countries and cultures, and to show curiosity about the different values and assumptions which inform the thinking and action of their colleagues from other countries. It requires a willingness to start by confronting complex problems, not from tried and tested positions and confident assertions of solutions, but from a recognition that we do not yet know the answers; and that a more provisional, questioning and experimental approach is needed, in which a variety of innovative approaches can be explored and tested, and lessons learned from mistakes as well as failures. It requires a willingness by councillors and officers to move out of the national and party political groupings in which the British abroad often seem to feel safer and more secure (superior?), and to risk talking, perhaps in French or Spanish, to people in other national delegations, and from other political parties. It involves a readiness to move beyond the over-certain binary polarisations (either/or; right/ wrong; left/right) which govern much British politics, management and thinking, into a much more fuzzy world of complexity, chaos and uncertainty in which action has to be taken under conditions of risk and uncertainty, and in which learning takes place through reflection on action. This stance is a long way from the traditions of oppositional politics (in which parties are clearer about what they are against than what they are for) and of modernist public administration (in which managers proceed on the basis of systems of rules and procedures derived from general principles). It is much closer to Popper's 'critical rationalism' in which:

> With each step forward, with each problem which we solve, we not only discover new and unsolved problems, but we also discover that where we believed that we were standing on firm and safe ground, all things are, in truth, insecure and in a state of flux.

Our conclusion is that transnational networking is a constructive response to the dilemmas of governance in a context of globalisation and Europeanisation, in which problems are increasingly complex and cross-cutting, and which therefore require responses which cut across the boundaries between nation states, different tiers and levels of government, and different spheres of society. Networking seems likely to emerge as a key part of a new paradigm for multinational, multilevel and multinodal governance within the emerging European polity. Transnational and European networking is already a familiar part of the practice of governance in many other European countries. Progress may be slower in the UK because of the rigidities of our (imperial?) political and managerial traditions, based upon a series of pendulum swings between state and market, hierarchy and competition. Networking provides the requisite variety for responding to a more global, complex and fluid environment.

About this study

We are grateful for the friendly support and lively stimulus given by the Director of the ESRC programme, Gerry Stoker, and by other colleagues in the programme and at the Local Government Centre at Warwick Business School. We particularly appreciate comments on previous drafts by LGC staff and visiting professors Nick Deakin, David Donnison, Mike Geddes, Jean Hartley and Steve Martin. We were greatly helped in the development of our ideas by a series of seminars with elected members and officers in the Warwick University Local Authorities Research Consortium, and with fellow academics from several universities in a parallel ESRC seminar series which we ran with Peter John (Southampton University) on 'Local and Regional Responses to European Integration'.

We situated our case studies of transnational networking in the context of structural changes not only in the pattern of governmental institutions, but also in the wider political economic and social context. This has allowed us to explain variations in the performance and effectiveness of different networks (for example, EURACOM and MILAN), not simply in terms of differences in their leadership capacities, or in their policy communities, but also, crucially, in the structural position of the industrial sectors with which they are concerned. Research on networking runs the danger of being overdetermined by interpersonal or interorganisational levels of explanation.

Contextualised case studies allow us to give due weight to these levels of analysis, while also taking into account the political economic context, and therefore of structural power and social relations as well as interpersonal and interorganisational relations.

We developed an unusually close and continuing dialogue with a working group of local authority policy-makers and practitioners, and a wider consortium and national network of local authorities, throughout the whole process of this research. This has provided us with a panel of users to help in the identification of the key issues and questions for the research, and to act as a sounding board against which to check our interim research findings. We have also developed a close dialogue with a number of researchers who act as advisers for the networks in our research. This has given us the opportunity sometimes to compare insider and outsider perspectives on the same situation, and has provided multifaceted accounts.

Within this methodological framework, we used a range of qualitative research methods to study networking as a process as well as networks as institutions, and in order to assess the 'significance' of this activity for policy-making and management in UK local authorities. These included participant observation at UK, transnational and supranational meetings of networks; semi-structured interviews with a wide range of key actors in the network, and also with other stakeholders not directly participating in the networks; shadowing of key actors (both politicians and officers) in the course of their 'networking'; focus group discussions with local authority councillors and officers; study of both official and unofficial and ephemeral documents; and testing of our research findings and interpretations with a panel of UK local authorities and experts from both the academic and policy communities.

13 The Private Financing of Public Infrastructure

David Heald and Neal Geaughan

Introduction

A valuable starting point for an overview of the private financing of public infrastructure is to adopt Hood's (1994) distinction between 'justifications' and 'explanations'. Justifications are those arguments mobilised in support of particular policies, whereas explanations are those – possibly overlapping – factors which can be identified as having been decisive in bringing about a particular policy change. The commentator often has to impose structure on a mass of documentation which rarely respects this distinction. Moreover, there might well be motivations ('unmentionables') which are deliberately left unspoken or understated. Dobek (1993) challenged the literature on UK privatisation which had claimed there was a lack of economic rationality behind certain aspects of the Conservative government's programme, and stressed that some of these features could readily be understood in terms of building political support and eroding the support of other parties.

The issues discussed in this chapter are relevant to the whole of the general government sector, not exclusively to local government. They are, however, highly relevant to local governance because of the way in which the traditional role of UK local government as a significant operator and provider of physical infrastructure has been severely challenged, in part for budgetary reasons and in part because of a changed outlook in central government as to the appropriate spheres of the public and private sectors. In the United Kingdom, central government possesses sufficient legislative and financial instruments to impose its wishes upon local authorities.

There are three influential factors worth emphasising in this introductory section. First, as globalisation and economic integration diminish the power of traditional macroeconomic levers, OECD governments have become more concerned about improving the competitiveness of their economies by means of investment in physical and human capital. The quantity and quality of investment in physical capital now receive more attention than its ownership. Evaluation of the effects of public infrastructure investment on private sector productivity is complicated by the way in which the extensive US literature on this topic has become intricately connected with partisan debates about federal spending. However, Munnell's (1992) survey takes these productivity benefits seriously.

Second, it is widely believed that the 1980s and 1990s have witnessed a neglect of the UK physical infrastructure, in comparison with that of other large European Union countries. Such comparisons are inevitably difficult, even without the political controversy and special pleading which have characterised UK debates. Reviewing the evidence, Heald (1997a) concluded that there were indeed grounds for concern.

Third, a clear pattern has been established that UK local authorities will in future have a more limited role, if any, in the provision of large physical infrastructure. There has been no attempt by central government to remove existing infrastructure facilities from local government ownership, though in cases when capacity has to be expanded (for example, a third Dartford crossing, a second Tyne tunnel and a second Forth bridge), it is now taken almost for granted that this will be privately financed. Without credit approvals (or the Scottish equivalent of capital allocations), neither individual local authorities nor joint boards could secure the financing. For reasons of public expenditure scoring, it is unlikely that such permissions would be granted, even if there had not developed a quasi-automatic central government presumption in favour of private financing. Significantly, the role of local authorities as provider tends not to be replaced by that as regulator – a transition often deemed to be one of the features of local *governance*. Where there is private sector financial involvement, there is predictable pressure for uniform national regulation. Local authorities might then become nothing more than another – albeit well-placed – local lobby, seeking the provision of facilities without incurring any financial responsibility for their viability.

The foregoing is vital background to the arguments about recourse to private financing of public infrastructure. The remaining sections of the chapter distinguish potentially good from indisputably bad arguments for private financing; consider the impact upon incentives and assess probable long-term effects; and delineate the policy issues which ought to be addressed systematically.

Before concluding this introductory section, it is useful to define some technical terms. A concession is the temporary granting by a public authority (concessioner) to another (usually private) body (concessionaire) of the right to construct, operate and levy third-party charges for a period defined either in years or in terms of some revenue or profit objective. At the end of that concession, the facility reverts to the ownership of the concessioner which can then either operate the facility itself, with or without third-party charges, or relet the concession by competition. This kind of contractual arrangement is long-standing in mainland France and francophone countries in, for example, the water and transport sectors. In terms of contemporary terminology, a concession is a BOOT scheme, standing for build, own, operate and transfer. An alternative model is the BOO scheme (build, own and operate), where reversion to the public authority does not occur (in, for example, the publicly owned Scottish water authorities).

Potentially good versus indisputably bad arguments

Of utmost importance is the need to distinguish between potentially good arguments (that is, those which, if true, can be shown to be influential or decisive) and indisputably bad arguments (that is, those which are either clearly flawed or solely advanced as policy alibi). When sifting such arguments, it is particularly important to guard against an artificial narrowing of the policy problem in a way which systematically excludes options, leaving the choice set empty except for the preferred option. It is in circumstances such as this that a conspicuously cost-ineffective option can easily be canvassed as the most cost-effective.

Potentially good arguments

The literature on infrastructure investment suggests four potentially good arguments. 'Potentially good' means that these arguments contain assumptions or predictions which, if verified, would lead to them carrying substantial force, to be weighed in the balance alongside other considerations.

First, it is contended that the narrower and clearer objectives of a private infrastructure provider will more satisfactorily resolve key principal–agent problems. For example, the civil engineering contractor will know that the private sector principal faces a bankruptcy constraint in a way that a public sector principal does not. Although the cost overruns on the Channel tunnel were notoriously large, it is certainly plausible that they would have been worse if the tunnel had been a joint Franco-British governmental project. This part of the argument focuses attention on the issue of cost containment at the construction stage. Another part of the argument relates to the relationship between the principal and the bankers who supply the finance. If the Channel tunnel had been a governmental project, it would have been far more difficult for the French and British governments to stand aside and watch the banks losing their money. Their respective Treasuries and central banks, concerned about their ability to finance large public sector borrowing requirements (PSBR), would have been much more worried about sovereign creditworthiness than about this specific project. The argument here is that a private sector principal will find it easier than a public sector principal to off-load risks.

There is clearly a measure of plausibility in this argument when applied to mega-projects such as the Channel tunnel, a project with a long gestation period (Holliday *et al.*, 1991). The charges faced by travellers will be lower than would have prevailed had there been no risk transfer to the suppliers of finance. On the other hand, there have to be doubts about whether a privately financed project such as the Channel tunnel would be replicable. An obvious point is that Eurotunnel was left exposed to a great deal of commercial risk because of the lack of constraints placed upon the cross-channel ferry operators, who have not melted away as may have been expected. In the case of such a huge project, it might well be worthwhile incurring a substantially higher cost of capital than would be the case if public funds were used, to guard against seriously adverse outcomes. If this argument holds, the relevant question becomes 'at what scale and innovativeness of projects do such net benefits disappear?' For example, would the argument apply to the second Severn crossing, or to a section of motorway, or to a new hospital? A key question is whether there is a strong element of replicability. This advantage of private involvement can be thought of in terms of reducing the total amount of risk by allocating risks to that party which is best able to manage each particular risk.

Second, as financial markets become more sophisticated and globalised, expertise in risk management grows and specific groups of financial investors may become specialists in bearing particular risks. Certain kinds of risk can be diversified away: for example, construction work on river crossings might confront unexpected geological difficulties in a proportion of cases. Those investors who finance many projects will be in a better position both to evaluate and to pool such risks. Again, this seems to point to a relative advantage for private financing in the case of atypical – as opposed to replicable – projects.

Third, it can be argued that private financing will make it easier to make user charges 'stick'. Heald (1991) showed that the crucial problem with the financing of the first Severn bridge was the lack of legislative provision for indexed tolls, a deficiency in the financial framework exacerbated by the laborious (and politically fraught) process of toll revision. Tolling can have two functions: to remunerate the costs of construction; and to act as a pricing signal. Unfortunately, these functions may conflict. There is much discussion in the literature on road-user charging about whether, in the absence of general road-user pricing, piecemeal pricing of a particular facility has beneficial or damaging consequences on road network utilisation. For example, tolls may divert traffic to unsuitable and environmentally sensitive roads on which there is no pricing mechanism. In the case of some tolled facilities, the marginal cost of an extra journey may be virtually zero, whilst in other cases it may be exceptionally high. Two arguments about the link between private financing and tolling deserve attention. There is some evidence that in the case of private financing more systematic consideration is given to toll regulation in advance of construction. Furthermore, those who advocate road pricing in general may believe that a dynamic benefit of private financing is that road users become more accustomed to the notion of tolling, and will be less hostile in future towards electronic tolling of the network as a whole.

Fourth, the combination of private financing and third-party charging might provide some protection against 'pork barrel' politics. The private sector would never have become involved, for example, in the financing of the Humber bridge (the construction of which was announced in the middle of the crucial 1966 Hull North parliamentary by-election); only an implausible parallel announcement of huge subsidies would have made the scheme attractive to private finance. Until February 1992, the interest which could not be serviced out of toll income was capitalised, with the result that the current debt of the Humber Bridge Board is £435 million. Since 1992, grants have been made under the Appropriation Acts to meet the annual shortfall. Early in the 1997–98 financial year, there will be a debt write-off under the terms of the *Humber Bridge (Debts) Act 1996* (Department of Transport, 1997).

What these four potentially good arguments have in common is that it should be possible in time to bring empirical evidence from the United Kingdom and overseas to bear on their validity. Because it is universally accepted that government can borrow more cheaply than the private sector, the only way that private financing is justifiable is if its use generates savings in capital and/or operating costs which cannot be achieved in any other way (for example, by fixed-price construction contracts and/or private management of the facility).

Indisputably bad arguments

Attention now turns to three arguments which are indisputably bad, either in the sense that they are logically flawed or that they have been abused. First, private finance enables projects (such as schools and hospitals) to be undertaken which the public sector could not afford (Hancock, 1993). Where there are no third-party payers, as in the case of schools and hospitals, the Exchequer will, in due course, have to meet the full service cost. Unless there are genuine efficiency gains arising from private sector involvement, this simply means the retiming of when the Exchequer incurs the cost (which will be higher than otherwise because of the excess financing costs). For this argument to have any credibility, it has to be postulated that the government temporarily lacks access to capital markets and that its intertemporal budget constraint bites more harshly in the present than it will in the future. Although there may be circumstances where this is plausible (for example, postwar reconstruction), the argument currently has no credibility. The motives for advancing this argument may themselves be dubious, whether aimed at drumming up business for financial institutions or attempting to mislead the public about affordability.

Second, there is frequently a 'nudge-and-wink' undercurrent to the advocacy of private finance, hinting that it represents a mechanism for manipulating public expenditure and PSBR numbers. What is frequently proposed is a cost-ineffective mechanism, on the grounds that this is the only option available. This line of argument exemplifies the danger highlighted earlier; almost anything can be made to look 'best' if the policy problem is formulated in sufficiently narrow terms. Decisions taken solely for public expenditure scoring are a manifestation of the dysfunctional consequences of the (inevitably) arbitrary lines which have to be drawn for statistical purposes. Despite the element of arbitrariness at the margin, public expenditure scoring rules have an important and legitimate function, in terms of recording what is happening to resource use in the economy. Respected commentators have questioned the motivations for private financing (Institute for Fiscal Studies, 1993). Governments undoubtedly do manipulate definitions to some extent, and the constraints imposed by the Maastricht rules about excessive deficits may lead to an increase in these manipulations (Heald and Geaughan, 1997). However tempting such manipulations may seem, they have opportunity costs, either in the form of cost-ineffective provision or reduced transparency about long-term affordability. It is sometimes argued that the failure to implement certain projects has large opportunity costs in the form of lost benefits. For this to be the case, it has to be held that either the total level of public expenditure is insufficient, or that its functional composition is seriously distorted. It is possible that politicians find taxing and borrowing such unpleasant subjects that they are willing to tie their own hands and then use cost-ineffective mechanisms. Even so, there is a strong case in public accountability for these circumstances to be rendered transparent.

Third, an argument which might have been classified as 'potentially good' is here classified as indisputably bad because it is consistently advanced in an insincere manner; it performs the function of policy alibi. This is the rhetoric that the UK government has stopped buying inputs or capital assets, and instead now contracts to buy outputs. In practice, there is very little interest in measuring outputs, much less in contracting to purchase them. The prominence given to this storyline is predominantly a means of keeping Private Finance Initiative (PFI) assets off the balance sheet, thereby avoiding the specific requirements of SSAP 21 (Accounting Standards Committee, 1984) and the spirit of FRS 5 (Accounting Standards Board, 1994). If genuine cases of output measurement and contracting begin to emerge, the classification of this argument could then be reconsidered.

Incentives and effects

It is clearly relevant to explore the nature of the incentives created by recourse to private financing for public projects, and to assess the likely effects of this policy innovation. Deserving particular emphasis is the way in which private finance may enable ministers to acquire capital assets without facing the budgetary discipline of having to compete for funds against the projects of other ministers within the framework of the Public Expenditure Survey, or of having to remunerate that capital by paying capital charges. There is a noteworthy contrast between the low profile of capital charging, introduced within the National Health Service in April 1991 (Heald and Scott, 1996) and now scheduled to be extended across central government as part of the Treasury's Resource Accounting and Budgeting package, and the remarkably high profile of the PFI. In the absence of third-party payers, the cost of the capital facilities and the associated operating costs become a charge upon public expenditure in future years. It is not difficult to imagine the attraction of such a mechanism to a Home Secretary seeking a dramatic expansion in prison capacity, or to an Education Secretary wishing to promise school modernisations and replacements, or to a Transport Secretary wanting to expand the road-building programme. Mechanisms such as shadow tolls as a means of remunerating the private constructors of toll-free (to the motorist) road sections are a device for posting bills to future taxpayers.

A number of effects can be identified, of which three are considered here. First, the size of the bills posted to the future is unlikely to be properly disclosed. One of the problems associated with new public management techniques is the greater emphasis placed upon commercial confidentiality as a justification for refusing to disclose financial information connected with public activities. Clearly, when organisations which have previously enjoyed monopoly status face competition, there are likely to be genuine concerns about unilateral disclosure of information potentially prejudicial to their competitiveness. More generally, PFI contracts are often surrounded by claims about commercial confidentiality, thereby raising two separate points about public accountability. The first point is that certain commitments may be given to the private consortium which are anti-competitive and/or undisclosed at the time of policy announcement; for example, the Scottish Office undertook to instruct the nationalised Caledonian Macbrayne to withdraw the ferry which served the same route as the Skye bridge and (at the very least) turned a blind eye to obstructions placed in the way of private ferries. Other possibilities are commitments not to upgrade competing road links without paying compensation, or even (as in Melbourne, Victoria) to reduce existing road capacity by lane elimination. In the case of health, there may be promises of ministerial pressure on a dominant health purchaser to buy from the NHS trust which has a new hospital development procured from a PFI consortium.

The other point is that, if recourse to such mechanisms became quantitatively significant, the margins of flexibility on public expenditure enjoyed by future Chancellors of the Exchequer could be severely eroded. Moreover, the financial penalties attached to policy change could escalate dramatically. This danger is exemplified by the recent dramatic downsizing of the roads programme which would have been much more difficult to implement had 1990s' mechanisms been extensively applied in the 1980s. Roads provide an interesting case because there is evidence that personalities matter: Margaret Thatcher's 'enormous roads programme' received less favour from John Major (Hogg and Hill, 1995, p. 119); and Dudley and Richardson (1996) concluded that the roads programme has been profoundly affected by certain ministers. The fact that there were 11 Cabinet Ministers for Transport in the period 1979–97 brought the Department within Bogdanor's (1996) observation that some departments 'are subject to a rate of [ministerial] turnover which is bound to militate against effective government'. Walker and Smith (1995) commented that in 1993 the Department of Transport was reported to have hoped that shadow-tolled roads would lead to the *additional* annual construction of £350 million of trunk roads. Astonishingly, 1998 was reported (p. 56) at that time to be seen as the target date for the electronic tolling of all UK motorways and trunk roads.

Second, ministers have indeed seen the PFI as a means of bringing capital spending forward in time. Unquestionably, this did happen in the case of the Skye bridge and, arguably, in the cases of the third Dartford and second Severn crossings. However, it is also possible that the time-consuming nature of the PFI process – a complaint regularly made in the financial and trade press – has delayed projects beyond the date at which they would have been progressed using conventional procurement (Institute for Health Services Management, 1997). Two factors can be identified: the sheer overload caused by the decision of the four Health Departments that all NHS trusts must pursue the PFI route; and the way in which PFI contracts raise issues beyond those involved in conventional procurement (for example, concerning contract lengths, the impact on neighbouring trusts and the expansion of private patient numbers). It is a matter of judgement as to whether such difficulties are inherent in the PFI as applied to the NHS or whether they are the set-up costs characteristic of a learning process. In any case, contracting for what are loosely called 'outputs' (for example, prison places, patients treated) commits ahead much more public spending than simply building a prison or a hospital, leaving levels of utilisation for later decision. A rather different point about timing was made by the Conservative MP Nicholas Budgen (1993) during a Treasury and Civil Service Committee hearing: he viewed much of the argument then for the PFI as really being about macroeconomic fine-tuning 'upwards', commenting that by the time of actual construction the Treasury would be mobilising counter-arguments in order to justify 'downwards' fine-tuning.

Third, in the case of project financing through the mechanism of third-party user charges, it is likely that greater weight will be attached at the stage of project design to revenue-generating potential, to the neglect of other costs (for example, environmental) and benefits (for example, non-user benefits through reduced congestion elsewhere). One of the interesting features of the Skye bridge is that the Scottish Office's evaluation revealed net benefits substantially below those achievable from other schemes within its roads programme. What differentiated the Skye bridge was the practicality of tolling. This example focuses attention back to the standard second-best concern in the public sector pricing literature, that piecemeal pricing might worsen resource allocation (Bös, 1985). Although this point applies to the piecemeal tolling of particular transport facilities irrespective of ownership, there is one reason for taking the issue more seriously in the context of private financing. Whereas a public operator is likely to have a complex range of motives (for example, meeting financing charges and promoting economic development), a private operator will – if unconstrained – wish to choose the profit-maximising toll. These more high-powered financial incentives may exacerbate the general dangers associated with piecemeal tolling. Quite apart from the technological and cost issues concerning widespread electronic tolling, it can be confidently predicted that concerns about traffic diversion to less suitable toll-free roads will feature prominently in UK debates. Ministers have unequivocally presented the case for tolls as a financing rather than capacity-rationing instrument, with the tolls being removed at some future date. Moreover, the political pressure to remove tolls from the Skye bridge has been fuelled by the large differential between tolls on different crossings and by the sense of unfairness that some crossings are toll-free. For instance, the Kessock, Cromarty and Dornoch bridges north of Inverness were regarded as integral parts of the A9 trunk road improvement, justified in part by the cost savings from route shortening.

Issues for debate and decision

Perrin (1984) crystallised a set of policy concerns which – in less articulate and elegant formulations – would mount in intensity over the subsequent ten years. At the level of popular debate, these concerns have in common an underlying fear that the UK's physical infrastructure was rapidly deteriorating, owing in part to government neglect. Before such questions can be systematically addressed, they all require precise – inevitably, rather technical – formulation. Using the terminology of academic accounting, Perrin sought to address four questions about the public sector capital stock:

(i)   is opportunity value being acted upon (that is, do decisions about the capital stock take full account of the value of assets in alternative use)?
(ii) is capital expenditure wisely decided and controlled (that is, do projects represent the best available value for money)?
(iii) is the capital stock being maintained?
(iv) is the cost of maintaining the capital stock being intertemporarily equitably shared (that is, are different generations carrying an appropriate share)?

As Perrin himself demonstrated, none of these questions is easy to answer. Capital charging has been promoted as a means of securing (i). On (ii), Flemming (1995) has been highly critical of the quality of much public sector investment, while Mayston (1993) addressed the differences between investment appraisal in the public and private sectors.

Behind each of the above questions often lies another set of questions. For example, in connection with (iii), there are conflicting notions of capital maintenance: Operating Capability Maintenance refers to the undertaking's ability to continue to produce a given level of output, whilst Financial Capital Maintenance refers to the maintenance of the financial purchasing power of the money invested by taxpayers in particular assets in public ownership (Byatt, 1986). Another consideration is that a significant part of the UK public sector has irrevocably been transferred to private ownership. As a consequence of conscious political choices by elected governments, there will inevitably be fewer public assets in 1997 than there were when Perrin was writing in 1984.

Nevertheless, these complications do not detract from the relevance of questions about what has happened to public sector net worth.

Privatisation can be viewed as a change in the public sector's asset portfolio, exchanging assets for cash. Indeed, if the private sector were better at managing certain assets than the public sector, then privatisation would lead to an increase in public sector net worth (at least before transactions costs and any one-off capital distribution to taxpayers). A recurrent concern, however, has been that insufficient attention has been given to the stewardship of continuing public assets, with excessive emphasis being placed on allowing the present generation to transform implicit asset holdings into cash. There is an obvious parallel in the cash distributions associated with demutualisation (Kay, 1991). With the public sector increasingly cast in the role of concessioner, it will be necessary to address the value of reversionary facilities when monitoring capital maintenance.

Question (iv) raises concerns about spreading the cost of public infrastructure assets across generations. There is a widely held view that assets inherited from earlier generations were in fact sold below their market value and privatisation proceeds used as a substitute for current taxes. Even if the PFI were shown to score well in efficiency terms, there would remain the issue of the present generation running down inherited assets but not then bequeathing paid-for assets to the next generation. Measurement in this area confronts formidable practical problems: for instance, the value of particular assets to future generations depends upon unpredictable factors such as future relative price changes and technological change. For example, the present generation places a much lower valuation on railway infrastructure than the Victorians might have expected, but a higher valuation on reservoirs and aquaducts. It is not easy to assess how future generations will view the motorway network. Hence, it is difficult to operationalise notions of intergenerational equity.

There are two high-level policy questions regarding infrastructure capital upon which attention should focus:

(a) the relative costs of service provision under different procurement models; and
(b) the extent to which contemporary political decision-makers face the true costs of their decisions.

In the former, the trade-off is primarily between the efficiency gains which are claimed for concession-type mechanisms and the higher financing costs faced by the private sector (Heald, 1997). Despite various changes of position about the use of private finance, the

Treasury has remained resolute in its view that the key to securing efficiency gains is to be found in the transfer of risk to the private sector. One of the difficulties confronting firm evaluation is likely to be the loss of credible public sector comparators, especially when it has been made abundantly clear that a publicly financed project would not be funded. Nevertheless, UK experience with explicit concession frameworks requires careful evaluation by the National Audit Office, both of concessionaire performance and of the specifics of each concession document (there are important differences in the calculations behind the determination of the reversion date). Curiously, there is contemporary media discussion of an extension of Eurotunnel's concession from 65 to 999 years as being 'costless'.

Moreover, it will be possible to absorb lessons from overseas experience of the use of a model which has received support from international bodies (OECD, 1987; European Conference of Ministers of Transport, 1989; Augenblick and Custer, 1990). In terms of post-evaluation, these schemes have the important advantages of being both large (justifying the cost) and reasonably free-standing (simplifying the factors which need to be included). Of vital importance will be the transparency of financial reporting and quality of disclosure by the concessionaire, particularly in those cases where concessions will eventually be retendered. Otherwise, genuine competition will not emerge and suspicions of corruption may develop, leading to a damaged reputation for the concession model.

Regarding the second question, as to whether present political decision-makers face the full costs of their decisions, there are grounds for serious reservations about private financing, except in those cases where there are third-party payers. One way to address these concerns is to allow private financing but to insist upon full disclosure of the present value of future commitments, score the capitalised value against the public expenditure control aggregate, and then exclude the payments when made. If shadow-tolled roads are indeed 15 per cent cheaper, as the Private Finance Panel (1997) has reported, they will be chosen in preference to conventional procurement. Unless due care is taken, efforts to impose discipline over public sector capital by means of capital charging will be undermined by access to lottery funds and to PFI assets. This is the area in which the distinction between justifications and explanations requires close attention; to cite one overseas study, Boorsma (1995) concluded that the motive for leasing in the Netherlands was almost always to avoid public expenditure controls. Bipartisan political support for the PFI has been portrayed by *The*

Economist (1995) as a warning to taxpayers, treating with suspicion the notion of doing good by stealth.

Conclusion

Given that the structure of this chapter has been designed to draw conclusions as the argument has progressed, it will suffice to conclude with two points. First, after remarkably lax control of public expenditure aggregates in 1991–92, the 1992–97 Parliament was notable for a series of highly restrictive Public Expenditure Surveys. Whereas much of this toughness was genuine, a significant sleight of hand was effected in the planned substitution of PFI-financed investment for conventional capital expenditure. For the years 1997–98 and 1998–99, the Treasury's (1996) plans include PFI-financed investment of, respectively, £2.51 billion and £3.65 billion. This raises two issues: burdens are being transferred forward through time (Treasury Committee, 1996), and, in the case that this PFI-financed investment fails to materialise, there would be an unintended shortfall in capital spending.

Second, apart from a number of high-profile schemes which would probably have been financed privately without the PFI ever having been conceived, there is an inescapable impression that so many people have been carried away with the rhetoric that the necessary learning process has stalled. The claim that the PFI 'has come a long way since its launch in November 1992, and the publication a year later of "Breaking New Ground"' (Treasury and Private Finance Panel, 1995) remains unproven. A further area for review by the National Audit Office should be the transactions costs, which appear to have been quite substantial. These are a resource cost to the economy and – presumably – will be factored in to the prices charged by private consortia to the public in its dual capacity as third-party payer and as the ultimate funder of government purchasers.

About this study

This project was titled 'Accounting for Infrastructure Assets: Financial Reporting, Project Finance and Concessions'. The project had two dimensions. The theoretical objective was to assess how UK accounting practice must develop in response to the emerging importance of the concession method of financing infrastructural development so that financial reporting systems generate meaningful and economically relevant information for a diverse set of users. The empirical dimension consisted of the preparation of accounting life histories of existing infrastructural facilities (notably, bridges and tunnels) both *during* their periods of local authority (joint board) or central government ownership and *after* their transfer into concessions, and for new facilities originating as concessions. The methods adopted were: theoretical investigation and reflection; the conducting of accounting case studies of existing facilities; fieldwork interviews with key actors in central and local government concerned with the water and transport sectors and with key actors in the finance sector; and fieldwork interviews with those involved in estuarial crossings and in the Scottish water sector. Certain outputs from the project have been referenced below: namely, Heald (1997a, b) and Heald and Geaughan (1997). The project contributed to the public debate about the PFI, in particular through: D. A. Heald 'The Private Finance Initiative: Value for Money and Public Expenditure Control', in Treasury Committee (1996), *The Private Finance Initiative*, 6th Report of Session 1995–96, HC 146 (London: HMSO) pp. 160–71. Empirical papers will subsequently be published on the accounting life histories of tolled infrastructure and on the use of private finance in the Scottish water industry.

14 Something Old, Something New

Jeffrey Stanyer

Introduction

The question 'how far do the experiences of the last two decades represent a new era in local governance?' is one which can only be answered by an analysis of the evidence of previous centuries. One or two decades are, on investigation, far too short a period for trends to reveal themselves. The reasons for this lie in the nature of time, which may contain several different patterns of flow (cycles, oscillations, fractures, 'noise', as well as trends) and several types of division into sections (years, decades, eras, ages); the longer the length of time considered, the less the chance of 'false friends', which creates the illusion that temporal characterisation is easy.

A 'lesson' in local governance history is a simple analytical generalisation, based on the past and relevant to the present and future, about the viability and suitability of distinct organisational forms and the characteristic behaviour associated with each, the verdict being divorced from any necessary connection with a public service or function. Of particular interest are the 'failures' and 'deformations' of policies inherent in each organisational form when employed as the method of local governance in a particular sphere of state activity. The 'lessons of history', however, are only worth learning if the person studying them ought to act differently after he or she has learned them.

This chapter first considers the failures and distortions often associated with local governance and puts them in historical perspective. Secondly, it reminds readers that there has long been a complex relationship between public and private organisations in the delivery of public services.

Policy failures

Failure through lack of compulsion

Failure occurs through lack of ability to coerce on the part of an organisation because it leads easily to avoidance behaviour in the widest sense. Truly private bodies have no powers to coerce their 'clientele' and if an apparently private organisation had powers of compulsion then it often used to be described as 'statutory' and would now be treated as a quango.

The private sector relies on individuals wanting to make use of their services and facilities, that is desiring the 'end product', and not being able to obtain it more easily in any other way. Unfortunately for many organisations the second condition often does not hold. An individual may avoid patronising a service point or facility by taking alternative action. Turnpike trusts were bedevilled by this: travellers chose other routes, joined the highway at an intermediate point or simply passed along the fields adjacent to it. Adaptive behaviour of these types has already been observed in relation to toll bridges and is widely expected to be a feature of any general road-charging scheme.

Without compulsion, income-maintenance schemes for old age and, to a lesser extent, unemployment, have struggled when an organisation cannot recruit from a sufficiently wide range of categories of individual to spread the risks in a stable manner. Anyone with a knowledge of friendly society and commercial insurance company history could have predicted the problems that the recent 'private pensions scheme' has encountered.

Failure because of fragmentation

A system of local governance is necessarily divided in two ways: into separate geographical areas and into separate organisations. The consequences are that it appears 'fragmented' when it fails to create universal geographical coverage, when it produces unacceptable variations in levels of service provision between areas, when adaptive behaviour on the part of the population, for instance 'voting with one's feet', thwarts the intentions of the policy-makers, and when technical reasons make the whole country the best area for administration. Local governance therefore always contains a potential for failure, but the size of the potential varies between organisational types.

The spatial diffusion of organisational forms over a period of time and the territorial expansion of individual organisations are clear evidence of the demand for geographical coverage. It is particularly acute in respect of public activities both because states do not like 'no-go' areas and because an individual's rights are abridged if he or she is excluded for a locational reason from the system of public provision. One reason for nationalising electricity was to provide this type of power everywhere, something a fragmented system could not do, hence the campaign for rural electrification in the immediate post-nationalisation decade.

Friendly societies organised on a local basis recognised the demand for geographical coverage and supported the search for work ('tramping') through a system of 'certificates' which enabled its members to obtain benefits when away from the area. The 1793 Act recognised this by exempting certificated individuals from the operation of the poor law settlement rules. But local societies were at a disadvantage compared with federations, and the movement grew most strikingly through amalgamations into the Manchester Unity of Oddfellows and the Ancient Order of Foresters. But this was still not enough and eventually (1909) it was thought desirable to create a public system of labour exchanges covering the whole country.

The experience of crime prevention and detection illustrates the problems of adaptive behaviour. There has always been a logical distinction between where criminals live and where crimes are committed. The two types of 'criminal area' have grown empirically further apart as personal mobility has increased. First the parish, then the town and then the region have become too restricted, and the state itself has been undermined as an area by the rise of European and global criminal networks.

Until the nineteenth century was well under way, both banking and the provision of currency (coins and notes) were largely or in part local activities. The individuals and organisations that carried out these functions were not in the public sector and would not be called 'governance' but some of the roles are now thought to be essentially part of central government for technical reasons. A single European currency would be carrying the process one step upwards – it will not end until the world adopts *Keynes's bancor*.

Deformation of policies

A political intervention produces a deformation of policy when widely held expectations of how a service will be provided are not realised in the ways that were expected. The word 'deformation' is used to indicate that the differences are observable and undesirable but leave the original recognisably part of the same universe.

Etzioni has identified distortion towards the measurable as a general phenomenon occurring when an organisation decides or is required to place greater emphasis on formal 'goal' achievement (Etzioni, 1964, pp. 8–10). 'Profit' is only one example; 'percentage of crimes solved' had the same effect in the eighteenth-century protection associations as in the late twentieth-century police forces.

Certain types of political directorate involved a specific measurable factor – monetary reward – and the application of this in education and the health services produced selectivity in service provision in the nineteenth century which has been replicated in the twentieth. Rewarding performance in the 'three Rs' had the same effect as 'league tables' today: it impoverished educational content and handicapped the apparently less able children. Commercial hospitals have always looked for the 'easy-to-treat' illnesses as well as the prosperous patients.

Some of the most striking examples in the first half of the nineteenth century are to be found within the system of local justice. Paying gaolers on the basis of prisoner-days led to the unnecessary and harmful incarceration of poor, retarded and mentally ill individuals and paying the private police working for protection associations by results led to numerous injustices.

Deformation through recruitment

One of the major weaknesses of recent discussions of republicanism and republican virtues is that they do not analyse highly relevant evidence from the history of local governance. If the essence of republicanism is the shouldering of public and civic duties by ordinary citizens – the Cincinnatus model – then eighteenth- and early nineteenth-century parish government are excellent sources for the corroboration or otherwise of general theories.

As Etzioni shows, there are three major leadership 'powers', to which there are corresponding motives of lower participants: coercion (fear), material incentives (calculation) and normative values (morality). Associated with each are patterns of recruitment to all levels of an organisation, including the political directorate, which involve one or more of the three types of motivation (Etzioni, 1961).

Coercion was widely used in local governance before the third decade of the nineteenth century and continued in some spheres for many decades afterwards. Individuals were coerced into being both leaders and workers in parish government. At the present time the principle survives only in jury service and community service as a form of punishment. It is rightly rejected as a method of recruiting both members of 'highway management' and road-menders. In fact most theories of local governance try to base themselves on notions of the local common good and the local public interest; that is, they espouse normative theories of motivation for local 'governors' of all types. The difficulty is excluding 'deviant' calculative involvement at all levels.

In policing the recruitment problem is encapsulated in the quotation from Juvenal: 'quis custodiet ipsos custodes?' (roughly 'who guards the guardians?') Every time the newspapers carry a story of a criminal forming or being employed by a private police organisation it should remind the reader of the eighteenth and nineteenth centuries when criminals often ran crime prevention and detection 'agencies' and dubious personalities achieved membership of watch committees.

Likewise news of heart attacks suffered by elderly men chasing burglars as part of a neighbourhood watch scheme should remind readers of all the problems of 'amateur' parish constables and the employment of decrepit substitutes who are unable and unwilling to tackle criminals.

Every recruitment system, therefore, contains a potential for deformation through the 'selection' of individuals with the wrong capacities and the wrong motivation. The research problem is to identify the causal links between recruitment processes and organisational forms.

Deformation through subsidarity

The supporters of subsidiarity believe that social responsibilities should be allocated to the lowest feasible geographical level appropriate to their organisation. This is basic to traditional political theories of decentralisation, to traditional management thinking and to the privatisation movement in the widest sense.

But what the experience of the past shows is that subsidiarity must always be considered in conjunction with additionality. The principle that help should be given to those who help themselves was a contributory consideration in the creation of specific grant systems in

decentralised administration and in the preference for 'supplementa-
tion' in welfare state systems. Grants of 100 per cent are virtually
costless to the recipient and the need to encourage members to work if
at all possible was central to friendly societies long before it was
adopted as the principle of 'less eligibility' by the state. It is found
most strikingly at the end of the twentieth century in the allocation of
lottery money to private and public organisations.

Good examples from the past are to be found in the private finance
of capital expenditure. It was not uncommon in the nineteenth century
for individuals to pay for the building of libraries, houses, schools and
even reservoirs for their locality. The gift of a facility, however, left the
payment of running costs to the local authority, so that there might be
reading rooms without many books, journals and newspapers. The
presentation by hospital friends of 'high-tech' equipment is not always
welcomed by the management (whether public or private) because its
running expenses are not funded by the donors. The National Trust
faces similar problems with donations of historic country houses. The
Private Finance Initiative repeats this dilemma because expenditure on
capital equipment generates new current expenditure which is in effect
mortgaged for the foreseeable future. The lesson is that capital investment and future current expenditure must be planned together.

Public and private organisations: a complex relationship

A clear lesson of history is that public and private organisations have
often been interlinked in the provision of public services. Learning
flows in both directions between public and private sectors. Mixed
economies of provision have a long history. Finally public and private
organisations have often in the past ended up 'needing' each other.

Learning processes work both ways

Discussion of one of the most misleading of all Thatcherite 'doctrines'
– the view that the public sector should always be learning from the
private sector, particularly in respect of organisational matters – can be
brief because this aspect of public–private relations has been considered elsewhere (Stanyer, 1992, 1993a). The transfer of ideas has been a
major feature of the history of organisational thinking, but because

many analysts have been and are 'speciesists' they have concentrated on only one category and thus the question of the import/export of ideas – systematically or erratically – has been ignored except as a subsidiary issue. One consequence of this is that there have been the crudest misrepresentations of the flow of ideas between the public and private sectors.

It is easy to show that both sectors learn from each other and that types of organisation within each sector learn from each other: 'private learns from private' and 'public learns from public'. These learning processes result in part from the extreme variability of behaviour discovered when individual organisations in each type are compared. Both personnel and financial management are good examples of where developments in thought and practice in the public sector ran ahead of or at least alongside their counterparts in the private sector. Slow progress and great variability are documented in personnel management (Northcott, 1950, p. 1), cost accounting (Edwards and Newell, 1991) and county financial management (Stanyer, 1993b, pp. 99–101, writing about Sir John Bowring as a member of Devon Quarter Sessions, 1860–72).

'Mixed economies' of service provision

The phrase 'the mixed economy of social welfare' has become common usage since the mid-1980s. It means that in the designated sphere there are organisations of different types, including both public and private, that make a contribution to the provision of services.

It is recognised that social welfare between, say, 1808 and 1845, was provided by both public and private organisations (Smith, 1997). In addition to county and parish organisation there were religious and non-religious charities, friendly societies, savings banks, estates and work-places, and capitalist bodies making a contribution to income maintenance, protection of the weak and disabled, homelessness and rehabilitation of offenders.

Virtually identical regimes can be found in education but what has not been recognised is that similar regimes were to be found, to take rarely considered examples, in the military, police, currency, banking and census administration. The elements of regimes can be represented in a standard manner which shows, first, how specific services are provided by a variety of organisational types, and second, how specific organisational types are involved in a variety of services.

Interestingly, the firm, which is an economic category and not an organisational form, can appear in many different legal guises. The consequence of this is that the phrase 'not-for-profit' as applied in the context of local governance is misleading, or at least unhelpful because it lumps together very diverse organisational forms and obscures the internal complexity of many organisations.

Public organisations bring into existence private organisations

In public–private sector relations the overlooked factor in enabling policies is the creation, through non-directed processes, of private by public organisations. In an enabling regime public authorities commission or contract with private individuals or organisations to provide specified public services. The commissions or contracts are usually renewable from time, and the process is intended to be competitive.

But as the supply system for troops in North America during the War of Independence showed, commissioning and contracting bring into existence new organisations, or cause the growth of existing ones, whose function it is to carry out the public service. A situation can soon arise where each needs the other – the supplier needs the contract and the enabler needs a supplier (Baker, 1971). The relationships that this

'Parental' organisational type

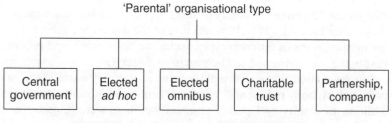

FIGURE 14.1   **Control of hospitals and education**

Trusts

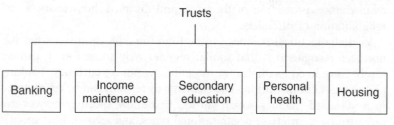

FIGURE 14.2   **Local functions of trusts**

engendered ranged from simple 'exploitation' to symbiosis. In the early nineteenth century, tax collection through contracting out assisted the establishment of individuals as country bankers. The tax receipts did not have to be paid into the Exchequer until several months after collection and during this period they could be lent at interest to others (Presnell, 1956). No study of the development of the private sector in any large urban area, such as Plymouth, is complete without analysis of the role of supplying and servicing institutions and depots – workhouses, asylums, hospitals, dockyards, naval bases, army camps, and so on – in bringing organisations into existence (Bishop, 1996).

The above examples are of adaptions to specific problems. A general 'enabling' stance was followed by the first county councils. As a speaker in the House of Commons debates on the 1888 legislation predicted, the one action that the first county councils did not want to do was to create a large administrative apparatus of their own: 'from his practical experience of county management, that one of the first things to which a County Board would look would be the curtailment, as best they could, of the expenses of a staff of officials' (Viscount Lymington, 1888, column 1283). The 'bureaucratic' form of county administration came into existence only very slowly and was not completed until the late 1940s (Stanyer, 1989).

Continuing problems

The system of local governance brought into existence in the last nineteen years has a number of serious problems inherent in it. Historical analysis identifies the 'needs for protection' created by organisations and these are easily observed today. Many of the problems arise from 'marriages' of particular organisational forms and specific public activities.

Protecting members against the organisations

The classic examples of protection of individuals against the organisation of which they are members are to be found in the 'Truck Acts'. The practice of part-payment of workers with vouchers that could only be cashed in company shops was made illegal because it was used to reduce wages and interfered very strongly with freedom of choice. Similar phenomena, resulting from a combination of two or more socioeconomic functions, are to be found in respect of 'tied cottages' and company pensions.

Often the protection needed is realistically protection against the political directorate, officers and other leaders of the organisation as individuals. The pursuit of private goals whilst formally working for an organisation is not a monopoly of lower participants; on the contrary the members in the best position to steal or misuse organisational assets, or to damage everyone else's interests, are the leaders.

Paternalism is also a danger against which rank-and-file members need protection. The requirement that 'the deserving poor' undertake religious observances threw doubt on the suitability of churches as welfare agencies. The imposition of leaders' moral and political values was a feature of trustee savings banks and may be a problem with housing associations and other trusts or trust-like local governance bodies where the leadership is not subject to an externally validated recruitment process.

Competition and the flight from competition

Pressures for both competition and the avoidance of competition create a sort of double helix in which the two forces swirl around each other producing mixtures of conflict and cooperation between organisations and organisational types.

To expect that insurance companies will not in the long run make use of genetic information in determining their strategies is like expecting building societies to ignore evidence about subsidence risks in different areas of a town. League tables in education are part of the competition between schools for pupils, hence policies for 'doctoring' the results from the selection of entrants through to the non-entry of weak candidates for examinations.

Competition will give an advantage to those who did and do adopt economically rational policies. But it is often recognised that unregulated competition is harmful to everyone in a particular sphere. Hence the insurance and friendly society worlds came together to promote actuarial science and turn its practitioners into a profession, in 1848 (Simmonds, 1948, ch. 1). Cooperation is often correctly thought to be right, as in this case, but collaboration can be regarded as a conspiracy by organisations against outsiders.

Power and interests of officers

The relations between the political directorate and 'top bureaucrats' have long been a topic in public administration and political studies in general. The question of the relative power of politicians and officials is repeated by every organisational form in addition to local government narrowly defined. Berle and Means (1932) focused on the board of directors and top managers, Burnham (1941) on managers as a class. The divorce of ownership and control was well known to the Fabians from the 1880s onwards, and Michels's (1915) 'iron law of oligarchy' describes the same phenomena in socialist parties and trade unions.

The lack of comparative analysis mentioned at the beginning of this chapter becomes acute at this point. Nineteenth-century history indicates that the earliest successful organisations of a particular type were dependent on the leadership of their paid staff, and studies of individual local authorities often pay tribute to the contribution of individual chief officers over a long period of time. But the role of the career motive, for instance in the growth of housing associations and charitable trusts, has been largely ignored.

The creation of 'policy networks'

The concepts of network and policy are metaphors for outcomes of the process of institutionalisation. If social activities are conceived as services then the central elements of a named network will be the appropriate public organisations at local, regional and central levels and the private bodies that have frequent dealings with them. The network is the set of relationships between these.

During the nineteenth and early twentieth centuries policy networks in this sense were coming into existence over long periods of time. At the start there was often a big and central contribution from private organisations, such as the Charity Organisation Society (1869, for personal welfare services in London) and the Royal Agricultural Society of England (1838), which attempted to provide the leadership and coordination that was missing from the system of public administration.

The same process can be seen to be unfolding today in respect of the physical environment, the cultural heritage and the protection of wildlife.

Complexity is always with us

One of the most common words used to describe the landscape of local governance in the 1990s was 'mess'. Other words and phrases, such as 'ambiguity', 'variability', 'crude categorisation', 'deviancy', 'flexible behaviour', 'hybridisation', 'discreteness' and 'wild stir', which have a similar connotation, were also widely used to refer to the confusion and unclarity that the researchers had found in their investigations. But the mess only appeared at the end of the presentations and in the subsequent discussions. What the study of the past teaches the student is that complexity, irregularity, 'deviant behaviour' and unpredictability are essential features of the local governance landscape, not passing phases created by the incompetence and mistakes of legislators.

About this study

Local governance has been organised in many different ways since 1801. The balances between different types of decentralised agency and between public and private bodies have changed many times and in several directions. The research looked first at the range of administrative agencies as their numbers and types have expanded and elaborated in the nineteenth and twentieth centuries. Second, consideration was given to the reasons that were adduced at the time for favouring one or other of the types as the means of carrying out public functions. The final objective was to see what light the past can throw on the experiences of the 1980s and early 1990s.

The methods were those of historical research, particularly those involving the use of public documents and publications by private individuals living at the time. These are supplemented by specialised analyses and case studies published in recent academic journals and monographs.

Bibliography

ACC/ADC/AMA (1997) *Crime – The Local Solution* (London: LGA).

ACC/ADC/AMA/LGMB (Association of County Councils, Association of District Councils, Association of Metropolitan Authorities, Local Government Management Board) (1996) *Survey of Community Safety Activities in Local Government in England and Wales* (Luton: LGMB).

Accounting Standards Board (1994) 'FRS 5: Reporting the Substance of Transactions', in R. M. Wilkins (ed.) (1996) *Accounting Standards 1996/97* (Milton Keynes: Accountancy Books) pp. 499–579.

Accounting Standards Committee (1984) 'SSAP 21: Accounting for Leases and Hire Purchase Contracts', in R. M. Wilkins (ed.) (1996) *Accounting Standards 1996/97* (Milton Keynes: Accountancy Books) pp. 205–60.

Adburgham, R. (1995) 'Support for a South West Body Growing', *Financial Times*, 9 March.

ADC (1990) *Promoting Safer Communities – A District Council Perspective* (London: ADC).

Adler, M., Munn, P. and Raab, C. (1996) *Devolved School Management* (Swindon: ESRC Report).

Adler, M., Petch, A. and Tweedie, J. (1989) *Parental Choice and Educational Policy* (Edinburgh: Edinburgh University Press).

Alexander, A. (1991) 'Managing Fragmentation – Democracy, Accountability and the Future of Local Government', *Local Government Studies*, vol. 17, no. 6, pp. 63–6.

Alter, C. and Hage, J. (1993) *Organisations Working Together* (London: Sage).

AMA (1990) *Crime Reduction: A Framework for the Nineties?* (London: AMA).

Amin, A. and Thrift, N. (1995) 'Institutional Issues for the European Regions: From Markets and Plans to Socioeconomics and Powers of Association', *Economy and Society*, vol. 24, no. 1, pp. 41–65.

Andrews, J. (1997) 'Colleges' Role in Economic Development', Fforwm Annual Conference, May 1997.

Armstrong, H. (1997) 'Five Sides to a New Leaf', *Municipal Journal*, 4 July, pp. 18–19.

Arnott, M., Raab, C., and Munn, P. (1997) 'Devolved Management: Variations in Response in Scottish School Boards', in C. Pole and R. Chawla-Duggan (eds), *Reshaping Education in the 1990's: Perspectives in Secondary Schooling* (London: Falmer).

Arthur, L. (1994) 'Higher Education Industrial Relations in Transition?' paper presented to the Employment Research Unit annual conference on 'The Contract State: The Future of Public Management', Cardiff Business School.

Audit Commission (1986) *Making a Reality of Community Care* (London: HMSO).

Audit Commission (1988) *The Competitive Council* (London: HMSO).

Augenblick, M. and Custer, B. C. (1990) *The Build, Operate and Transfer ('BOT') Approach to Infrastructure Projects in Developing Countries* (Washington, DC: World Bank).

Bache, I. (1992) *Bypassing the Centre: Assessing the Value of UK Local Authority Participation in EC Transgovernmental Coalitions*, unpublished MA thesis, International Studies Department, University of Sheffield.

Bache, I. George, S. and Rhodes, R. (1996) 'The European Union, Cohesion Policy, and Subnational Authorities in the United Kingdom', in L. Hooghe (ed.), *Cohesion Policy and European Integration* (Oxford: Oxford University Press).

Baker, N. (1971) *Government and Contractors: The British Treasury and War Supplies 1775–1783* (London: Athlone Press).

Ball, M., Harloe, M. and Martens, M. (1988) *Housing and Social Change in Europe and the U.S.A.* (London and New York: Routledge).

Ball, S. J. (1993) *Education Reform: A Critical and Post-Structural Approach* (Buckingham: Open University Press).

Ball, S. J., Bowe, R. and Gewirtz, S. (1994) 'Competitive Schooling, Values, Ethics and Cultural Engineering', *Journal of Curriculum and Supervision*, vol. 9, no. 4, pp. 350–67.

Ball, S. J., Bowe, R. and Gewirtz, S. (1995) 'Circuits of Schooling: A Sociological Explanation of Parental Choice of School in Social Class Contexts', *Sociological Review*, vol. 43, no. 1, pp. 52–78.

Barnes, M. (1997) *Care, Communities and Citizens* (Harlow: Addison Wesley Longman).

Barnes, M. and Shardlow, P. (1996a) 'Effective Consumers and Active Citizens: Strategies for Users' Influence on Services and Beyond', *Research, Policy and Planning*, vol. 14, no. 1, pp. 33–8.

Barnes, M. and Shardlow, P. (1996b) 'Identity Crisis? Mental Health User Groups and the "Problem" of Identity', in C. Barnes and G. Mercer (eds), *Exploring the Divide: Illness and Disability* (Leeds: The Disability Press).

Barnes, M. and Wistow, G. (1994) 'Achieving a Strategy for User Involvement in Community Care', *Health and Social Care in the Community*, vol. 2, pp. 347–56.

Barnes, M., Harrison, S., Mort, M., Shardlow, P. and Wistow, G. (1996) 'Citizens and Officials in Health and Social Care', *Local Government Policy Making*, vol. 23, no. 1, pp. 9–17.

Barrett, S. and Hill, M. (1984) 'Policy Bargaining and Structure in Implementation Theory: Towards an Integrated Perspective', *Policy and Politics*, vol. 12, no. 3, pp. 219–40.

Bassett, K. (1996) 'Partnerships, Business Elites and Urban Politics: New Forms of Governance in an English City?', *Urban Studies*, vol. 33, no. 3.

Benington, J. (1994) *Local Democracy and the European Union: The Impact of Europeanisation on Local Governance*, Research Report No. 6 (London: Commission for Local Democracy).

Benington J. (1998) 'Risk and Reciprocity: Local Governance within Civil

Society', in A. Coulson (ed.), *Trust and Contract in the Public Services* (Bristol: Policy Press).

Benington, J. and Geddes, M. (1996) *Partnerships to Promote Social Cohesion: The European Union Dimension*, Research Monograph, Dublin, European Foundation for the Improvement in Living and Working Conditions.

Benington, J. and Harvey, J. (1994a) 'Spheres or Tiers? The Significance of Transnational Local Authority Networks', in *Contemporary Political Studies, 2* (Belfast: Political Science Association).

Benington, J. and Harvey, J. (1994b), 'Spheres or Tiers?', *Local Government Policy Making*, vol. 20, no. 5, pp. 21–30.

Benington, J. and Harvey, J. (1995) 'The Europeanisation of Local Governance: The Significance of Transnational Networks?', paper to ESRC Seminar on Local Governance, Exeter University, September 19–20.

Benington, J. and Harvey J. (1998) 'Transnational Local Authority Networking: Passing Fashion or New Paradigm' in D. Marsh (ed.), *Comparing Policy Networks* (Buckingham: Open University Press), pp. 149–66.

Benington, J. and Taylor, M. (1993) 'Changes and Challenges facing the UK Welfare State in the Europe of the 1990s', *Policy and Politics*, vol. 21(2), pp. 121–34.

Bennett, R. *et al.* (1994) *Local Empowerment and Business Services* (London: UCL Press).

Benson, J. K. (1982) 'A Framework for Policy Analysis', in D. Rogers, D. Whitten and Associates, *Interorganisational Co-ordination* (Ames, Ill.: University of Chicago Press).

Benyon, J. (1986) 'Policing in the Limelight', in J. Benyon and C. Bourn (eds), *The Police: Powers, Procedures and Proprieties* (Oxford: Pergamon Press).

Best, M. (1990) *The New Competition: Institutions of Industrial Restructuring* (Cambridge: Polity Press).

Bhaskar, R. (1975) *A Realist Theory of Science* (Brighton: Harvester).

Birchall, J. (1996) 'Decentralisation of Local Government Services: Some Emerging Paradigms', paper presented to the International Symposium of New Frontiers of Theories and Practices in Local Government, Honolulu, November 1996.

Bishop, P. (1996) 'Buyer–Supplier Linkages in the Defence Industry: The Case of Devonport Dockyard', *Area*, vol. 28, no. 1, pp. 78–88.

Blackburn, R. (1992) 'Small Firms and Subcontracting: What Is It and Where?', in P. Leighton and A. Felstead (eds), *The New Entrepreneurs: Self-Employment and Small Business in Europe* (London: Kogan Page).

Bogdanor, V. (1996) 'Ministerial Chairs', *Guardian*, 23 July.

Boorsma, P. B. (1995) 'Leasing in the Public Sector, with Special Reference to the Netherlands', *Public Finance*, vol. 50, no. 2, pp. 182–200.

Bös, D. (1985) 'Public Sector Pricing', in A. J. Auerbach and M. Feldstein (eds), *Handbook of Public Economics: Volume 1* (Amsterdam: North-Holland) pp. 129–211.

Brown, S. (1997) 'Educational Change in the UK: A North–South Divide', in C. Pole and R. Chawla-Duggan (eds), *Reshaping Education in the 1990's: Perspectives on Secondary Schooling* (London: Falmer).

Brunnsson, N. and Olsen, J. (1993) *The Reforming Organisation* (London: Routledge).

Budgen, N. (1993) 'Oral Question', in Treasury and Civil Service Committee, *Private Finance for Public Projects: Minutes of Evidence, Wednesday 17 February 1993*, HC 508-i of Session 1992–93 (London: HMSO) Q. 8–9.

Bullock, A. and Thomas, H. (1997) *Schools at the Centre: A Study of Decentralisation* (London : Routledge).

Bulmer, M. (1987) *The Social Basis of Community Care* (London: Allen & Unwin).

Burns, D., Hambleton, R. and Hoggett, P. (1994) *The Politics of Decentralisation* (London: Macmillan).

Byatt, I. C. R. (chair) (1986) *Accounting for Economic Costs and Changing Prices: A Report to HM Treasury by an Advisory Group*, Vols I and II (London: HMSO).

Cabinet Office (1996) *Competitiveness: Helping Business to Win* (London: Office of Public Service).

Callierès, Francoise de [1716] (1963) *On the Manner of Negotiating with Princes* (Washington: University of America Press).

Castells, M. (1996) *The Rise of the Network Society* (Oxford: Blackwell).

Clarke, A. (1994) 'Leisure and the New Managerialism: From Public Missionary to Private Profit', in J. Clarke, A. Cochrane and E. Mclaughlin (eds), *Managing Social Policy* (London: Sage).

Clarke, J., Cochrane, A. and McLaughlin, E. (eds) *Managing Social Policy* (London: Sage).

Clarke, J. and Newman, J. (1997) *The Managerial State* (London: Sage).

Clarke, K. (1991) Speech to the North of England Educational Conference, November (quoted in Fitz *et al.* (1993) p. 13).

Clarke, R. V. (1995) 'Situational Crime Prevention', in M. Tonry and D. Farrington (eds), *Building a Safer Society: Strategic Approaches to Crime Prevention* (Chicago, Ill.: University of Chicago Press).

Clarke, R. V. and Hough, M. (eds) (1980) *The Effectiveness of Policing* (Farnborough: Gower).

Clegg, S. (1990) *Modern Organisations* (London: Sage).

Cohen, J. and Rogers, J. (eds) (1995) *Associations and Democracy* (London: Verso).

Cooke, P. and Morgan, K. (1993) 'The Network Paradigm: New Departures in Corporate and Regional Development', *Environment and Planning D*, vol. 11, pp. 543–64.

Cooke, P. and Morgan, K. (1998) *The Associational Economy: Firms, Regions and Innovation* (Oxford: Oxford University Press).

Cordingly, P. and Kogan, M. (1993) *In Support of Education: The Functioning of Local Government* (London: Kogan Page).

Crime Concern (1992) *Family, School and Community: Towards a Social Crime Prevention Agenda* (Swindon: Crime Concern).

Daft, R. and Lewin, A. (1993) 'Where are the Theories for the "New" Organisational Forms?', *Organisation Science*, vol. 4, no. 4, pp. i–vi.

Davis, A., Ellis, K. and Rummery, K. (1997) *Accessing Assessment: Disabled People's Experiences of Assessment for Community Care Services* (Bristol: The Policy Press).

Deakin, N. and Michie, J. (1997) 'The Theory and Practice of Contracting', in

N. Deakin and J. Mitchie (eds), *Contracts, Cooperation and Competition* (Oxford: Oxford University Press).

Deakin, N. and Walsh, K. (1994) 'The Enabling State: The Role of the Markets and Contracts', paper presented to the Employment Research Unit Annual Conference on The Contract State: The Future of Public Management, Cardiff Business School.

Deem, R. (1997) 'The School, the Parent, the Banker and the Local Politician: What We Can Learn from the English Experience of Involving Lay People in the Site Based Management of Schools?', in C. Pole and R. Chawla-Duggan (eds), *Reshaping Education in the 1990's: Perspectives on Secondary Schooling* (London: Falmer).

Deem, R., Brehony, K. and Heath, S. (1995) *Active Citizenship and the Governing of Schools* (Buckingham: Open University Press).

Department of the Environment (1987) *Housing – the Government's Proposals*, Cm. 214 (London: HMSO).

Department of the Environment (1989) Local Government Research Seminar, London.

Department of Health (1989) *Working for Patients: Self-Governing Hospitals*, Working Paper 1 (London: Department of Health).

Department of Trade and Industry (1992) *One Stop Shops For Business* (London: DTI).

Department of Transport (1997) *Transport: The Government's Expenditure Plans, 1997–98 to 1999–2000*, Cm 3606 (London: Stationery Office).

Desveaux, J. (1995) *Designing Bureaucracies* (Stanford: Stanford University Press).

DHSS (1971) *Better Services for the Mentally Handicapped* (London: HMSO).

DHSS (1975) *Better Services for the Mentally Ill* (London: HMSO).

DiMaggio, P. and Powell, W. (1991) 'Introduction', in W. Powell and P. DiMaggio (eds), *The New Institutionalism in Organisational Analysis* (Chicago, Ill.: University of Chicago Press).

Dobek, M. M. (1993) 'Privatization as a Political Priority: The British Experience', *Political Studies*, vol. 41, no. 1, pp. 24–40.

Doeringer, P. *et al.* (1987) *Invisible Factors in Local Economic Development* (Oxford: Oxford University Press).

Doogan, K. (1997) 'The Marketization of Local Services and the Fragmentation of Labour Markets', *International Journal of Urban and Regional Research*, vol. 21, no. 2, pp. 296–302.

Doogan, K. (1998 forthcoming) 'The Impact of European Integration on Labour Market Institutions', *International Planning Studies*, vol. 3.

Drucker, J. and Macallan, H. (1994) 'Sub-contracting – What is in a Name?', paper presented to the 'Work Employment and Society in the 1990s. Changing Boundaries and Changing Experiences' WES conference, September 1994.

Dryzek, J. S. (1996) 'The Informal Logic of Institutional Design', in R. E. Goodin (ed.), *The Theory of Institutional Design* (Cambridge: Cambridge University Press).

Duclaud-Williams, R. (1993) 'The Governance of Education: Britain and France', in J. Kooiman (ed.), *Modern Governance: New Government–Society Interactions* (London: Sage).

Dudley, G. and Richardson, J. (1996) 'Promiscuous and Celibate Ministerial Styles: Policy Change, Policy Networks and British Roads Policy', *Parliamentary Affairs*, vol. 49, no. 4, pp. 566–83.

Dunleavy, P. (1994) 'The Globalization of Public Services Production: Can Government be the "Best in the World"?', *Public Policy and Administration*, Summer, pp. 36–63.

Dunleavy, P. (1995) 'Policy Disasters: Explaining the UK's Record', *Public Policy and Administration*, vol. 10, no. 2, pp. 52–70.

Echols, F., McPherson, A. and Willams, D. (1990) 'Parental Choice in Scotland', *Journal of Education Policy*, vol. 5, no. 3.

Economist (1995) 'Cooking the Books', 28 October.

Edwards, J. R. and Newell, E. (1991) 'The Development of Industrial Cost and Management Accounting before 1850: A Survey of the Evidence', *Business History*, vol. 33, no. 1, pp. 35–57.

Ellwood, S. (1996) *Cost–Based Pricing in the NHS* (London: Chartered Institute of Management Accountants).

Emery, F. E. and Trist, E. L. (1965) 'The Causal Texture of Organisational Environments', *Human Relations*, vol. 18, pp. 21–32.

Escott, K. and Whitfield, D. (1995) *The Gender Impact of CCT in Local Government* (Manchester: EOC).

Etzioni, A. (1961) *A Comparative Analysis of Complex Organizations* (Glencoe: Free Press).

Etzioni, A. (1964) *Modern Organizations* (Englewood Cliffs, NJ: Prentice–Hall).

Etzioni, A. (1995) *The Spirit of Community, Rights, Responsibilities and the Communitarian Agenda* (London: Fontana).

European Commission (1991) *Ex-Ante Evaluation of Community Support Programmes and Dependent Programmes for the Objective 2 Areas of South Wales and Bremen* (Brussels: DGXVI).

European Conference of Ministers of Transport (1989) *Systems of Road Infrastructure Cost Coverage*, Round Table 80 (Paris: OECD).

Fairbrother, P. (1994) *Politics and the State as Employer* (London: Mansell).

Farnham, D. and Horton, S. (1992) 'Human Resource Management in the New Public Sector: Leading or Following Private Employer Practice?', *Public Policy and Administration*, vol. 7, pp. 42–55.

Farnham, D. and Horton, S. (1996) *Managing the New Public Services*, 2nd edn (London: Macmillan).

Ferlie, E., Ashburner, L., Fitzgerald L. and Pettigrew, A. (1996) *The New Public Management in Action* (Oxford: Oxford University Press).

Finlay, I., Holmes, S. and Kydd, L. (1997) 'Institutional Boundary Management: Experiences of Scottish Colleges Since Incorporation', *Developing FE, FEDA Report*, vol. 1, pp. 81–106.

Fitz, J., Halpin, D. and Power, S. (1993) *Grant-Maintained Schools: Education in the Market Place* (London: Kogan Page).

Flemming, J. (1995) 'Can the Private Finance Initiative Stand the Strain?', *Public Finance Foundation Review*, no. 5, pp. 1–3.

Flynn, R., Williams, G. *et al.* (1996) *Markets and Networks: Contracting in Community Health Services* (Buckingham: Open University Press).

Fortune, P. (1995) 'Forging Ahead?', *Business Directions*, September/October.
Foster, D. (1993) 'Industrial Relations in Local Government', *Political Quarterly*, vol. 64 no. 1, pp. 49–59.
Fox, A. (1974) *Beyond Contract: Work, Power and Trust Relations* (London: Faber).
Fox, C. and Miller, H. (1995) *Postmodern Public Administration* (Thousand Oaks, Calif.: Sage).
Frances, J. *et al.* (1991) 'Introduction', in G. Thompson, J. Frances, R. Levačić and J. Mitchell (eds), *Markets, Hierarchies and Networks: The Co-ordination of Social Life* (London: Sage).
Friedman, M. (1989) 'Feminism and Modern Friendship: Dislocating the Community', *Ethics*, vol. 99, pp. 275–90.
Garland, D. (1996) 'The Limits of the Sovereign State: Strategies of Crime Control in Contemporary Society', *British Journal of Criminology*, vol. 36, no. 4, pp. 445–71.
Garmise, S. (1997a) 'Making a Difference? Regional Government, Economic Development and European Regional Policy', *International Planning Studies*, vol. 2, no. 1, pp. 63–81.
Garmise, S. (1997b) 'Region-Building? The Impact of European Regional Policy on the Development of the Regional Tier in the UK', *Regional and Federal Studies* (forthcoming).
Garmise, S. and Rees, G. (1997) 'The Role of Institutional Networks in Local Economic Development: A New Model of Governance?', *Local Economy*, vol. 12.
Garmise, S. *et al.* (1996) 'Networks and Local Economic Development: Evidence from South East Wales and the West of England', Papers in Planning Research Number 160, Department of City and Regional Planning, Cardiff University.
Gewirtz, S., Ball, S. J. and Bowe, R. (1995) *Markets, Choice and Equity in Education* (Buckingham: Open University Press).
Glatter, R., Woods, P. and Bagley, C. (eds) (1977) *Choice and Diversity in Schooling: Perspectives and Prospects* (London: Routledge).
Goodin, R. (1996) 'Institutions and Their Design', in R. Goodin (ed.), *The Theory of Institutional Design* (Cambridge: Cambridge University Press).
Goodlad, R. (1993) *The Housing Authority as Enabler* (London: Longman).
Gouldner, A. (1957/58) 'Cosmopolitans and Locals: Towards Analysis of Latent Social Roles', *Administrative Science Quarterly*, vol. 2, pp. 281–302, 444–80.
Government Office–South West (1995) *Annual Report, 1994/95* (Bristol: GO–SW).
Government Office–South West (1996) *Annual Report, 1995/96* (Bristol: GO–SW).
Granovetter, M. (1973) 'The Strength of Weak Ties', *American Journal of Sociology*, vol. 78, no. 6, pp. 1360–81.
Granovetter, M. (1985) 'Economic Action and Social Structure: The Problem of Embeddedness', *American Journal of Sociology*, vol. 91, pp. 481–510.
Grant, W. (1989) *Pressure Groups, Politics and Democracy in Britain* (Oxford: Philip Allan).

Grant, W. (1992) 'Models of Interest, Intermediation and Policy Formation Applied to an Internationally Comparative Study of the Dairy Industry', *European Journal of Policy Research*, vol. 21, pp. 53–68.

Grant, W. (l993) 'Pressure Groups and the EC: An Overview', in S. Mazey and J. Richardson (eds), *Lobbying in the EC* (Oxford: Oxford University Press) pp. 27–46.

Halpin, D., Powers, S. and Fitz, J. (1997) 'Opting into the Past? Grant Maintained Schools and the Reinvention of Tradition', in R. Glatter *et al.*

Hancock, D. (1993) 'More Private Funding for Public Projects', *Observer*, 10 January.

Hansard (1997) *Parliamentary Debates*, House of Commons Official Report, 2 June 1997, columns 49–50.

Harrigan, K. R. and Newman, W. H. (1990) 'Bases of Organisational Co-operation: Propensity, Power and Persistence', *Journal of Management Studies*, vol. 27, no. 4, pp. 417–34.

Harris, C. (1994) 'What Does Privatization Mean to Employees? A Case Study of Two Water plcs', paper presented to the Employment Research Unit annual conference on 'The Contract State: The Future of Public Management', Cardiff Business School.

Harrison, S. (1991) 'Working the Markets: The Purchaser/Provider Split in English Health Care', *International Journal of Health Services*, vol. 21, no. 4, pp. 623–36.

Harrison, S., Barnes, M. and Mort, M. (1997) 'Praise and Damnation: Mental Health User Groups and the Construction of Organisational Legitimacy', paper for presentation to the JUC/PAC conference 'Understanding Governance', Sunningdale, 1–3 September.

Hartley, J. (1994) 'Case Studies in Organisational Research', in C. Casell and G. Symon (eds), *Qualitative Methods in Organisational Research* (London: Sage) pp. 208–29.

Harvey, D. (1996) *Justice, Nature and the Geography of Difference* (Oxford: Blackwell).

Heald, D. A. (1991) 'Accounting for the Severn Bridge', *Financial Accountability and Management*, vol. 7, no. 4, pp. 267–307.

Heald, D. A. (1997a) 'Accounting and Accountability for Infrastructure', in I. Lapsley and R. M. S. Wilson (eds), *Explorations in Financial Control* (London: International Thomson) pp. 214–39.

Heald, D. A. (1997b) 'Privately Financed Capital in Public Services', *Manchester School*, vol. 65, no. 4, pp. 568–98.

Heald, D. A. and Geaughan, N. (1997) 'Accounting for the Private Finance Initiative', *Public Money and Management*, vol. 17, pp. 11–16.

Heald, D. A. and Scott, D. A. (1996) 'NHS Capital Charging after Five Years', in A. Harrison (ed.), *Health Care UK 1995/96* (London: King's Fund) pp. 131–40.

Held, D. (1987) *Models of Democracy* (Cambridge: Polity Press).

Hennessy, P. (1989) *Whitehall* (London: Secker & Warburg).

Hirschman, A. (1970) *Exit, Voice and Loyalty* (Cambridge, Mass.: Harvard University Press).

Hirschman, A. (1991) *The Rhetoric of Reaction* (Cambridge, Mass.: Harvard University Press).

Hirschman, A. (1995) *A Propensity to Self-Subversion* (Cambridge, Mass.: Harvard University Press).

Hirst, P. (1994) *Associative Democracy* (Cambridge: Polity Press).

Hogg, S. and Hill, J. (1995) *Too Close to Call: Power and Politics – John Major in No. 10* (London: Little, Brown).

Hoggett, P. (1991) 'New Management in the Public Sector?', *Policy and Politics*, vol. 19, no. 4, pp. 234–56.

Hoggett, P. (1994) 'New Modes of Control in the Public Sector', paper presented to the Employment Research Unit annual conference on 'The Contract State: The Future of Public Management', Cardiff Business School.

Hoggett, P. (1996) 'New Modes of Control in the Public Service', *Public Administration*, vol. 74, no. 1, pp. 9–32.

Hogwood, B. (1995) *The Integrated Regional Offices and the Single Regeneration Budget*, Commission for Local Democracy, Research Report No. 13 (London: CLD Ltd).

Holliday, I., Marcou, G. and Vickerman, R. (1991) *The Channel Tunnel* (London: Belhaven Press).

Home Office (1984) *Circular 8/84: Crime Prevention* (London: HMSO).

Home Office (1991) *Standing Committee on Crime Prevention: Safer Communities: The Local Delivery of Crime Prevention Through the Partnership Approach* (London: HMSO).

Home Office (1992) *Home Office Response to the Report: 'Safer Communities – The Local Delivery of Crime Prevention Through the Partnership Approach'* (London: Home Office).

Hood, C. (1994) *Explaining Economic Policy Reversals* (Buckingham: Open University Press).

Hood, C. (1995) 'Contemporary Public Management: A New Global Paradigm', *Public Policy and Administration*, vol. 10, no. 2, pp. 104–227.

Hood, C. and James, O. (1996) 'Reconfiguring the UK Executive: From Public Bureaucracy State to Re-regulated Public Service?', paper presented to ESRC Conference, 'Understanding Central Government: Theory into Practice', University of Birmingham, 16–18 September.

House of Lords (1996) *Rebuilding Trust*, Volume 1, Report, Select Committee on Relations Between Central and Local Government (London: HMSO).

Hoyes, L., Lart, R., Means, R. and Taylor, M. (1994) *Community Care in Transition* (York: Joseph Rowntree Foundation).

Humber Bridge (Debts) Act 1996, Ch. 1 (London: HMSO).

Hyder, M. (1984) 'Implementation – the Evolutionary Model', in D. Lewis and H. Wallace (eds), *Policies into Practice* (London: Heinemann).

Incomes Data Services (1995) *Pay in the Public Services: Review of 1994; Prospects for 1995*, IDS Ltd, London, February, p. 45.

Institute for Fiscal Studies (1993) *Tax Options for 1993: The Green Budget*, Commentary No. 33 (London: Institute for Fiscal Studies).

Institute for Health Services Management (1997) *Building Services and Servicing Buildings: The Private Finance Initiative in the NHS* (London: IHSM).

Jessop, B. (1994) 'The Transition to Post-Fordism and the Schumpeterian Workfare State', in R. Burrows and B. Loader (eds), *Towards a Post-Fordist Welfare State* (London: Routledge).

Johnson, H. and Riley, K. A. (1995) 'The Impact of Quangos and New Government Agencies on Education', in F. F. Ridley and D. Wilson (eds) *The Quango Debate* (Oxford: Oxford University Press) pp. 106–18.

Jones, T. *et al.* (1994) *Democracy and Policing* (London: Policy Studies Institute).

Jordan, G. (1990) 'Policy Community Realism versus "New" Institutional Ambiguity', *Political Studies*, vol. 38, pp. 470–84.

Jordan, G. (1994) *The British Administrative System* (London: Routledge).

Kay, J. A. (1991) 'The Economics of Mutuality', *Annals of Public and Cooperative Economics*, vol. 62, no. 3, pp. 309–18.

Keane, J. (1988) *Democracy and Civil Society* (London: Verso).

Keeling, D. (1972) *Management in Government* (London: Allen & Unwin).

Kettl, D. (1993) *Sharing Power Public Governance and Private Markets* (Washington, DC: The Brookings Institution).

Kickert, W. J. M., Klijn, E. H. and Koppenjan, J. F. M. (eds) (1997) *Network Management in the Public Sector* (London: Sage).

King, D. (1995) 'From the Urban Left to the New Right: Normative Theory and Local Government', in J. Stewart and G. Stoker (eds), *Local Government in the 1990s* (London: Macmillan).

King's Fund (1980) *An Ordinary Life* (London: King's Fund).

Klijn, E., Koopenjan, J. and Termeer, K. (1995) 'Managing Networks in the Public Sector', *Public Administration*, vol. 73, pp. 437–54.

Klijn, E.-H. and Van Der Pennen, T. (1992) 'Changes in Local Housing Policy', Networks RISBO-paper B10 (Rotterdam: Rotterdam Institute for Sociological and Public Administration Research).

Knight, J. (1992) *Institutions and Social Conflict* (Cambridge: Cambridge University Press).

Kooiman, J. (1993) 'Governance and Governability: Using Complexity, Dynamics and Diversity', in J. Kooiman (ed.) *Modern Governance* (London: Sage).

Kramer, R. and Tyler T. (eds) (1996) *Trust in Organisations: Frontiers of Theory and Research* (London: Sage).

Kumar, K. (1993) 'Civil Society', *British Journal of Sociology*, vol. 44, no. 3.

LARIA (Local Authorities' Research and Intelligence Association) (1994) *Research for Policy: Proceedings of the the 1994 Annual Conference of LARIA* (Newcastle upon Tyne: LARIA).

Larson, A. (1992) 'Network Dyads in Entrepreneurial Settings: A Study of Governance Exchange Relationships', *Administrative Science Quarterly*, vol. 37, pp. 76–104.

Le Grand, J. (1990) *Quasi-markets and Social Policy* (Bristol: SAUS/University of Bristol).

Leach, S. and Stoker, G. (1997) 'Understanding the Local Government Review: A Retrospective Analysis', *Public Administration*, vol. 75, no. 1, pp. 1–20.

Leach, S., Stewart, J. and Walsh, K. (1994) *The Changing Organisation and Management of Local Government* (London: Macmillan).

Levačić R. (1991) 'Markets and Government: An Overview', in G. Thompson, J. Frances, R. Levačić and J. Mitchell (eds), *Markets, Hierarchies and Networks: The Co-ordination of Social Life* (London: Sage).

Levačić, R. (1995) *Local Management of Schools: Analysis and Practice* (Buckingham: Open University Press).

LGMB (Local Government Management Board) (1993) *CCT Information Service, Survey Report No. 8*, December.

Liddle, M. and Gelsthorpe, L. (1994) *Inter-Agency Crime Prevention: Organising Local Delivery*, Police Research Group Crime Prevention Unit Paper 52 (London: Home Office).

Liebfried, S. and Pierson, P. (eds) (1995) *European Social Policy: Between Fragmentation and Integration* (Washington DC: Brookings Institution).

Lister, R. (1995) 'Dilemmas in Engendering Citizenship', *Economy and Society*, vol. 24, no. 1, pp. 1–36.

Lloyd, C. and Seifert, R. (1995) 'Restructuring in the NHS: Labour Utilization and Intensification in Four Hospitals', *Work, Employment and Society*, vol. 9, no. 2, pp. 359–78.

Lowndes, V. (1993) *Networks and Inter-organisational Relationships: Conceptual Frameworks*, Working Paper, INLOGOV, Birmingham University.

Lowndes, V. (1995) 'Citizenship and Urban Politics', in D. Judge, H. Wolman and G. Stoker (eds), *Theories of Urban Politics* (London: Sage).

Lowndes, V. (1996a) 'Varieties of New Institutionalism: A Critical Appraisal', *Public Administration*, vol. 74, no. 2, pp. 181–97.

Lowndes, V. (1996b) 'Locality and Community: Choices for Local Government', in S. Leach and H. Davis (eds), *Enabling or Disabling Local Government* (Buckingham: Open University Press).

Lowndes, V. (1997) 'Change in Public Service Management: New Institutions and New Managerial Regimes', *Local Government Studies*, vol. 23, no. 2, pp. 42–66.

Lowndes, V. and Riley, K. (1998) *Networks and Networking* (London: Local Government Management Board).

Lymington (Viscount) (1888) *House of Commons Hansard*, 13 April.

McKeown, P. and Connolly, M. (1992) 'Education Reform in N. Ireland: Maintaining the Distance', *Journal of Social Policy*, vol. 21, no. 2, pp.211–32.

McKeown, P., Donnelly, C. and Osborne, B. (1997) 'School Governing Bodies in N. Ireland: Responses to Local Management of Schools', in C. Pole and R. Chawla-Duggan (eds), *Reshaping Education in the 1990's: Perspectives on Secondary Schooling* (London: Falmer).

Mackintosh, M. (1997a) 'Economic Culture and Quasimarkets in Local Government: The Case of Contracting for Social Care', *Local Government Studies*, vol. 23, no. 2, pp. 80–102.

Mackintosh, M. (1997b) 'Trading Work: Discourses of Exchange in the Economic Culture of Local Government', *Public Policy and Administration*, vol. 12, no. 2, pp. 17–31.

McLaughlin, E. and Murji, K. (1995) 'The End of Public Policing? Police Reform and the "New Managerialism"', in L. Noakes, M. Levi and M. Maguire (eds), *Contemporary Issues in Criminology* (Cardiff: University of Wales Press).

McPherson, A. and Raab, C. (1988) *Governing Education: A Sociology of Policy since 1945* (Edinburgh: Edinburgh University Press).

Macneil, I. (1980) *The New Social Contract: An Enquiry into Modern Contractual Relations* (New Haven, Conn.: Yale University Press).

Malpass, P. (1990) *Re-shaping Housing Policy: Subsidies, Rents and Residualisation* (London: Routledge).

Malpass, R. (1994) 'Policy Making and Local Governance: How Bristol Failed to Secure City Challenge Funding (Twice)', *Policy and Politics*, vol. 22, no. 4, pp. 301–12.

March, J. and Olsen J. (1989) *Rediscovering Institutions* (New York: Free Press).

Marks, G. (1993) 'Structural Policy and Multilevel Governance in the EC', in A. W. Carfruny and G. G. Rosenthal (eds), *The State of the European Community. Volume 2: The Maastricht Debates and Beyond* (London: Lynne Rienner) pp. 391–410.

Marks, G., Hooghe, L. and Blank, K. (1996) 'European Integration from the 1980s: State-Centric v. Multi-Level Governance', *Journal of Common Market Studies*, vol. 34, no. 3, pp. 342–78.

Marsh, D. and Rhodes, R. (eds) (1992a) *Policy Networks in British Government* (Oxford: Clarendon Press).

Marsh, D. and Rhodes, R. (eds) (1992b) *Implementing Thatcherite Policies: Audit of an Era* (Buckingham: Open University Press).

Marsh, D. and Smith, M. (1995) 'The Role of Networks in an Understanding of Whitehall: Towards a Dialectical Approach', Political Studies Association Annual Conference, University of York, vol. 37, pp. 76–104.

Martin, J., Ranson, S., McKeown, P. and Nixon, J. (1996) 'School Governance for the Civil Society: Redefining the Boundary Between Schools and Parents', *Local Government Studies*, vol. 22, no. 4, pp. 210–28.

Mawson, J. and Spencer, K. (1997) 'The Government Offices for the English Regions', *Policy and Politics*, vol. 25, no. 1, pp. 71–84.

Mayston, D. (1993) 'Public and Private Sector Project Appraisal: A Comparative Evaluation', in A. Williams and E. Giardini (eds), *Efficiency in the Public Sector: The Theory and Practice of Cost–Benefit Analysis* (Aldershot: Edward Elgar) pp. 3–25.

Mazey, S. and J. Richardson, (l993a) *Lobbying in the European Community* (Oxford: Oxford University Press).

Mazey, S. and Richardson, J. (l993b) 'Interest Groups in the European Community', in J. Richardson (ed.), *Pressure Groups* (Oxford: Oxford University Press).

Mills, M. (1992) 'The Case of Food and Health and the Use of Network Analysis', in D. Marsh and R. Rhodes (eds), *Politics in British Government* (Oxford: Oxford University Press).

Mintzberg, H. (1979) *The Structuring of Organizations* (Englewood Cliffs, NJ: Prentice-Hall).

Monnier, E. (1997) 'Vertical Partnerships: The Opportunities and Constraints which they Pose for High Quality Evaluations', *Evaluation*, vol. 3, no. 1, pp. 110–18.

Morgan, K. (1996) 'Learning by Interacting: Inter-Firm Networks and Enterprise Support', in OECD (ed.) *Networks of Enterprises and Local Development* (Paris: OECD) pp. 53–66.

Morgan, K. (1997a) 'The Learning Region: Institutions, Innovation and Regional Renewal', *Regional Studies*, vol. 31, no. 5, pp. 491–503.

Morgan, K. (1997b) 'The Regional Animateur: Taking Stock of the Welsh Development Agency', *Regional and Federal Studies*, vol. 7, no. 2.

Morgan, K. and Rees, G. (1994) 'Vocational Skills and Economic Development: Building a Robust Training System in Wales', Occasional Paper, Department of City and Regional Planning, Cardiff University.

Morgan, K. and Roberts, E. (1993) 'The Democratic Deficit: A Guide to Quangoland', Papers in Planning Research Number 144, Department of City and Regional Planning, Cardiff University.

Mort, M. and Harrison, S. (1996) 'User Involvement as a Technology of Legitimation: Representation, Participation and Incorporation', paper presented at joint sessions of European Consortium for Political Research, Oslo, 4 April.

Mort, M., Harrison, S. and Wistow, G. (1996) 'The User Card: Picking Through the Organisational Undergrowth in Health and Social Care, *Contemporary Political Studies*, vol. 2 (Belfast: Political Studies Association) pp. 1133–40.

Moss Kanter, R., Stein, B. and Todd, D. (1992) *The Challenge of Organizational Change* (New York: Free Press).

Mouffe, C. (1992) *Dimensions of Radical Democracy: Pluralism, Citizenship, Community* (London: Verso).

Mouffe, C. (1993) *The Return of the Political* (London: Verso).

Munn, P. (ed.) (1993) *Parents and Schools: Customers, Managers or Partners* (London: Routledge).

Munnell, A. H. (1992) 'Infrastructure Investment and Economic Growth', *Journal of Economic Perspectives*, vol. 6, no. 4, pp. 189–98.

Nicholson, H. (1950) *Diplomacy* (Oxford: Oxford University Press).

Nixon, J. and Ranson, S. (1997) 'Theorising "Agreement": The Bases of a New Professional Ethic', *Discourse: Studies in the Cultural Politics of Education*, vol. 18, no. 2.

Nixon, J., Martin, J., McKeown, P. and Ranson, S. (1996) *Encouraging Learning: Towards a Theory of the Learning School* (Buckingham: Open University Press).

Nixon, J., Martin, J., McKeown, P. and Ranson, S. (1997a) 'Confronting "Failure": Towards a Pedagogy of Recognition', *International Journal of Inclusive Education*, vol. 1, no. 2.

Nixon, J., Martin, J., McKeown, P. and Ranson, S. (1997b) 'Towards a Learning Profession: Changing Codes of Occupational Practice Within the New Management of Education', *British Journal of Sociology of Education*, vol. 21, no. 1, pp. 5–28.

North, D. (1990) *Institutions, Institutional Change and Economic Performance* (Cambridge: Cambridge University Press).

Northcott, C. H. (1950) *Personnel Management*, 2nd edn (London: Pitman).

OECD (1987) *Toll Financing and Private Sector Involvement in Road Infrastructure Development* (Paris: OECD).

OECD (1995) *Governance in Transition: Public Management Reforms in OECD Countries* (Paris: PUMA/OECD).

Oliver, M. (1996) *Understanding Disability: From Theory to Practice* (London: Macmillan).

Osborne, D. and Gaebler, T. (1992) *Reinventing Government* (Reading, Mass.: Addison-Wesley).

Ostrom, E. (1986) 'An Agenda for the Study of Institutions', *Public Choice*, vol. 48, pp. 3-25.

O'Toole, B. and Jordan, G. (eds) (1995) *Next Steps Improving Management in Government?* (Aldershot: Dartmouth).

O'Toole, L. (1986) 'Policy Recommendations for Multi-Actor Implementation: An Assessment of the Field', *Journal of Public Policy*, vol. 6 no. 2, pp. 181–210.

Painter, C., Rouse, J., Issac-Henry, L. and Munk, L. (1996) *Changing Local Governance: Local Authorities and Non-Elected Agencies* (Luton: Local Government Management Board).

Painter, J. (1991) 'Compulsory Competitive Tendering in Local Government: The First Round', *Public Administration*, vol. 69, pp. 191–210.

Pateman, C. (1992) 'Equality, Difference, Subordination: The Politics of Motherhood and Women's Citizenship', in G. Bock and S. James (eds), *Beyond Equality and Difference. Citizenship, Feminist Politics, Female Subjectivity* (London: Routledge).

Patterson, A. and Pinch, P. (1995) "Hollowing Out" the Local State: Compulsory Competitive Tendering and the Restructuring of British Public Sector Services', *Environment and Planning A*, vol. 27.

Penney, D. and Evans, J. (1997) 'When "Breadth and Balance" Means Balancing the Books: Curriculum Planning in Schools Post ERA', in C. Pole and R. Chawla-Duggan (eds), *Reshaping Education in the 1990's: Perspectives on Secondary Schooling* (London: Falmer).

Perrin, J. (1984) 'Accounting for Public Sector Assets', in A. Hopwood and C. Tomkins (eds), *Issues in Public Sector Accounting* (Oxford: Philip Allan) pp. 61–84.

Peters, G. (1993) 'Managing the Hollow State', in K. Eliassen and J. Kooiman (eds), *Managing Public Organisations* (London: Sage).

Peters, T. (1993) *Liberation Management* (New York: Knopf).

Phillips, A. (1993) *Democracy and Difference* (Cambridge: Polity Press).

Pinch, S. (1994) 'Labour Flexibility and the Changing Welfare State', in R. Burrows and B. Loader (eds), *Towards a Post-Fordist Welfare State* (London: Routledge).

Polanyi, K. (1944) *The Great Transformation* (New York: Rinehart).

Pollitt, C. (1993) *Managerialism and the Public Services* (Oxford: Blackwell).

Pollitt, C. (1995) 'Justification by Works or by Faith? Evaluating the New Public Management', *Evaluation*, vol. 1, no. 2, pp. 133–54.

Pollitt, C., Birchall, J. and Putman, K. (1998) *Decentralising Public Service Management* (London: Macmillan).

Pollitt, C., Hanney, S., Packwoods, Roberts, S. and Rothwell, S. (1997) *Trajectories and Options: An International Perspective on Finnish Public Management Reform* (Helsinki: Ministry of Finance).

Powell, W. (1990) 'Neither Markets nor Hierarchy: Network Forms of Organization', in L. Cummings and B. Shaw (eds), *Research in Organizational Behavior*, Volume 12 (Greenwich: JAI Press) pp. 295–336.

Powell W. (1991) 'Neither Market Nor Hierarchy: Network Forms of Organisation', in G. Thompson, J. Frances, R. Levačić and J. Mitchell (eds),

Markets, Hierarchies and Networks: The Co-ordination of Social Life (London: Sage).

Powell, W. (1996) 'Trust-based Forms of Governance', in R. M. Kramer and T. Tyler (eds), *Trust in Organisations: Frontiers of Theory and Research* (London: Sage).

Power, S., Halpin, D. and Fitz, J. (1997) 'The Grant Maintained Schools Policy: The English Experience of Self-Governance', in C. Pole and R. Chawla-Duggan (eds), *Reshaping Education in the 1990's: Perspectives on Secondary Schooling* (London: Falmer).

Pratchett, L. and Wingfield, M. (1996) 'The Demise of the Public Service Ethos', in L. Pratchett and D. Wilson (eds), *Local Democracy and Local Government* (London: Macmillan).

Presnell, L. S. (1956) *Country Banking in the Industrial Revolution* (Oxford: Clarendon Press).

Pressman, J. and Wildavsky, A. (1984) *Implementation*, 3rd edn (Berkeley: University of California Press).

Prior, D., Stewart, J. and Walsh, K. (1995) *Citizenship: Rights, Community and Participation* (London: Pitman).

Private Finance Panel (1997) *DBFO Roads Deliver Better Value for Money*, Press Release.

Purnell, S. (1995) 'Drive for Privatized Services is in Trouble', *Daily Telegraph*, 24 April.

Putnam, R. (1993a) *Making Democracy Work* (Princeton, NJ: Princeton University Press).

Putnam, R. (1993b) 'The Prosperous Community: Social Capital and Public Life', *The American Prospect*, no. 143, pp. 35–42.

Ramon, S. (ed.) (1991) *Beyond Community Care: Normalisation and Integration Work* (London: Macmillan).

Ranson, S. (1988) 'From 1944 to 1988: Education, Citizenship and Democracy', *Local Government Studies*, vol. 14, no. 1, pp. 1–19.

Ranson, S. (1992) *The Role of Local Government in Education* (Harlow: Longman).

Ranson, S. (1994) *Towards the Learning Society* (London: Cassell).

Ranson, S. (1995) 'From Reforming to Restructuring Education', in J. Stewart and G. Stoker (eds), *Local Government in the 1990s* (London: Macmillan).

Ranson, S., Martin, J. and Nixon, J. (1997) 'A Learning Democracy for Co-operative Action', *Oxford Review of Education*, vol. 23, no. 1, pp. 117–31.

Ranson, S., Martin, J., McKeown, P. and Nixon, J. (1996) 'Towards a Theory of Learning', *British Journal of Educational Studies*, vol. 44, no. 1, pp. 9–26.

Rao, N. (1990) *The Changing Role of Local Authorities* (London: Policy Studies Institute/Joseph Rowntree Memorial Trust).

Rees, G. and Thomas, M. (1994) 'Inward Investment, Labour Market Adjustment and Skills Development: Recent Experience in South Wales', *Local Economy*, vol. 9, pp. 48–61.

Reid, B. (1995) 'Interorganisational Networks and the Delivery of Local Housing Services', *Housing Studies*, vol. 10, no. 2, pp. 133–49.

Reiner, R. (1992) *The Politics of the Police* (Hemel Hempstead: Harvester Wheatsheaf).

Rhodes, R. A. W. (1981) *Control and Power in Central–Local Government Relations* (Aldershot: Gower).

Rhodes, R. A. W. (1986) *European Policy Making, Implementation and Subcentral Government* (Maastricht: European Institute of Public Administration).

Rhodes, R. A. W. (1988) *Beyond Westminster and Whitehall* (London: Allen & Unwin).

Rhodes, R. A. W. (1990) *Local Government in a Changing Social and Economic System: A Comment on Stoker's Research Agenda*, Political Studies Association of the United Kingdom Annual Conference, University of Durham.

Rhodes, R. A. W. (1991a) *Local Governance* (Swindon: ESRC).

Rhodes, R. A. W. (1991b) *ESRC Research Initiative on 'Local Governance'*, Political Studies Association of the United Kingdom Annual Conference, University of Lancaster.

Rhodes, R. A. W. (1991c) *Local Governance* (Swindon: Economic and Social Research Council, Society and Politics Research Development Group).

Rhodes, R. A. W. (1992) 'Beyond Whitehall: Researching Local Governance', *Social Sciences*, no. 13, p. 2.

Rhodes, R. A. W. (1994) 'The Hollowing-Out of the State', *Political Quarterly*, vol. 65, pp. 138–51.

Rhodes, R. A. W. (1995) 'The Institutional Approach', in D. Marsh and G. Stoker (eds), *Theory and Methods in Political Science* (London: Macmillan).

Rhodes, R. (1996) 'The New Governance, Governing without Government', *Political Studies*, vol. 44, no. 4, pp. 652–67.

Rhodes, R. A. W. (1997a) 'Shackling the Leader? Coherence, Capacity and the Hollow Crown, in P. Weller, H. Bakvis and R. A. W. Rhodes (eds), *The Hollow Crown: Countervailing Trends in Core Executives* (London: Macmillan) pp. 198–223.

Rhodes, R. A. W. (1997b) *Understanding Governance* (Buckingham: Open University Press).

Rhodes, R. A. W. and Marsh, D. (1992a) 'Policy Networks in British Politics: A Critique of Existing Approaches', in D. Marsh and R. A. W. Rhodes (eds), *Policy Networks in British Government* (Oxford: Oxford University Press).

Rhodes, R. A. W. and Marsh, D. (1992b) 'New Directions in the Study of Policy Networks', *European Journal of Policy Research*, vol. 21, pp. 181–205.

Rhodes, R. A. W. and Marsh, D. (1992) 'Thatcherism: An Implementation Perspective' in Marsh and Rhodes (ed) *Implementing Thatcherite Policies* (Buckingham: Open University Press).s

Rhodes, R. A. W., Bache, I. and George, S. (1996) 'Policy Networks and Policy Making in the European Union: A Critical Appraisal', in L. Hooghe (ed.), *Cohesion Policy and European Integration* (Oxford: Clarendon Press).

Riley, K. A. (1993) 'The Abolition of the ILEA: Some Implications for the Restructuring of Local Government', *Public Money and Management*, April–June, pp. 57–60.

Riley, K. A. (1997) 'Changes in Local Governance – Collaboration Through Networks: A Post-16 Case Study', *Educational Management and Administration*, vol. 25, no. 2, pp. 155–67.

Riley, K. A., Walsh, K., Lowndes, V. and Woollam, J. (1995) 'An Approach to the Study of Networks', paper to ESRC Conference on Networks, Cardiff, May.

Roche, M. (1992) *Rethinking Citizenship. Welfare, Ideology and Change in Modern Society* (Cambridge: Polity Press).

Sabel, C. (1993) 'Constitutional Ordering in Historical Context', in F. Scharpf (ed.), *Games in Hierarchies and Networks* (Boulder, Co.: Westview Press).

Sartori, G. (1997) *Comparative Constitutional Engineering*, 2nd edn (London: Macmillan).

Sayer, A. (1984) *Method in Social Science – a Realist Approach* (London: Hutchinson).

Schmitter, P. C. (1996) 'Examining the Present Euro-Polity with the Help of Past Theories', in G. Marks, F. Scarpf, P. Schmitter and W. Streeck, *Governance in the European Union* (London: Sage).

Secretaries of State for Health, Social Security, Wales and Scotland (1989) *Caring for People: Community Care in the Next Decade and Beyond* (London: HMSO).

Secretaries of State for Health, Wales, Northern Ireland and Scotland (1989) *Working for Patients*, CM555 (London: HMSO).

Sieber, S. (1981) *Fatal Remedies: The Ironies of Social Intervention* (New York: Plenum).

Simmonds, R. C. (1948) *The Institute of Actuaries, 1848–1948* (Cambridge: Cambridge University Press).

Sinden, A. (1995) 'Telecommunications Services: Job Losses and Spatial Restructuring in Britain, 1989–1993', *Area*, vol. 27, no. 1, pp. 34–45.

Smith, B. (1985) *Decentralisation: The Territorial Dimension of the State* (London: Allen & Unwin).

Smith, L. (1997) 'The Early County Asylums in the Mixed Economy Care, 1808–1845', paper to the Conference on Insanity, Institutions and Society, Exeter.

Smith, M. (1995) 'UK Electricity: Takeovers Redraw Industry Map', *Financial Times Survey*, 14 November 1995.

Smith, M. J. (1993) *Pressure, Power and Policy* (Brighton: Harvester).

Stanyer, J. (1989) *The History of Devon County Council 1889–1989* (Exeter: Devon Books).

Stanyer, J. (1992) 'Public–Private Sector Relations as Inter-Organisational Interaction', paper to the Seminar on Recent Research in Public–Private Sector Relations (Keele: Political Studies Assocation).

Stanyer, J. (1993a) 'An Historical Perspective on the Public–Private Distinction', paper to the Panel on Comparative Public–Private Sector Relations (Leicester: Political Studies Association).

Stanyer, J. (1993b) 'Struggling with the Intractable: Sir John Bowring and the Reform of Devon Quarter Sessions', chapter 8 in J. Youings (ed.), *Sir John Bowring: Aspects of His Life and Career* (Exeter: The Devonshire Association).

Stanyer, J. (1994) 'Forgetting the Nineteenth Century: The Lessons of the Organisation of the Police', *Strategic Government*, vol. 2, no. 1, pp. 35–45.

Stewart, J. (1988) *A New Management for Housing Departments* (Luton: Local Government Training Board).

Stewart, J. (1992) *The Rebuilding of Public Accountability* (London: European Policy Forum).

Stewart, J. (1993) 'The Limitations of Government by Contract', *Public Money and Management*, July–September, pp. 7–12.

Stewart, J. D. and Stoker, G. (1988) *From Local Administration to Community Government*, Series 351 (London: Fabian Society).

Stewart, J. D. and Stoker, G. (1989) *The Future of Local Government* (London: Macmillan).

Stoker, G. (1990) *Local Government in a Changing Social and Economic System Towards Research Agenda*, Political Studies Association of the United Kingdom, University of Durham.

Stoker, G. (1991) *The Politics of Local Government*, 2nd edn (London: Macmillan).

Stoker, G. (1995) 'Regime Theory and Urban Politics', in D. Judge and H. Wolman (eds), *Theories of Urban Politics* (London: Sage).

Stoker, G. (1996a) *The ESRC Local Governance Programme: An Update* (Glasgow: Department of Government, University of Strathclyde).

Stoker, G. (1996b) 'Memorandum', Rebuilding Trust. Volume II: Oral Evidence and Associated Memoranda, House of Lords Select Committee on Relations Between Central and Local Government, Session 1995–6, HL Paper 97–I (London: The Stationery Office) pp. 168–83.

Stoker, G. (1997a) 'Local Government in Britain After Thatcher', in J. Erik-Lane (ed.), *Public Sector Reform* (London: Sage).

Stoker, G. (1997b) 'The New Forms of Local Governance', in M. Chisholm, R. Hales and D. Thomas (eds), *A Fresh Start for Local Government* (London: CIPFA).

Stoker, G. (1998a) 'Governance as Theory: Five Propositions', *International Social Science Journal*, pp. 17–28.

Stoker, G. (1998b) 'Public Private Partnerships and Urban Governance', in J. Pierre (ed.), *Partnerships in Urban Governance: European and American Experience* (London: Macmillan) pp. 34–51.

Stoker, G. and Mossberger, K. (1994) 'Urban Regime Theory in Comparative Perspective', *Government and Policy*, vol. 12, pp. 195–212.

Stoker, G. and Mossberger, K. (1995) 'The Post-Fordist Local State: The Dynamics of its Development', in J. Stewart and G. Stoker (eds), *Local Government in the 1990s* (London: Macmillan).

Stone, C. (1989) *Regime Politics: Governing Atlanta, 1946–1988* (Lawrence: University of Kansas Press).

Stone, C. (1993) 'Urban Regimes and the Capacity to Govern: A Political Economy Approach', *Journal of Urban Affairs*, vol. 15, pp. 1–28.

Stone, C. (1995) 'Political Leadership and Urban Politics', in D. Judge, G. Stoker and H. Wolman (eds), *Theories of Urban Politics* (London: Sage).

Stones, R. (1992) 'Labour and International Finance 1964–1967', in D. Marsh and R. Rhodes (eds), *Policy Networks in British Government* (Oxford: Oxford University Press).

Streeck, W. (1995) 'From Market Making to State Building? Reflections on the Political Economy of European Social Policy', in S. Liebfried and P. Pierson (eds), *European Social Policy* (Washington, DC: Brookings Institution) pp. 389–431.

Thompson, G., Frances, J., Levačić, R. and Mitchell, J. (1991) (eds), *Markets, Hierarchies and Networks: The Co-ordination of Social Life* (London: Sage).

Thompson, G. (1993) 'Network Co-ordination', in R. Maidment and G. Thompson (eds), *Managing the United Kingdom* (London: Sage) pp. 51–74.

Tjosvold, D. (1986) 'The Dynamics of Interdependence in Organisations', *Human Relations*, vol. 39, no. 6, pp. 517–40.

Treasury (1996) *Financial Statement and Budget Report 1997–98*, HC 90 of Session 1996–97 (London: Stationery Office).

Treasury and Private Finance Panel (1995) *Private Opportunity, Public Benefit: Progressing the Private Finance Initiative* (London: Treasury).

Treasury Committee (1996) *The Private Finance Initiative*, HC 146 of Session 1995–96 (London: HMSO).

Tyler, T. T. and Degoey, P. (1996) 'Trust in Organisational Authorities', in R. M. Kramer and T. Tyler (eds), *Trust in Organisations: Frontiers of Theory and Research* (London: Sage).

Urry, J. (1987) 'Society, Space and Locality', *Environment and Planning D: Society and Space*, vol. 5, pp. 435–44.

Van Waarden, F. (1992) 'Dimensions and Types of Policy Networks', *European Journal of Policy Research*, February.

Waldegrave, W. (1993) *The Reality of Reform and Accountability in Today's Public Services* (London: Public Finance Foundation).

Walker, C. and Smith, A. J. (1995) *Privatized Infrastructure: The BOT Approach* (London: Thomas Telford).

Walker, J. (1987) 'Local Politics and the Local Labour Market', *Local Economy*, vol. 2, no. 3, pp. 181–99.

Walsh, K. (1995) *Public Services and Market Mechanisms* (London: Macmillan).

Walsh, K. and Davis, H. (1993) *Competition and Service: The Impact of the Local Government Act 1988* (London: HMS0).

Walsh, K., Lowndes, V., Riley, K. and Woollam, J. (1995) 'Institutional Change, Public Service Management and Citizenship', *Strategic Government*, vol. 3, no. 1, pp. 38–54.

Walsh, K., Lowndes, V., Riley, K. and Woollam, J. (1996) 'Management in the Public Sector: A Content Analysis of Journals', *Public Administration*, vol. 74, no. 2, pp. 315–24.

Watson, A. (1982) *Diplomacy* (London: Eyre Methuen).

Weatheritt, M. (1993) 'Measuring Police Performance: Accounting or Accountability?', in R. Reiner and S. Spencer (eds), *Accountable Policing: Effectiveness, Empowerment and Equity* (London: Institute of Public Policy Research).

Welsh Affairs Committee (1995) *Wales in Europe* (London: HMSO).

Welsh Affairs Committee (1997) *Further Education in Wales* (London: HMSO).

Welsh Office (1995) *People and Prosperity: An Agenda for Action in Wales* (Cardiff: Welsh Office).

West of England Initiative (1995) *Proceedings of the Annual Conference on Regional Government and the South West* (Swindon: WEI).

Western Daily Press (1996) 'Hobbled in the Race for Jobs', 11 July.

Western Daily Press (1997) 'Partners in Success Win Praise at Euro Event', 1 April.

Western Development Partnership (1994) *Economic Development Strategy for the Avon Area* (Bristol: WDP).

Whitely, R. (1992) 'The Social Construction of Organisations and Markets: The Comparative Analysis of Business Recipes', in M. Reed and M. Hughes (eds), *Rethinking Organisation* (London: Sage) pp. 120–45.

Williamson, O. (1993) 'Calculativeness, Trust and Economic Organisation', *Journal of Law and Economics*, vol. XXXVl, pp. 453–86.

Williamson, O. E. (1985) *The Economic Institutions of Capitalism* (New York: Free Press).

Wistow, G., Knapp M. *et al.* (1994) *Social Care in a Mixed Economy* (Buckingham: Open University Press).

WLGA (Welsh Local Government Association) (1996) *Evidence to House of Lords Select Committee on Relations Between Central and Local Government* (Cardiff: WLGA).

Wolfensberger, W. (1972) *The Principle of Normalization in Human Services* (Toronto: National Institute on Mental Retardation).

Wolfensberger, W. (1983) 'Social Role Valorization: A Proposed New Term for the Principle of Normalization', *Mental Retardation*, vol. 21, no. 6, pp. 234–9.

Wulf-Mathies, M. (1995) *Community Structural Policies and Employment* (Brussels: DGXVI).

Yin, R. K. (1994) *Case Study Research: Design and Methods*, revised edition, (Beverly Hills, Calif.: Sage).

Index